THE IMPERIAL WAR MUSEUM
BOOK OF
THE WESTERN FRONT

MALCOLM BROWN

BCA

LONDON NEW YORK SYDNEY TORONTO

This edition published 1993
by BCA by arrangement with
SIDGWICK & JACKSON LTD

ISBN 0 283 061405

1 3 5 7 9 8 6 4 2

A CIP catalogue record for this book is available from
the British Library

Typeset by Parker Typesetting Service, Leicester
Printed and bound in Great Britain by
BPCC Hazell Books Ltd
Member of BPCC Ltd

HALF-TITLE
'Funking it'. Anzac Troops taking shelter in funk holes during a gas
alarm, Ypres Salient, 30 September 1917. (E(AUS) 840)

FRONTISPIECE
Men of 'B' Company, 1st Scots Guards, in the trenches, October
1915. (Q 17390)

CN 2359

CONTENTS

Author's acknowledgements vi

Preface vii

Foreword: The Western Front ix

PART ONE: MOVEMENT
Introduction to Part One 3
Advance to Mons 5
From Mons to the Aisne 13
Casualty of the Great Retreat 21
First Ypres and Entrenchment 25
Killed in Action at First Ypres 34
A Nurse at First Ypres 36

PART TWO: DEADLOCK
Introduction to Part Two 43
First Winter, and the Christmas Truce 44
The Trenches 50
The Guns 58
'Rest' – and Rest 64
First Battles 69
The Battle of Loos 77
Wounds, 'Blighty ones', Fatalities 87
'If your number's on it . . .': Religion and
    Fatalism 91
Executions at Dawn: from the Diary of an
    Assistant Provost-Marshal 97
'Smile, boys, smile': Soldiers' Humour 99
A French Artist with the BEF 103
The 'No Man's Land' War: Patrols and
    Raids 104
The Somme: Hard Knocks, Hard Lessons 111
'All in a day's work': The Death of
    Captain Geoffrey Donaldson 116
The Australians at Pozières 119
Unhappy Warriors 122

'Stellenbosched': Nightmare of a
    Brigadier-General 125
First Tanks 131
'Over the Top' 134
The 'Bomb-proof' Canadian 140
Winter, and the German Withdrawal 145
Diary of a Battalion Runner 150
Entertainments, for the troops, various 154
Arras: A Senior Staff Officer's View 159
Liaison Officer with the Portuguese 165
Messines, June 1917 169
The Treatment of Prisoners 176
The First Day of Third Ypres 182
'Only Murder': A Stretcher-Bearer during
    Third Ypres 186
The War in the Air 189
The Battle of the Menin Road 192
'Great Days These': The View from
    Passchendaele 198
Cambrai: Hopes Raised, Hopes Deferred 200

PART THREE: BREAK-OUT
Introduction to Part Three 205
The 'Kaiser's Battle': First Impact 206
The March Retreat 213
'Backs to the Wall' 221
A World of Rare Women 228
Americans 233
The Last Hundred Days: I 238
The Last Hundred Days: II 249
Endings 258
The Changing Face of Ypres 260

An Afterword on Attitudes 262

Index of Contributors 271
General Index 272

AUTHOR'S ACKNOWLEDGEMENTS

This is the second book to have resulted from my association with the Imperial War Museum. I am most grateful to the Museum's staff from Director-General downwards for the benign and generous manner in which I have been accepted in their midst, so that though I am strictly speaking an alien I feel more and more like an insider – with an insider's privileges while still retaining an outsider's independence. In view of this, my acknowledgements are not so much formal and general as particular and personal. My first thanks must go to Roderick Suddaby and all the members of his Department of Documents: Philip Reed (now at the Cabinet War Rooms), Nigel Steel, Simon Robbins and Stephen Walton, not forgetting David Shaw and Wendy Lutterloch. Next, my thanks go to Jane Carmichael and the staff of the Department of Photographs, all of whom have been most helpful but among whom I must give special mention to Hilary Roberts and to Ron Brooker and his colleagues of the Photographic Darkrooms, notably David Price, Greg Brinklow and Greg Smith. Among the staff of the Department of Art I must single out Michael Moody, Jenny Wood and Pauline Allwright; among the staff of the Department of Exhibits and Firearms I should like to name Diana Condell and Mike Hibberd; while among many helpful members of the Department of Printed Books particular thanks should go to Sarah Paterson, Mary Wilkinson and Angela Wootton. I am also grateful to Roger Smither and Paul Sargent of the Department of Film. A vital service was discharged by Peter Simkins, the Museum's historian, whom I thank most sincerely for his expert reading of the text in its final stage and his valuable and valued comments on a subject about which his knowledge is virtually second to none. Dr Christopher Dowling, who is responsible for the Museum's publishing programme, has supported and encouraged the project throughout, while Suzanne Bardgett, General Editor of the *Imperial War Museum Review*, assisted by reading much of the manuscript in its first draft. As in the case of my earlier volume, *The Imperial War Museum Book of the First World War*, I am especially grateful to the Director-General, Dr Alan Borg, for contributing a Preface.

I have also been conscious throughout of the enthusiastic backing of my publisher, William Armstrong, who invited me to undertake the book. My warm thanks go to him, and also to those who have seen the book through its editing and production stages, notably Helen Gummer, Peter Hull and the designer Peter Ward.

Most importantly of all I must express my profound gratitude to the people whose vivid and memorable accounts and descriptions I have been privileged to use as the basis of this history. Their names, and the names of the copyright holders who have kindly allowed me to quote from them, appear in the Index of Contributors at the end of the book.

All illustrations have been taken from the Museum's collections, except that on page 49, reproduced by courtesy of John Frost Historical Newspapers and the 1991 photograph on page 261 by Dr. A. J. Lane.

PREFACE

The Western Front holds a unique place in the historical consciousness of the nation. Still, when we think of the First World War, we think of the Western Front and it is Flanders fields that springs to mind, even though many fell in other corners of foreign fields. The Ypres Salient and the Somme have become peculiarly British battle-fields, although there were troops of many nations there. Moreover there was life – and of course death – on the Western Front both before and after the infamous set-piece battles in the trenches.

This book, like its predecessor *The Imperial War Museum Book of the First World War*, is firmly based on the Museum and its collections. Indeed, it was while working on the earlier book that Malcolm Brown came to realize that the depth and richness of the holdings in our Department of Documents demanded a separate and additional volume on the Western Front. The collections of letters and diaries he has used, all of which are available for students and scholars to work on, reveal something of this range. In fact there is much more than is revealed here, especially as the author has chosen to use only immediate eyewitness accounts. These have the vivid strength of actual experience, but there are many other records held by the Museum which were written up by the participants in retrospect. Some of these later reports are among the classics of twentieth-century literature, such as Sassoon's *Memoirs of an Infantry Officer* or Sherriff's *Journey's End* (the manuscript of both are held by the Museum), but descriptions set down at the time have a different ring, more pragmatic than philosophical.

The First World War has now effectively joined the mainstream of history, rather than being a tributary fed by the continuing memories of those who took part in it. Each year the number of surviving veterans decreases and they will soon be gone altogether. Yet their words and the images of their Western Front live on in the pages of this book. I hope readers will be encouraged to visit the Museum, either to browse in the public galleries or to delve in the research departments; as a record of human experience our collections are difficult to match.

Alan Borg
Director-General
Imperial War Museum

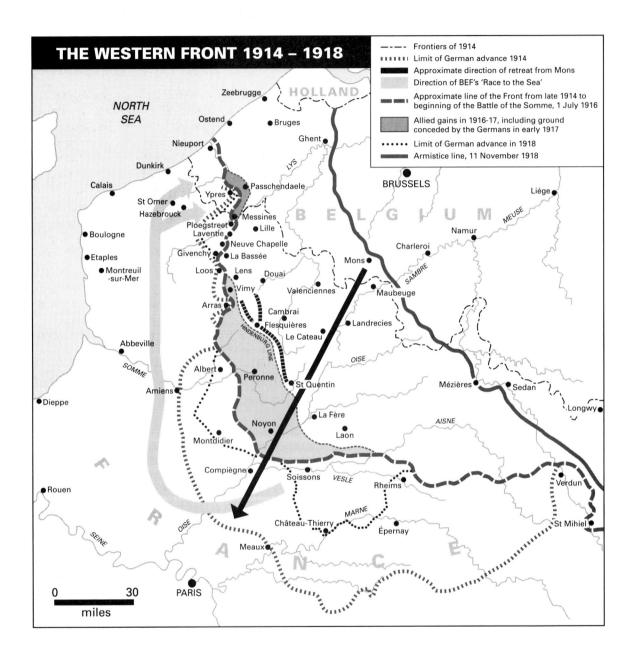

THE WESTERN FRONT 1914 – 1918

Legend:

- –·–·– Frontiers of 1914
- ।।।।।। Limit of German advance 1914
- ▬▬▬ Approximate direction of retreat from Mons
- ▬▬▬ Direction of BEF's 'Race to the Sea'
- ▬▬▬ Approximate line of the Front from late 1914 to beginning of the Battle of the Somme, 1 July 1916
- Allied gains in 1916-17, including ground conceded by the Germans in early 1917
- ······ Limit of German advance in 1918
- ▬▬▬ Armistice line, 11 November 1918

NORTH SEA

HOLLAND

Zeebrugge
Ostend
Bruges
Nieuport
Ghent
Dunkirk
Calais
Passchendaele
Ypres
St Omer
Hazebrouck
Messines
BRUSSELS
Liége
B E L G I U M
MEUSE
Boulogne
Ploegstreet
Laventie
Lille
Namur
Etaples
Neuve Chapelle
Charleroi
Montreuil
-sur-Mer
Givenchy
La Bassée
Loos
Lens
Douai
Mons
SAMBRE
Maubeuge
Vimy
Valenciennes
Arras
Cambrai
HINDENBURG LINE
Flesquières
Le Cateau
Landrecies
Abbeville
SOMME
Albert
Peronne
St Quentin
OISE
Mézières
Sedan
Dieppe
Amiens
La Fère
Longwy
Noyon
Laon
AISNE
Montdidier
Compiègne
Soissons
VESLE
Rheims
Verdun
Rouen
Château-Thierry
MARNE
Épernay
St Mihiel
Meaux
SEINE
OISE
F R A N C E

0   30
miles

PARIS

FOREWORD: THE WESTERN FRONT

Of all the theatres in which the First World War was fought there is no doubt that for the British, the French, the Americans and the principal enemy, the Germans, the Western Front was the most important. Basically, it was there that the war was lost and won. But it was also there that another issue was opened up – that of the nature of warfare itself, for what took place there between 1914 and 1918 seemed so horrific, and was in human terms so costly, that it has left a permanent scar on the imagination and attitudes of later generations.

When people use the term 'Western Front', what is being referred to, nearly always, is the war of the trenches. Strictly speaking, however, the Western Front opened with the first shots of August 1914 and closed with the Armistice of November 1918. This is the span covered by this book, but, necessarily, the bulk of it is devoted to the period of trench warfare, which began in earnest in late 1914 and became moribund (though it was far from extinct) with the great German offensive of March 1918.

Trench warfare was all the more disturbing because it was unexpected, so that those involved in it saw it not only as a monstrosity but also as an aberration. There was certainly no general perception in 1914 that the war in the west would degenerate into a head-to-head confrontation between fixed positions. All the armies involved had planned for a campaign of movement; instead they found themselves enmeshed in a static struggle between increasingly sophisticated and ever denser defence systems. In effect, they were drawn into a new, industrialized version of old-style siege warfare, except that this was a siege without walls, with sandbags substituting for battlements and No Man's Land fulfilling the role of the mediaeval moat. Each line of trenches became, as it were, a flattened fortress, a horizontal Troy.

That metaphor is not entirely frivolous in that the essence of the four years which followed entrenchment was the search for some kind of wooden horse; indeed the original wooden horse was itself in effect a technical response to a stalemate war. The Germans who flinched at the sight of the tanks at Flers-Courcelette in the Battle of the Somme in 1916 could have been forgiven if they saw that new weapon in such terms. They themselves found their equivalent in the successful penetration methods, such as their use of groups of *Sturmtruppen* (Stormtroopers) pushed forward before the moment of attack, which they employed when they finally broke the trench-lock in March 1918. New developments of various kinds – including major advances in artillery techniques and infantry tactics – crucially helped the final sweep to victory of the Allies in 1918.

With hindsight, it can be seen that trench warfare was virtually inevitable. The sheer power of the new mass-produced weaponry now available gave the armies no alternative but to go to ground. For this was to be above all an artillery war, and to a lesser extent a war of the machine-gun, against which the obvious response was to create defences for protection. And the more each army acquired its necessary reinforcements and its ever-burgeoning units of support, the more the temporary positions they occupied on entrenchment acquired the air of permanence. It was as though two giants of equal strength were trapped facing each other in an underground tunnel with no way back.

The situation produced an understandable nostalgia in those who remembered the dash and movement of earlier wars. Thus the first British Commander-in-Chief, Field Marshal Sir John French, whose reputation had been won on the South African veld, could, writing in May 1915, deplore the 'tremendous *crust* of defence' which the Germans had been forming and consolidating throughout the previous winter and state, with a touch almost of romantic longing:

How I should love to have a real good 'go' at them

in the open with lots of cavalry and horse artillery and run them to earth. Well! It may come.*

The zone of the trenches became more than a geographical location, a piece of territory assigned for close fighting. It became a thing of itself. It acquired its own personality. In a memoir written just after the war a former conscript soldier described his awareness of it from behind the lines:

> I gazed in an eastward direction. All the snow had melted, the fields, the bare trees and hedges, were steeped in warm sunlight. In the distance there was a gentle slope crowned by a long line of poplars. Beyond the poplars, about eight miles away, there was something I did not see, although I knew it was there – a stupid, terrible and uncouth monster that stretched in a zigzag winding course from the North Sea to the Alps. It was strangely silent at that hour, but I was fascinated by it and thought about it harder and harder, in spite of myself. I became increasingly conscious of it, and it grew upon me until it seemed to crush and darken everything beneath its intolerable weight.†

If it was a monster, it was a Hydra, a thing with many heads, and also with innumerable limbs. Over the years the Western Front grew and developed until it became a society, a world on its own, a temporary alternative civilization – except that that is an incongruous word to use about a form of human activity devoted by definition to mass destruction. Its ramifications stretched far behind the fire-step and the machine-gun post, to the artillery lines, the billet villages, the supply dumps, the training-grounds, the casualty clearing stations, the base hospitals, the veterinary establishments, not to mention the baths (often brewery vats) to which the troops came from time to time to be deloused. And the estaminets and the brothels, one might add, and the towns and cities away from the war zone into which men could occasionally escape for a taste of quasi-normal life. It also had its postal and transport systems, its own labour organization, its canteens, its concerts, its burial force. More, and crucially, at all levels from brigade to GHQ it had its Staff personnel. Overall, indeed, far more men were engaged in administration and organization than in fighting. One consequence of this was that there could be a strong resentment on the part of those who risked their lives against those who were thought to be having an easy life at the base. Thus Captain Arthur Gibbs MC, an officer in the Welsh Guards, could refer in some heat, in a letter of 30 April 1918, to the compilation of a list of so-called 'Sturmtruppen' (British ones in this case, not German), i.e., officers who had been in the Army from the beginning but had never been in the trenches with their regiments and had thus had 'a real soft job for the whole of the war'. Yet those who were responsible for what we could now call the infrastructure of the front also had their stout defenders. For underneath the criticism, which was often focused on the red-tabbed young officers who rode around on fine horses in the entourage of senior generals, was a realization that somehow the whole multifarious operation of keeping an Army at war did actually work and get things done. Thus as early as November 1915 Major C. E. L. Lyne, an officer of the Royal Field Artillery, could write approvingly of 'the vast organization necessary for carrying on the war. One appreciates it without realizing it.'

It will have been noticed that the above description applies to the British zone of the Front only, which is, and properly – the Imperial War Museum being the supreme source of material about the British role in the First World War – the subject of this book. In addition, of course, the French, the Germans and, on a much smaller scale, the Belgians had their own sectors and civilizations. Mention of which fact offers the opportunity to make a point frequently forgotten by British readers, that for most of the war the French were by a long way the senior partner in the Franco-British alliance, maintaining several hundreds of miles of trench-lines whereas the British never held more than about a hundred, and that only for a brief period in 1918. This had consequences often overlooked: when, for example, battles continued longer than might

---

*Richard Holmes, *The Little Field Marshal*, Jonathan Cape 1981, p. 294.

†F. A. Voigt, *Combed Out*, first published 1920, republished Jonathan Cape 1929, pp. 64–5.

have seemed sensible from a British point of view, this was almost always because of pressure from the French. The British High Command was never in the position of fighting its own private war.

The Western Front has, of course, been portrayed many times – so why a new book about it? What gives this volume a special validity is that it presents its subject through evidence which, in virtually every case, is in public print for the first time. It is as though long after an election or a referendum a mass of unopened ballot-boxes had been found in a hitherto locked room; the overall result might not be affected but some adjustments to previously accepted views might possibly be required. To give just one example: it is surely of interest that a brave and intelligent infantry officer (soon to be killed in action) could have written *as early as September 1914* – i.e., under two months after going to France with the British Expeditionary Force – that he hoped the outcome of the present fighting might be a speedy Waterloo which would keep the peace for fifty years, by which time the profession of soldiery might be seen as a thing of the past. Moreover, he believed he was not recording a personal, deviant attitude, but a 'really universal feeling against war' among many of his fellows. So much for the general assumption that serious questions about the war's carnage were not asked until the articulate civilian-soldiers of Kitchener's Army had had their blooding on the Somme in 1916.

There is another significant way in which this volume strikes a different note among current books about the First World War. Very early I took the strategic decision to use – except in the case of a small number of clearly declared exceptions – only evidence produced *at the time* as source material, and to ignore memoirs or interviews from a later date. I did this despite a widely held view that what was written by soldiers during the war, particularly in letters to loved ones back home, was almost always so anodyne as to give no real conception of what was actually taking place. I have not found this to be so. Undoubtedly many men *were* reticent, wishing to spare their families the harsher details, but equally there were many who made no bones about telling them how it was, and in the case of

diaries there was no such sanction anyway. There have been numerous books in recent years using, often very effectively, the reminiscences of living veterans, so there is a strong case for making this one in a different mode. This is not to claim that contemporary evidence is automatically better or more true – letters and diaries written just after an event can be as fallible as evidence offered many decades later – but there is often a vigour and a muscle about their accounts not matched by the later memoir or recording. One other consequence of this decision is that, as it happens, there are a substantial number of fatalities among the book's contributors. This is how it should be, for it is surely not right that the description of a war should be left only to its survivors. Not a few of those who came through the great 1914–18 conflict have looked back on it as the time of their lives. For too many soldiers quoted in this book it was the time of their deaths. I look on this book as offering an important opportunity to give these largely forgotten men their voice.

In adopting this policy, I have had to ignore some excellent works of reminiscence and also some very remarkable sound recordings which the IWM has been energetically collecting in recent years. For these, I am sure, the time will come, but this present volume is, I believe, the better and the more valuable a contribution to the literature of the war, for the sharp focus that has been adopted. One other positive consequence of this policy is that a notable absentee from this book is General, Colonel, Sergeant or Private Hindsight. This is not to say that the men quoted here do not have their strong views and opinions; they do and they express them vigorously. But their views are of the time, not massaged by later assumptions or reappraisals.

If there is a keynote text among the mass of letters and diaries which I have consulted it is a sentence written in 1914 by an officer who is much quoted here and who was not among the survivors at the Armistice: Captain, later Major, Harry Dillon, DSO MC. On 23 September that year he wrote a very frank account of events on the Aisne front, and then made this comment on what he had written:

I don't know if some of this letter is a bit gruesome

but I can tell you there are a good many things which I have not and could not put on paper, but I think it is a mistake to gloss everything over so that people at home should imagine war lightly as a sort of picnic.

This is surely a significant statement. Dillon plainly saw there was no virtue in simply piling horror on horror – there were limits; but he also saw that there was a great virtue in conveying the reality of events in a manner which would leave the reader far from the scene in no doubt as to the nature of the war to which he was giving his support and which was being fought in his name. It is men like Dillon, consciously or unconsciously adopting this viewpoint, who have made this book possible. Their names appear in the List of Contributors at the end of the book, a list which is, in a real sense, a roll of honour.

As has already been implied, the war of the Western Front falls into three principal phases. I have reflected this in the book. The first phase, dealt with in Part One, Movement, covers the period from the beginning of the war until the end of the first fast-moving battles – i.e. from August to November 1914. The second phase, which is dealt with in Part Two, entitled Deadlock, covers the period of trench warfare from the end of 1914 to the German spring attacks of 1918. The final phase, dealt with in Part Three, Break-out, covers the period from March to November 1918.

Some subjects have been omitted because they were dealt with at length in my earlier volume, *The Imperial War Museum Book of the First World War*, which contained much material about the Western Front. Thus for example there is only a token section about the air war, chaplains are discussed only in relation to fatalism, and women in the medical role are represented only by one brief section in Part One; on the other hand in Part Three there is a section on women as WAACS – i.e. members of the Women's Army Auxiliary Corps. In short this book is intended to complement its predecessor rather than to repeat it.

With regard to quotations, these are reproduced verbatim whenever possible, but obvious errors have been corrected and minor confusions have been clarified. As a general rule it has not been thought necessary to indicate where the original text has been abridged.

MALCOLM BROWN

BACKGROUND NOTE

The British Expeditionary Force (BEF) of regular troops and reservists which left for France in August 1914 consisted of I Corps (1st and 2nd Divisions) and II Corps (3rd and 5th Divisions). The 4th Division arrived in time to assist at Le Cateau, while the 6th joined during the Battle of the Aisne: these then became III Corps. The 7th Division arrived in time to be drawn into the First Battle of Ypres. An Indian Corps and the first units of the Territorial Army (originally a part-time force raised for home defence) also came into action at this time. 1915 saw the arrival of the first divisions of Kitchener's citizen army of volunteers; these would play an increasingly important role. In the later years of the war, however, the principal reinforcement troops of the BEF were conscripts.

The BEF was constituted into two Armies on Christmas Day 1914, with General Sir Douglas Haig appointed to command First Army, and General Sir Horace Smith-Dorrien Second Army. This number would eventually grow until by 1917 there were five Armies in the field. The BEF's first Commander-in-Chief was Field Marshal Sir John French. He was succeeded by Haig in December 1915, the latter holding this position to the end of hostilities, though he did not become a Field Marshal until January 1917.

Other 'Empire' countries which contributed in the British zone of the Western Front were Canada, Australia, New Zealand and South Africa, with forces from all these countries gaining impressive reputations for their fighting skill. Portugal also sent a somewhat less effective expeditionary force in 1917.

Armies usually consisted of four Corps, which in turn consisted of three or four divisions. Throughout the war troops moved and fought in divisions but lived and thought in smaller units, such as battalions (infantry) or batteries (artillery). Normally there were four (later three) battalions in a brigade, and three brigades in a division. An infantry battalion at full complement consisted of up to a thousand men, of whom thirty were officers. Battalions were subdivided into companies, platoons and sections.

GHQ (General Headquarters) was established at St Omer in October 1914 but from March 1916 to April 1919 was at Montreuil, just inland from the main British base and training ground at Etaples.

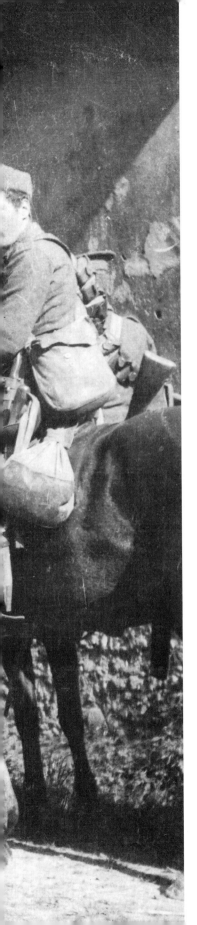

PART ONE

MOVEMENT

August – November 1914

This constant marching is a tremendous physical strain, and is trying for nerves as well. The men are doing it with their usual wonderful efficiency, but many have fallen out, and when we are retiring that means that they are probably captured. Poor fellows! However, I suppose that is the fortune of war.

Captain James Paterson
1st Battalion, South Wales Borderers
5 September 1914

We have been, I assure you, in the hottest of places and people who have themselves been through South Africa describe the same as being a mere picnic compared with what this war has been up to the present. We have been on the move incessantly and attacking and retiring and advancing the whole time.

Lieutenant Neville Woodroffe
1st Battalion Irish Guards
c. 13 September 1914

Part of the 5th Cavalry Brigade during the Mons Retreat, August– September 1914.
(Q 60698)

INTRODUCTION TO PART ONE

It could be said that the Western Front came into existence as soon as the Germans opened hostilities in Western Europe by their invasion of Belgium on 4 August 1914. The German intention was to strike through that country at their prime enemy, France; the fact that Belgium's integrity had been guaranteed by the British by a treaty signed in 1839 was the trip-wire that brought Britain into the war, though Britain was also linked to France by the understanding, established in 1904, known as the *Entente Cordiale*. In response the French themselves attacked, throwing substantial forces eastwards against the heavily defended provinces of Alsace-Lorraine (which they had lost to Germany in the Franco-Prussian War of 1870–71 and now wanted back), where they would make few gains and suffer appalling losses. Meanwhile Britain ordered its stand-by Expeditionary Force (the BEF) to the continent to assist the French and Belgians. These were long-anticipated moves and (except in the case of neutral Belgium) followed detailed plans on all sides, Germany's being a modified version of that devised between 1897 and 1905 by a former Chief of the German General Staff, Count Alfred von Schlieffen.

In briefest outline, the Germans struck with seven armies ranged north to south, the northernmost ones swinging round faster than the southernmost in a massive semicircular movement of which the original aim was to overrun Paris on both sides and then sweep eastwards to divide France's forces in two. This, the Germans hoped, would secure them the French capital, break France's will to resist, and bring about a speedy victory before their enemy on their eastern flank, Russia, could lumber into action. In the event, they lost impetus partly thanks to the activities of Belgian *franc-tireurs* and the resistance offered by the Belgian forts of Liège and Namur, but also because of their diversion of troops from their right wing to invest Antwerp. The right wing was vital to the whole German strategy, but now the current German Chief of the General Staff, von Moltke, opted to reinforce the less important left wing. This decision was just one symptom of a loss of grip, and of nerve, on von Moltke's part which arguably lost the Germans the campaign and certainly lost von Moltke his job – and his reputation.

As the invaders moved on through Belgium and into France, they met increasing French opposition, which, together with the efforts of the BEF at Mons and Le Cateau, put a further brake on an advance that soon began to show signs of running out of steam through sheer physical exhaustion. A successful counter-attack was launched by the French Generals Lanrezac and Franchet d'Esperey, following which the Germans decided to rein in their advance to the north of Paris. This shift in the axis of the German right wing has been well described as 'the last of a series of fatal modifications to the Schlieffen Plan'.* As they swung east they made themselves vulnerable to a determined flank attack by the French, who, again with British help, crucially fought them to a standstill at the Battle of the Marne.

The Germans retreated but then dug themselves in on the heights overlooking the valley of the Aisne, after which a brief unexpected preview of trench warfare took place, lasting several weeks. Subsequently, with the Germans marching first, both sides attempted a series of outflanking movements until there were opposing forces spread out in roughly parallel lines over some 450 miles from the Swiss border to the Channel coast. During this period the British redeployed at their own request from the Aisne region to the area of northern France and Belgium – near to the Channel ports – which they were to make theirs for the next four years.

There followed a major attempt by both sides

---

*Peter Simkins, *World War I: The Western Front*, Military Press 1991, p. 27.

to strike a decisive blow in the area around Ypres in Belgium. No clear victor having emerged, the armies settled into lines of defence, and the long deadlock of the trenches began.

Part One tells the story of the BEF's arrival in France, of the Battle of Mons, of the Great Retreat that followed, of the first taste of trench warfare on the Aisne, and of the touch-and-go battle of late 1914 which was to become famous as the First Battle of Ypres. There are three sections on individuals: a Staff Sergeant who went into hiding after Mons, an officer of the Irish Guards killed at First Ypres, and a professional nurse who served at a Casualty Clearing Station within earshot of that battle.

Advance to Mons

It began in euphoria. When Sergeant William Edgington and his comrades of D Battery, Royal Horse Artillery, landed at Le Havre in mid-August, they received an enthusiastic reception from the French population, who, his diary records, 'smothered us with flowers (and kisses)'. The *entente* between the British and the French, it seemed, could not have been more *cordiale*, but inevitably there were rich opportunities for comedy, even farce. It was perhaps significant that Captain James Paterson, Adjutant of the 1st South Wales Borderers, which unit had recently returned from India, found that the crowds of soldiers and workmen waiting at the Havre quayside reminded him of Baluchistanis, for French seemed the least available *lingua franca* as his battalion established itself ashore. His Quartermaster, Wilson, went immediately into action without the slightest concern for linguistic barriers. 'Can't speak a word of French and does not want to,' Paterson noted in his diary; 'manages to carry on with English and Arabic picked up in Egypt some twenty-five years ago. Nobody understands a word he says, but he does not care a damn – excuse me.' Similarly when a day or so later a French lady, eager to offer accommodation to the arriving allies, attempted to communicate this to an ordinary Tommy of Paterson's battalion, the latter answered with 'a mixture of English, Welsh and Urdu'. The lady's efforts, Paterson added, had involved 'showing him [the Tommy] various beds and things, and naturally this had led to misunderstandings'. It was a situation that almost called for a Feydeau. Happily when Paterson arrived on the scene, both parties had dissolved into fits of laughter.

However, 'beer and cigarettes', both of which were readily available, seemed to mean the same to both nationalities, as did – it was a concept that would become a craze, a cult, almost a religion, over the next four years – 'souvenirs'; Paterson observed that some soldiers were dispensing, to selected demoiselles and in return for kisses, the 'SWBs' from their shoulder straps. Likewise Sergeant Bert Reeve, 16th Battery, Royal Field Artillery, found 'everyone shaking hands and wanting souvenirs, cap badges, belts, etc.' when on his second evening at Le Havre he went for a walk in the town proper, 'previous visit only docks and boulevards'. He also recorded in his diary: 'Had a 5 cent ride on tram. French beer very pale and light.'

If there was beer for the men, there was stronger stuff for the officers. Lieutenant Rowland Owen, 2nd Battalion, Duke of Wellington's Regiment, wrote to his parents on 22 August: 'We are living in great luxury, drinking enormous quantities of the wine of the country and eating food beautifully cooked by an aboriginaless' – a term which presumably referred to a genuine *citoyenne* of Le Havre, rather than to an outback Australian who happened to have taken up residence in the chief port of

LA GUERRE EUROPÉENNE de 1914
117 - NANTES- La première toilette du brave soldat anglais à son débarquement
First washing in french water

A contemporary French postcard picturing the 'brave English soldier' at a first washing of clothes at Nantes, one of several ports of entry used by the BEF, soon after disembarkment in 1914. (Q 90849)

Normandy. One evening Captain Paterson's kindly hostess promised her SWB guests 'a bottle or two of twenty-four-year-old wine' with dinner, which turned out to be a very acceptable *prunelle* – plum brandy. But to all ranks hospitality seemed limitless. Sapper Hugh Bellew, member of a signal company of the Royal Engineers attached to GHQ, was clearly delighted: 'Every night we went out and were treated everywhere we went, would not let us pay for a thing.' A day or two later his diary comments were still positive – 'Up to now living like fighting cocks, the bread here beats English bread' – but there were drawbacks: 'Properly fed up with French tobacco, would give anything for a gold flake.' However, this was a small fly in much good ointment.

It was the same at Boulogne. The diary of Lieutenant T. S. Wollocombe, Adjutant of the 4th Battalion, Middlesex Regiment, includes this description:

> The whole town turned out to a man to cheer us on with shouts of 'Huway, huway!' and 'Vive l'Angleterre' and 'Les Allemands, Wugh!', followed by a sign with the hand drawn across the neck as if to cut it. They were most enthusiastic and at a halt they brought us plums, beer and water for the men.

Wollocombe noted that there was admiration as well as welcome in the attitude of the Boulogne population:

> They were surprised at the way the men kept in step as French troops are not encouraged to do this.

This is a not insignificant observation, in that one thing that was to distinguish the British Army on the Western Front throughout the war was a sense of its innate quality and worth. Without this it would not have survived the troughs and setbacks of the years to come nor emerged in 1918 as arguably the best troops in action on any front of the war. But on the road to this excellence there would be many painful experiences and hard lessons, and few of the first into the fight would be there to enjoy the consummation.

The breezy atmosphere continued as the BEF moved northwards towards the future fighting zone, with cheering crowds, more kisses, and free gifts of all kinds at the stations. Captain Paterson summed it all up in one sentence:

Really France is very nice, what with the food and the ladies, bless them!

But this hectic cheerfulness could not last. There was serious business ahead, as Paterson was well aware:

There will be a sad change when we get on the march again and nearer the enemy.

Sunday, 23 August, witnessed the turning-point, the collision between euphoria and reality. Belgium produced the setting, and the small commercial and industrial town of Mons provided the name, for the first British engagement of the war.

German Cavalry – much feared in the early phase of the war – seen riding out of the Citadel at Ham, Germany. (Q 42054)

On the previous day, the 22nd, Wollocombe's 4th Middlesex was feeling its way somewhat uncertainly towards Mons. Together with his CO, Wollocombe rode on ahead of the battalion, halting several miles short of the town at a village called Mesvin, where they discussed the situation with their advanced guard cavalry commander, Lieutenant Whittle of the 15th Hussars. Whittle had little to impart 'except that our protective cavalry were in touch with the Uhlans who had bolted at the sight of our cavalry and were being followed up.' (This was possibly a case of rumour rather than fact, for the Uhlans, Germany's élite lancer units, were to feature in numerous reports at this time, often when they were seen and somewhat more frequently when they were not – the alarming thought of horsebacked Prussians with plumed helmets erupting at speed over the horizon being in everyone's mind.) Wollocombe found that the Belgian villagers were 'tremendously excited to think that an English battalion was coming through', and judged from the lavishness of their welcome (chocolates were much in evidence, among numerous other gifts) that they were capable of even outdoing the French in hospitality. But the overwhelming civilian mood was one of sheer fear 'at the name of "*Les Allemands*"' – the Germans. '"*Ou sont les Allemands?*" they continually asked us with expressions of terror in their faces.' They would have been even more alarmed, as indeed would Wollocombe and his fellow-officers, had they realized that at that moment the German First Army was, in Cyril Falls' expressive simile, coming south at the British 'like a bull with head down'.

Everybody was aware, however, that the Germans were not far off. Wollocombe waited at Hyon, two miles from Mons, while the CO went off on a further reconnaissance, and when the latter came back for a change of horse and a much-needed meal, he brought yet more stories indicating the presence of enemy outriders in the vicinity:

> We heard that 9 prisoners, Uhlans, had been captured by our Cavalry – one wounded and brought back to a cross roads just in front of one of our Company's Headquarters. We were all very excited about this capture: the first we had heard of – German prisoners, and Uhlans too! However we never saw them.

The next move was to Mons itself, where the 4th Middlesex and their fellow units of 9th Brigade were ordered to take up a defensive line on the north and west flanks of the town:

> This gave us 4 canal bridges and 2 railway level crossings to hold. There were a lot of buildings on our side of the railway which were placed in a state of defence by the RE [Royal Engineers].
>
> We had had a very trying day and were all glad of a night's rest. This was the first night in the open and luckily it was a beautiful one, quite warm and there was not even any dew, which means of course rain; and rain we got the next day. It was not hard, but drizzled all the time from about 6 a.m. to 10 a.m. when the battle of Mons started.

The battle began to the ringing of church bells for Sunday mass; churchgoers were hurrying to worship in their Sunday black as the first

A patrol of 18th Hussars chatting with the local population on the outskirts of Mons attempting to get information about the Germans, 21 August 1914. (Q 83053)

shells flew. 'We were very soon subjected to very heavy shell fire,' wrote Wollocombe, 'but nothing was heard of the enemy's infantry for about 2 or 2½ hours.' It was not until about one o'clock that the German infantry, attacking en masse, appeared in the defenders' sights. They were met by the disciplined rifle-fire of the well-trained British battalions, releasing their bullets at fifteen rounds a minute with a consistency that made the Germans think that they were marching against machine-guns. Such machine-guns as there were – two per battalion – also joined in the affray and, Wollocombe noted, there was 'tremendous execution', but despite this the Germans' attack was making gains:

> We got a message from Brigade Headquarters about 2.15 as follows: 'Did you get my [signal] 46 re destroying bridges. Please inform if they have been destroyed or not.'
>
> The CO dictated the answer which was to the effect that the order had arrived too late and the Germans were already in possession of them. I can remember having a good pull at my water bottle after this message had gone off. It was about the first time in the day that my thoughts had been off the day's work, and I can remember how the sun was shining and how hot I was, and I even had time to think that a battle was a wonderfully exciting thing when it is in progress.

Not far off on the British front, at St Ghislain, the 120th Battery, Royal Field Artillery, was also in action. One of its senior NCOs, Sergeant Albert George, subsequently described the abrupt transformation of a quiet Sunday morning into a scene of violence and destruction in a diary account remarkable for its detail and precision:

> In St Ghislain the people were just going and coming from the different churches and the scene was very peaceful. At 10 a.m. we put our gun in action behind the Mons Canal on a small hill about 500 yards to the right front of the

Town Hall. All the gunners were busy barricading and digging gun-pits and about 11.15 when they were almost finished the order 'Action' came down and everybody went to their different duties and also we were very pleased to have a go at the Germans. About 11.20 a.m. four shells came whizzing through the air and all four dropped in the town terrifying the people who started screaming and running in all directions and a panic started but our presence soothed them a great deal. At 11.30 a.m. our battery opened fire and the war began in earnest.

All the while the German shells were dropping all around us, but they could not at first find our Battery. At 12 noon the Germans found a good target, the town hall and the church spire, and we counted over a dozen holes in the dome of the town hall and half a dozen through the church and as the church was in the middle of the town the Germans could not help hitting a house or something. At about 12 noon also the German infantry were advancing upon us and things were beginning to look unpleasant, as we had to fire alternately at the infantry and guns, as our infantry had not arrived. At about 12.15 the German gunners found our battery and things were beginning to get very hot for us and the shells were dropping all round us but not causing serious damage to us only ploughing up the ground and killing civilians. The Germans were advancing so rapidly that we were firing at the low range of 600 yards and every shell killing dozens as they were advancing in close order. Our Major seeing how things were going kept sending down cheery messages but every man was too intent upon his work to take much notice or feel afraid of the German shells.

At 1.0 p.m. seeing that the only way to save the Battery from being captured or killed our Major ordered us to get ready to retire and at 1.15 p.m. we retired into the town behind the town hall. When we had been in the town about half an hour the civilians began to regain their courage and come out of their houses and shops and they readily gave us wine and sandwiches, fruit, boiled eggs and bread and butter, but we refused most of it as we felt too sick and down-hearted to eat, so we all had a very poor Sunday dinner. Some of the men were drinking beer to try to drown their miseries, but our Captain fell the battery in and threatened to shoot the first man he saw taking wine or beer from the villagers. This order might seem severe, but he said, 'It might be drugged or poisoned and that we must not disgrace the British Army.'

At 2.30 p.m. our Infantry had taken up their position and as the firing had died down somewhat our Major resolved to have another go at the Huns so we went into action again. All that afternoon we kept the Huns at bay although they were about ten to one.

With such odds, however, there could only be one outcome:

We started to retire at 7.0 p.m. with four guns out of six; as we were galloping through the villages infantrymen with ammunition wagons and water carts left them and their horses and ran after our wagons so as to get away as soon as possible. The civilians also were shouting and screaming and running in hundreds and little children were crying piteously, it was an awful ending to an awful day. We thought of Sunday in England and of what our friends were doing and we all envied them.

That night we camped about 11.30 p.m. near Dour but we all slept with

our boots and clothes on and all the horses had their harness on. That night the sky was lit up by many houses which the Huns had set on fire in order to watch our movements.

The remnants of Lieutenant Wollocombe's 4th Middlesex spent the night in a corn-field near Mesvin, from which they had advanced the previous day. In Mesvin itself they had been warmly welcomed by the surviving villagers, despite the fact that they were now marching away from the Germans and not towards them.

Although thirsting for information about 'Les Allemands', they did not forget to produce biscuits, chocolates, water, fruit, bread and all sorts of things for the men, who were retiring, like a beaten army, through their village. They bore no malice.

However, although the BEF had plainly suffered a setback, Wollocombe felt that there were grounds for confidence. The Germans had not had it all their own way, and they had revealed professional weaknesses that could obviously be exploited:

The battle showed that the enemy was not led but driven, and that well-directed fire would mow them down at very little risk to the firers, as they did not aim but shot anyhow and without troubling to put their rifles to their

Soldiers of the German 47th Infantry Regiment, part of Crown Prince Wilhelm's Fifth Army, advancing through north-eastern France, August 1914. (Q 53422)

shoulders; that they had not been taught to use the rifle; that their firing was distinctly erratic, and was one result of their iron discipline, which enabled their officers to drive them on and make them shoot as they went along without them bothering how or where they shot.

The battle also gave the impression that the enemy, although in vastly superior numbers, had very little push or plan of action, and did not try to make any use of cover. If they had had a proper plan they should have pushed us back in a quarter of the time they did, but they simply relied on their weight of numbers, which must have been 9 to 1. In consequence of this and their neglect of cover, they must have lost about 10 to 1 in casualties, and had they not had their artillery to support them, they must have lost 20 or perhaps 30 to 1, for nearly all our casualties were by shell fire. The value of machine-guns was a revelation to all of us, and though ours had done good work, the enemy's had too, and they had lots of them.

Our men, instead of being downcast, were much impressed with the superiority of their rifle fire and extended order manoeuvring over the enemy's fire and movements 'en masse'. The casualties had been awful and the thought of those we had left behind were dreadful, but we knew all along that we should have to retire, and knew that it could not be helped.

Whether ahead of 23 August retirement was considered inevitable by those involved is debatable, but it had undoubtedly become inevitable by the end of that dramatic day. About 1 a.m. on the 24th, Lieutenant-General Sir Archibald Murray, Chief of the General Staff, issued verbal orders to the staff officers of the I and II Corps and of the Cavalry Division, for what was to become famous in history as 'the retreat from Mons'. The verdict of the British official historian is clear and uncompromising: 'No other course was possible; for on the right of the BEF all the French were retiring, and on its left wing there was nothing except for French Territorial division near the coast, also in retreat.'*

*Brigadier-General Sir James E. Edmonds: *A Short History of World War I*, OUP 1951, p. 29 (referred to hereafter as Edmonds, *Short History*).

From Mons to the Aisne

'All ranks are very much depressed owing not only to the fact of continually retiring,' Sergeant William Edgington noted under the date 27 August, 'but at the total lack of any information. We appear to be simply driven blindly back.'

It was Edgington who had recorded that during the euphoric arrival of his Royal Horse Artillery brigade at Le Havre only ten days previously he and his colleagues had been smothered in flowers and kisses. All this must have seemed far in the past as his 1st Cavalry Division began its hurried journey southwards within hours of the conclusion of the encounter at Mons.

> Monday 24th: Moved at daybreak and after what seemed to us wandering aimlessly about the country, came into action (great confusion), lost my cap, teams came up without orders, both my wagons overturned. Retired further back later and took up position at the edge of cornfield and got heavily shelled, difficulty in getting out of action. Big fight this day having had to assist 5th Division who were in difficulties.
>
> Tuesday 25th: A very hot trying day Germans seemed to be all round us. We came into action at 8.00 against Infantry and drove them back, my gun jammed.
>
> Wednesday 26th: Inhabitants fleeing from Germans. Marched early in the morning without orders but were en route to Ligny when we found we were on the flank of a big fight. Came into action against retiring Infantry and did good work.

The 'big fight' referred to under 26 August was the battle of Le Cateau. The British II Corps, acting without orders and on the personal decision of its commander, General Sir Horace Smith-Dorrien, turned on the pursuing enemy and delayed his advance with a vigorous rearguard action which allowed the BEF to make good its escape. Le Cateau was to become a subject of much controversy and was to pave the way for Smith-Dorrien's fall from favour in 1915, but the accepted verdict is that it was a vital as well as a courageous feat of arms. For many of those involved, however, it was one more confusing episode in a period of confusion, but at least losses were being inflicted on the Germans as well as the British. The following is from the description by the Artillery Sergeant, Albert George, of the events of Wednesday 26 August:

> We awoke at dawn eager for the fray and by 9 a.m. we were in action with our brigade but our shells were falling short so our Captain received orders to pick up a new position. At 1.0 p.m. we started for our new position about two miles away and while we were advancing shells and rifle bullets whizzed all round us but our Captain said, 'Follow me men' and we couldn't refuse. We got into action with the 3rd and 4th Divisions about 1.30 p.m. just as the Huns were getting the range on the 6th Battery RFA, several shells of the Huns

**A scene of retreat.
Exhausted Infantrymen
on the march.** (Q 109707)

hitting the guns and wagons and killing most of the gunners. We found that for about two miles to our right and left was British artillery and we knew then it would be an artillery duel. Every gun of our army was firing as fast as possible and by reports we did awful damage but the German guns were 10 to 1 so you can imagine which had the best chance. All our gunners stuck it as long as possible, but we were being gradually beaten by force and numbers.

The battle in progress was more of a nineteenth- than a twentieth-century one in that it was fought virtually on an open field with guns in view of guns – a phenomenon that was soon to disappear, indeed had already officially disappeared, from the artillery textbooks. Meanwhile the participants had an extensive view of the action in a manner reminiscent of the battles of the Napoleonic Wars or the Crimea. This is also from George's account, a passage which reaches beyond vivid description towards accusation of outright panic on the part of some of the British side:

We could see ammunition wagons trying to replenish getting about half-way to the gun, then a couple of shells would burst blowing the drivers and horses to smithereens, it was a terrible sight but the last two days had made us used to it. About 3.30 p.m. the Germans were advancing upon us so rapidly that the General Staff could see it was useless trying to stop the furious advance, so a General Retirement was ordered and it was every man for himself. The retirement was a scandalous sight in the History of Britain, but it will never be published. In our hurry to get away guns, wagons, horses, wounded men were left to the victorious Germans and even our *British Infantrymen* were throwing away their rifles, ammunition, equipment and running *like hell* for their lives, mind you not one Infantryman was doing this, but thousands, and not one Battery running away, but the whole of the British Expeditionary Force that took part in the Battle of that fatal Wednesday 26 Aug at Le Cateau.

The retreat continued, lack of sleep, lack of orders and general confusion turning the process into a sustained nightmare. This is from an account written for his parents by Lieutenant Rowland Owen, 2nd Battalion The Duke of Wellington's Regiment:

The march to St Quentin was a marvellous sight – everybody completely exhausted – staff officers and generals asleep bent double in motors – men asleep over horse's necks and on wagons and on limbers and all along the roadside – personally I slept on the march and kept crashing into the corporal in front at any checks. When eventually a halt was called, before we got strung out again, I went plumb asleep, I was woken by someone shouting 'fall in'; so I fell in; and after marching a short way I began to wake up to the fact that things were a bit strange, and I found I was with the Middlesex Reg – quite a different division.

Captain A. H. Habgood, RAMC, with the 3rd Field Ambulance, 3rd Division, also kept a detailed diary of the retreat which confirms the sense of confusion and fatigue suggested by Lieutenant Owen:

I was dog-tired, half asleep and dreaming at times; the reality of the event became obscured; only the physical discomfort was apparent and uppermost in my mind; I felt that we should soon have to chuck it and go home to tea.

There was a general absence of orders; many officers and detachments asked us the way to their units; we did not know, and the only answer we got from the staff officers we encountered was 'Get on', so we followed the rest.

Caught up in the retreating tide were thousands of Belgians and French desperately trying to escape, with what belongings they could carry by hand or pile on carts. They could be a considerable hazard if their shambling progress coincided with outbreaks of fighting. 'The civilians created a deuce of a discord every time a volley was fired or a shell burst near,' Sergeant Bert Reeve noted on 25 August, though he admitted they had some reason for their panic; 'it certainly was a bit startling what with the noise of battle and the shouting and the searchlights and houses on fire.' But the pathetic aspect of their situation was evident too and created much sympathy among the British. 'It would make you weep', Sapper Hugh Bellew noted under 27 August, 'to see the refugees who have lost everything trekking along, little children and women crying.'

Inexorably the retreat went on. This is from Sergeant Reeve's entry for Sunday 30 August, one week after Mons:

March, march, march, all the blessed day. Halt! dismount – mount, and then dismount. Halted long enough to get the water for tea, all but boiling and then of course we get the order to shift. The irony of the thing was that after going half a mile we halted for an hour at a spot where we couldn't make tea. The infantry were falling out in dozens and we put as many on our vehicles as

possible, making our own men walk. It was a terrible hot day, the hottest we have had so far. Circled round the town of Soissons, which looks a big place from what I could see of it from the heights above it. We camped in a cornfield about two miles W of the town. Had our breakfast, dinner and tea combined, after which I had a three days shave and a sponge bath. At 10 p.m. got the right side of a good stew and went to bed alongside a hay stack.

Opposite: Soldiers of the XI Hussars resting in the Forêt d'Ermenouville, 2 September 1914. Captain the Hon. C. Mulholland in the foreground. (Q 51224)

As August ended and still the retirement continued Sergeant Edgington and his RHA comrades were rapidly becoming dispirited:

September 1: All ranks grumbling about the suppression of information. We know that we are marching towards Paris covering the retreat of the whole army, and we hear such rumours as 'The French have shifted the Govt. to Bordeaux', 'Our base has been shifted to Nantes', which all seems to point to disorder and all we get from the officers is that the mythical French Cavalry Corps should now be here, but nothing ever turns up.

Horses are now beginning to suffer from the want of proper rations and continued marching, sore backs and breasts getting very prevalent.

In fact the rumour regarding the French government was one day ahead of events; it left for Bordeaux on 2 September. The idea of falling back on Nantes also had substance, in that Sir John French had become so concerned for his force that he had proposed to remove it westward and re-embark it not at Nantes but at the neighbouring port of St Nazaire and had had to be deterred from doing so by a personal visit to the Commander-in-Chief's headquarters by the Secretary of State for War, Lord Kitchener. French had been firmly reminded of his duty to his Allies as well as to his own army; there was no question of its being withdrawn from the field, certainly not at a time of such high tension and danger.

In fact, the enemy's advance was about to lose its vigour and to rein in to the north of Paris, while the French, with some help from the BEF, were to deliver the crucial setback to Germany's plans known to history as the Battle of the Marne. The invading force found itself not attacking but attacked; outmanoeuvred, and with its men suffering increasingly from fatigue, the German military leadership now found it was their turn to order a retreat. On 6 September Sergeant Edgington noted, with evident relief:

March at 9 a.m. East: great joy in the change of direction after continually marching South.

Sergeant Reeve recorded the event in more matter-of-fact terms:

Sun. 6 Sept. Moved off at 5 a.m. Scheme changed and we are now advancing on to German flank, whose front has been changed to meet the 5th French Army. We came across them about 11 a.m. and came into action. Believe we have done very well.

Captain Paterson's diary for this period gives a brisk but inevitably confused impression of the battle as seen from the point of view of a battalion in perpetual movement. He also noted an early instance of a phenomenon which would be replicated many times in the months ahead, casualties from 'friendly fire':

> Wednesday, 9 September: Battle of the Marne. Push off again to take the Bridge at Nogent, which after some delay we find to be unoccupied by enemy.
>
> Our Cavalry, which is already across the river, is fired on by RA [Royal Artillery] – silly asses. It is quite obvious they are not the enemy. Advance again North. Sound of large battle on our left, i.e. West. We find eighteen Cavalry[men] wounded by our guns. The officer of RA responsible ought to be shot in my opinion. We move North and still North and finally bivouac at Le Thoulet. All the villages are broken and signs of the retreating enemy are met with everywhere. Dead horses, graves, etc. Nasty sights. An occasional hole where a shell has dropped with perhaps some blood about it. Ugh! There is a certain amount of fighting with our advance guards and the Germans and we see ambulances coming back full of wounded. However, one is accustomed to such sights. Thursday, 10 September. Get off at 8 a.m., raining, very nasty. Get news at 10.30 that the Germans, who are retiring from West to North-East, are crossing our front and we push on. Our divisional cyclists come in for it and are shelled at 1,000 yards. Several killed and wounded, about twenty. General Findlay, CRA [Commander Royal Artillery], 1st Division, hit on the head by shrapnel bullet, was not dead when last we heard.
>
> Push on and come nasty close to high explosive German shells about the village of Priez, where we halt.
>
> Orders then come to move to Sommelmans and billet, which we do. Find on arrival that the interpreters have given us a very good meal.
>
> Just before turning in comes news of General Findlay's death. Poor fellow.

The Battle of the Marne, in the words of the official historian, 'was the great turning-point of the war. It made a German victory impossible. Our enemy had lost the benefit of getting his blow in first by means of superior speed of mobilization and rapidity of advance through neutral territory. Such an advance could never recur; he might gain a compromise peace; but he could never win.' For a brief time, indeed, it seemed as if victory might be there for the grasping, that the Germans might be forced back over their frontiers only weeks after they had left them. But to the north of the valley of the Marne lay the valley of the Aisne, with commanding heights on its northern bank the defensive potential of which the Germans could not fail to see. They dug themselves in and turned to await the Allied advance, and for a few short weeks a form of siege warfare was adopted by both sides which became, as it turned out, a foreshadowing of events to come. What was to be known as the Battle of the Aisne was, in essence, a dress rehearsal for the war of the trenches, and it was loathed from the moment it began by all participants. This was not the kind of war for which they had joined the colours; it was squalid, it was bloody, and it left grim reminders of the horror of what was happening in places from which they could not be decently removed. 'At 4 a.m. I relieved the Guards in their trenches,' wrote Captain Harry Dillon, a company commander of the 2nd Battalion Oxfordshire and Buckinghamshire Light Infantry, on 18 September; 'hundreds of German dead and wounded lie in thick clusters within a few yards but we cannot come out and collect them.'

The new style of warfare also entailed the maintaining of hastily prepared fixed positions in which men were peculiarly vulnerable to artillery fire (gunners had all the time in the world to register on their targets) or to attacks by snipers, so that they could be 'killed in action' when doing nothing more offensive than cleaning a rifle or writing a letter home. Captain Paterson inveighed angrily on Sunday 20 September:

> We sit still in our trenches. Every now and then a man is knocked out with nothing to shoot at. One does not mind losing men when one is doing something, but to sit still and be knocked over one by one without seeing a soul is trying.

And on Thursday 24 September:

> If I am to be killed let it be in the heat and rush of an advance and not by a dirty sniper who waits his chance for perhaps hours.

A daily ration of three to four hours of shell fire was not uncommon, as Lieutenant Rowland Owen reported in a letter of the same date. He added:

> When I get home I hope you will not take it amiss if I dive under the sofa when the servants slam the attic door, or fall down flat in New Street when I hear an errand boy whistling, as these things are rather apt to get on one's nerves. I find the danger of these shells is that when one does at long last come under a bit of rifle fire, in one's delight one treats it as child's play, although it must be far more dangerous. Some of the enemy are only about sixty yards away from our position, and the rest about 300 yards. There are snipers all over the place, in the woods and up trees; and they carry on a hearty old shoot all day.

In some units morale was plummeting. Sergeant T. H. Cubbon of the 15th Hussars noted on 3 October:

> Stood to at 3.30 relieved by C Company at 5.30. Then went into dugouts again. Rations ¼ loaf, piece of cheese and 1 lb jam to 6 men. Can't get a drop of water, it's terrible as there is nothing to drink not even when we are in the wood. The position beginning to make every one feel fed up. Have been here since 14 Sept, 20 days, and there seems to be no change of position. Have already had men shooting themselves, including Capt. G------, Dr S------, Pte M----. Stayed in dugouts until dark. Then went into trenches as last night. From 1 o'clock had 3 hours heavy artillery and rifle fire poured into us.

The enemy was now a near neighbour. Thus Captain Dillon, also on 3 October:

> I went out the other night a little way and one could hear them talking quite close. I could not see them from my place as there is a slight rise in front but where I am tomorrow I am only 500 yards off and amuse myself having pots at them if they put up their heads. If they pot back I can walk along the bottom of the trench a little further on.

The fighting on the Marne and the Aisne meant much work for the Royal Army Medical Corps. In the first stage of the Aisne battle Captain A. H. Habgood's 9th Field Ambulance entered the village of Vailly and found a church full of wounded. What he saw drew from him a grim and vivid description:

> Inside the church which was lit by candles, there were about two hundred men lying upon straw and mattresses of all sorts; they lay in the aisles, the chancel, the lady chapel and the altar steps.
>
> Rifles and equipment were stacked in the porch, and the 'lightly' wounded sat in groups on church chairs, placidly eating, drinking and smoking; in tattered khaki with dirty faces and scrubbly beards they looked like scarecrows.
>
> Most of the wounds had been caused by shells and some of the men had been hit a day or two before they could be brought in; their wounds were already festering, and the air of the church was bitter with the sickening stench of gangrene.
>
> Many of the men were quiet, but some were shouting in delirium; others groaning, praying, cursing and crying monotonously for water and morphia.

Time did not endear the area of the Aisne to the British, even though there were frequent doldrum stretches without much action. Trenches were not what this war was meant to be about. Captain Arthur Maitland, 2nd Battalion Essex Regiment, wrote to his 'dear M. & F.' on 30 September:

> I spent my day and night in a trench. I have got a hole, partly burrowed out and partly roofed over with branches, just big enough to lie down, it is rather monotonous. I get out for meals but I have to be with my guns day and night as we are in the most forward trench waiting for the attack that never comes, as a matter of fact I think our position is too strong for the Germans' liking, they shell us constantly but we laugh at them from our burrows like rabbits. I couldn't tell you why we are fixed like this but we shall be very glad when we move forward again as this cave life is not to our liking.

On the same day Lieutenant Owen wrote to his parents in remarkably similar terms:

> We are now living in a wood in little rabbit scratches, roofed over with straw – I am getting terribly sick of it.

Equally scathing was Captain Harry Dillon. When his division finally moved away in mid October he dismissed the Aisne trenches with the telling understatement:

> Anyhow it is not the sort of place you would have selected for a honeymoon.

Casualty of the Great Retreat

The Retreat from Mons left many men behind; stragglers, the exhausted or those who were overtaken while carrying out their duties. In the last category was Frederick Thornton, a Staff Sergeant in the Army Ordnance Corps, attached to the 1st Battalion Loyal North Lancashire Regiment in 1st Division. He was working on regimental equipment at a place called Morbaix when he was advised to leave, as the Germans were expected to occupy the village in a few hours. 'I did not believe it,' he later admitted. 'I stayed on, and the result was that the Germans arrived before the end of the day, and there was no time to clear out.' He decided, however, not to surrender, but to go into hiding in the hope of escaping to continue his war.

On 29 September 1914 a letter was sent to his wife from Red Barracks, Woolwich, signed by the Officer in charge of Army Ordnance Corps Records, in reply to an enquiry posted by her the day before. Its key sentence read:

Madam,

I beg to acknowledge the receipt of your communication of the 28th instant, and in reply I regret to inform you that a report has been received from the British Expeditionary Force to the effect that your husband No. 1011 Armourer Staff Sgt. F. R. Thornton, Army Ordnance Corps (attached 1st Bn. Loyal North Lancs Regt) is reported as 'missing'.

Mrs Thornton heard no more for many months. In the absence of information to the effect that her husband had become a prisoner of war, it was assumed that he was dead. She was already in possession of her widow's pension papers when on 28 May 1915 she received a telegram originating from Rotterdam with the brief message: 'Safe. Fred.'

Her husband, with a Corporal from the same unit, had been befriended by a French farming family named Legrand, and had escaped through Belgium to neutral Holland with the aid of the network associated with Prince Réginald and Princess Marie de Croy, one of the two escape organizations which functioned at this time in collaboration with Nurse Edith Cavell. From there he returned to England where he was able to resume his army career. Before leaving the farm he wrote an account of his various adventures since Mons which he left with the Legrands, the intention being that they should send it to his wife to England at the end of the war. If the escape were successful it would be superfluous; if on the other hand Thornton failed to get through, in particular if he lost his life in the attempt, the letter would tell his story. The following is an abbreviated version of the letter which was written on 28 April:

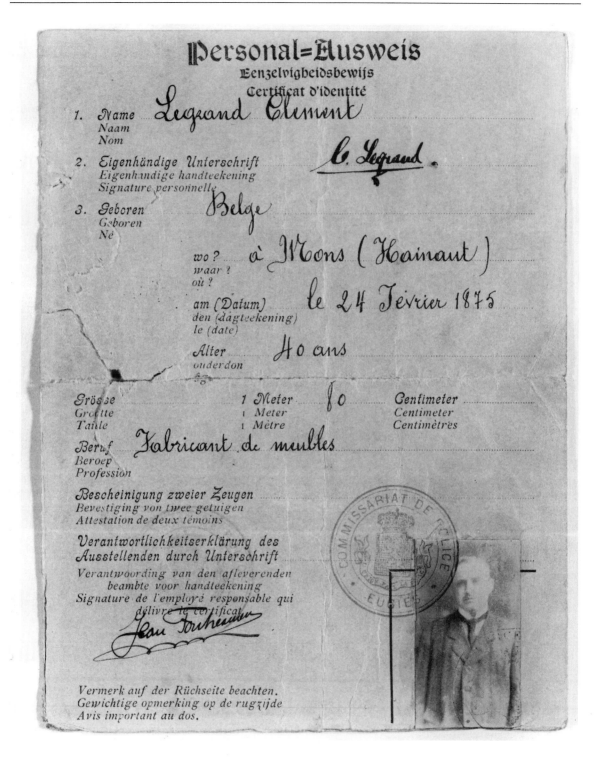

The false identity document issued to Clement Legrand, furniture maker and native of Mons, aged 40; alias Staff Sergeant Frederick Thornton of the British Expeditionary Force, aged 33. (HU 63277A)

My own dearest wife

It is just eight months since we came to this house. A lot of our troops have been cut off the same as us. These people have been so good to us. But the anxiety has been very great. I am always thinking of the Baby and you, and praying that you are all right. About two months after we came here an English lady came to see us. She lives about a mile from here. They have done all they can for us and let us have some books to read. We thought the War would have been over by this time. Since we came here we have learned to speak a little French and can now well understand what they tell us. The Germans are all around us, a lot of them have been staying in the next village to us. It is an anxious time for the people we are staying with as if we were caught here they would burn the farm, and the poor old people would be severely punished.

When we first came here we used to go out in the fields for walks and sometimes into the villages. Once we went to a village, and were looking at a German motor lorry that had broken down and had been left there when some Germans came through on bicycles. The foolish people in the village very nearly gave us away by staring at us. Of course we were not in uniform. When we saw them we walked quietly away, and got back safe. Another time we were in a house, and some Germans drove up in a motor car and we escaped out of the back and over the fields. The Germans got to know that there were some English and French soldiers still in the villages, and they made a proclamation saying the people were not to have us in their houses or to give us anything to eat, and they came and searched a lot of houses. Two poor soldiers of the Connaught Rangers that had been wounded and were staying in Hospital in this village had to leave. That was in November. The poor fellows had nowhere to go. These people put them up for two nights and then they went and stopped in a hut in the fields. We used to take them over their food. Soon after this (3 Dec) the Germans got to know about us, and we had to clear. Somebody must have given us away, for they asked in the village for the farm of M. Legrand and five of them came along on motor bikes, but instead of coming here they stopped at a house about 200 yards away, and there happened to be four French soldiers there having their breakfast. In the meantime we had gone, and stopped in a little hut that was used for duck shooting close to a river. We stayed there ten days without budging, and these people brought us our food. We had no fire, but a spirit stove so did not do so bad for we had plenty to eat with hot milk and coffee. When things had quietened down we came back to the farm, and have been like prisoners ever since, we only go out when it is dark, and have to hide every time anyone comes to the house.

We have heard from the English people of a chance that may turn out well, and that is to go through Belgium and over the frontier into Holland. They say a lot of English soldiers have got back to England that way, so we are going to try our luck. We have to go from here through the Forest of Mormal and into Belgium, where we go to a house and they get us passports and take a photo which they use for the passport. Then we go through Mons and Brussels, it is about sixty miles from here to Brussels, and then we go north till we get over the frontier into Holland. It is very dangerous but we must chance it. We have people go with us as guides on different stages of the journey. I pray we shall be successful. If so you will have heard from me ere this reaches you, if not I hope that the worst that will happen is that we shall be treated as prisoners of war.

The old people told us we could stop here till the war ended, but it is too dangerous, we might be given away any day. They have been extremely good to us, never been short of food or tobacco. They are going to post this letter after the war is over, and then you can tell them the news. I have only had 10 shillings pay since I left England, so you can send them something out of the pay I have to come. God knows they deserve something for all they have done for us.

So now my love, I think I have told you all. I am reserving the postscript to let you know the date I start on the journey to try and reach you. And now I conclude (Let Father and all know) God Bless you. I pray the day will soon come when I shall be with you. *With all my love to you and Baby*, and all my prayers. Always and for ever your loving and devoted

XXXXXXXXXXXXXX Husband Fred

The letter was given to a staff officer in the 32nd Division in November 1918; as it happens the covering note posted with it was dated 11 November, Armistice Day. By then the Legrands had received a message from Thornton from England so it was known that he had in fact returned safe home. Thornton's letter is a tribute not only to his own courage but to that of the French family which ran great risks in giving him and his comrade help and sustenance while under enemy occupation.

First Ypres and Entrenchment

On 10 October Captain James Paterson noted in his diary 'the curious thing that we have been given maps of the North-West of France and South of Belgium and that we have been asked whether we have sufficient horses to move our Transport.' This raised an encouraging prospect. 'I wonder if we shall move to Belgium. I hope so, as we are all sick of this village and valley and neighbourhood.' The time would come when certain parts of Belgium and North-West France would have a far more sinister reputation than was ever attached to the region of the Aisne, and the names of places such as Ypres, Armentières, Arras and Albert would resound in British history long after those associated with the first experience of trench warfare had been largely forgotten. The British were in fact about to enter into what was to become their special sector of the Western Front, but in October 1914 this was hidden in the future and Flanders seemed to offer fresher fields.

The possibility of a change of ground had already been recorded two days previously by Sergeant Edgington, with a remarkably accurate statement of the basic reason:

> There seems to be no doubt that we are moving to the left flank to anticipate the Germans who are supposed to be making a dash for the coast.

The fact was that neither the Germans nor the Allies had been content with the stalemate on the Aisne. It was plainly absurd to settle into an attritional slogging-match in one sector when open ground beckoned on either side, particularly in the strategically important areas to the north and west. The result was what was to become known as the 'Race to the Sea', but which was in essence a determined attempt by each side to outflank the other, with the Germans making the initial moves and a halt being called only when the Channel coast prevented further deployment.

With hindsight it can be seen that, unless one side managed an outright victory, the end product of all this would simply be stalemate on a grander scale – a log-jam, as it were, from the coast to the Franco-Swiss frontier – but it took several weeks before this became apparent. These weeks took a high toll. At the end of them the BEF of 1914 had almost ceased to exist, while the French, who bore more of the brunt of the fighting than the British, and the Germans had suffered equally appalling losses. Germany, sensing that her golden opportunity was slipping away, flung untrained volunteer regiments, many of them raised from young students, into the battle; ardent but ill-led, they advanced *en masse* in the manner which had so amazed the British at Mons. The following is from a diary written by an Infantry private, H. J. Milton, probably of the 2nd Battalion, Highland Light Infantry, during the first days of what was to become known as the First Battle of Ypres:

The so-called 'Race to the Sea': XI Hussars on the march north-west from the Aisne, in the Doullens district, 9 October 1914. (Q 51150)

British Field Artillery on the move near Ypres, 1914. An image of dash in an area soon to be associated with deadlock. (Q 60750)

Thurs 22 Oct: The enemy charged about 7 or 8 p.m. after they had fired a big farm next to our trench, to show us up and help them direct their fire. After it got ablaze they charged up to within 50 yards of our firing line and we simply mowed them down, our fire was terrific during this time, the enemy were simply running into death, they gave great yells after they started but very few got back as far as we could make out. The screams were terrible.

Captain Harry Dillon's 2nd Oxford and Bucks Light Infantry faced the same attack; two days later he described it for his family:

It came with a suddenness that was the most startling thing I have ever known. A great grey mass of humanity was charging, running for all God would let them, straight on to us not 50 yards off. Everybody's nerves were pretty well on edge as I had warned them what to expect, and as I fired my rifle the rest all went off almost simultaneously. One saw the great mass of Germans quiver. In reality some fell, some fell over them, and others came on. I have never shot so much in such a short time, could not have been more than a few seconds and they were down.

Then the whole lot came on again and it was the most critical moment of my life. Twenty yards more and they would have been over us in thousands, but our fire must have been fearful, and at the very last moment they did the most foolish thing they possibly could have done. Some of the leading people turned to the left for some reason, and they all followed like a great flock of sheep. I don't think one could have missed at the distance and just for one short minute or two we poured the ammunition into them in boxfuls. My rifles were red hot at the finish.

The firing died down and out of the darkness a great moan came. People with their arms and legs off trying to crawl away; others who could not move gasping out their last moments with the cold night wind biting into their broken bodies and the lurid red glare of a farm house showing up clumps of grey devils killed by the men on my left further down. A weird awful scene; some of them would raise themselves on one arm or crawl a little distance, silhouetted as black as ink against the red glow of the fire.

At this time Captain James Paterson's South Wales Borderers were at Langemarck to the north of Ypres, where they witnessed similar mass attacks and wrought the same terrible havoc. 'They get simply cut to pieces,' he noted on the 22nd, 'and then up come more. Their casualties can't last, that is one thing.' Then later that day there was a development of a different kind; the launch of a sustained attempt by German artillery to wipe Langemarck from the map. The battalion's headquarters – where Paterson, as Adjutant, was based – had been in the town, but sensing a heavy bombardment coming on they moved to the open country in the rear. Steadily the German bombardment intensified. Deeper into the war, destruction of the kind Paterson then recorded would become common-place, but in these early months it could seem a dreadful vandalism:

There we sat and saw the total destruction of the village. The Germans went for the church spire until the whole church was in flames and falling to pieces, and then they turned their attention to the rest of the town and simply blew it to pieces. I went in the evening to see it. Practically every house ruined and all round the church on fire. A wonderfully awful sight in the night with the church one glowing mass and showers of sparks coming up as some house fell in somewhere in the town. There was absolutely no reason for the continued bombardment. Of course, if we use buildings we can't expect to keep their shells off them; but this was such wanton destruction. They went at the church and continued at it long after the spire, which of course might have had one of our Artillery or observation officers in it, was blown away. Up to a very late hour they went at it, and now the nice little place is simply one ruin. We moved all the inhabitants out on the night of the 21st, but the poor cows and pigs suffered a lot. What a war!

Saturday, 24 October. Bombardment continuing all day. Last night the French 17th Division relieved our 2nd Division on our right. I suppose the 2nd Division is wanted to help on our extreme left, which I believe is hard pressed.

All the prisoners we have taken have been either old men or boys of fifteen to twenty. They can't have a man left in Germany now, I should think. And to think that we haven't started with all our hundreds of thousands which are in the making. They are beaten I am sure; they must be beaten, and I have no doubt that they will be beaten properly.

Paterson's last diary entries are under this date, 24 October; he was wounded while carrying orders for his CO on 29 October, and died on 1 November, becoming one more statistic in the long casualty lists of 1914.

To the south of Ypres Sergeant Edgington's RHA Battery had been engaged with the enemy on and off since arriving from the Aisne. 'Came into action early, E of Messines-Wytschaete Road,' he had written on 16 October, adding the choice detail (he had served in India): 'The natives from the houses just in rear of the guns kept us supplied with hot soup and coffee, in exchange for which we gave them all our empty cartridge cases.' But at that stage the Germans seemed to be short of guns, 'so between whiles we ran races etc. to enliven things up a bit.' By the end of the month, however, there was no need for athletics to keep the gunners in fighting trim. On the 30th, now further north at St Eloi, he wrote:

A very violent cannonade started early in the morning from the enemy, and all our guns were firing on different targets. About midday the 129th started to retire through our guns, and the 5th Lancers having been shelled out of their trenches, the whole brigade was ordered back, my section remaining in action all night close in front of St Eloi. We lost about 1½ miles of ground. The London Scottish were billeted in the village having been brought up by motor buses.

This account reveals much about the parlous condition of the BEF at this time. The London Scottish was a Territorial battalion – a unit of former part-time soldiers sent to France for non-combatant purposes it was now poised to go into action [see p. 30]. The 5th Lancers was a regiment of Cavalry, fighting in trenches as dismounted infantry.

Captain Valentine Fleming, Member of Parliament, was serving as a squadron commander with another Cavalry regiment, the Queen's Own Oxfordshire Hussars, which found itself required to play a similar role. So far their time in France had been little more than a 'tour of the

principal French watering places', followed by a fortnight hanging about Dunkirk and St Omer ('*very* dull'), but all this was abruptly changed. Fleming (father of the writers Peter and Ian Fleming) described what happened next in a letter to a fellow officer in England:

> On 30 Oct. at 4.30 p.m. raining like hell and v. cold we were told to saddle up and move off at 6, we got off at 6.30, marched all night to Neuve Eglise, 35 miles, had a hurried breakfast and were put at 8.30 a.m. on the 31st to dig a line of reserve trenches behind Messines. (They produced spades, picks etc. from somewhere.) Then De Lisle [in command of the 1st Cavalry Division] appeared and told us to advance up the hill and occupy a line of trenches on the right of Messines. This was disagreeable as projectiles of every variety were exploding with a disquieting regularity all over the ground of our advance. We also had to leave our coats and tools. Off we went, over some very holding ground, three squadrons in a succession of rushes in extended lines, the regularity of which was soon disturbed by the wire! (Never move without nippers on the Sam Browne belt!) *Luckily* we had no one hit – I can't think why – which put some heart into the men. On arriving at the indicated position we found only trenches for one squadron, the other two lay about in the open scratching themselves in with bayonets. We had 4 or 5 wounded, and lay there, getting occasional blows off at Gs, at about 800 yards off, under a really *very* heavy fire, only luckily all the shrapnel burst just behind us, and the B. Marys just in front, so though *horribly* frightened, we weren't hurt. There we stopped (*v. hungry*) till 11 p.m. We couldn't move about to get food as they had two Maxims nosing on our line of retirement pretty continuously till dark. When relieved we were given 1 hrs rest and then put on a Barricade in Messines with the 4th DGs [Dragoon Guards] and the 18th Hussars. This

A long way from home: Indian troops at the First Battle of Ypres. A contingent of 129th Baluchis in the vicinity of the Hollebeke Château, near Ypres, 28 October 1914. (Q 56324; photograph by General Gough)

The London Scottish were the first Territorials to see action. On 31 October with the vaguest of orders and no preparation they charged the enemy near Messines. 'Battalion mustered about 300 strong' wrote Private Sam Ross in his pocket diary. '800 went up. It's bitter.' The photograph, in which Ross is indicated by an arrow, shows one of the depleted companies marching to La Clytte, where the battalion finally mustered some 350 short of its final strength. (Q 56313)

was frightening, all the houses were burning, the Gs. were only about 500 yards away, and had a gun with which they kept blowing shrapnel at the Barricade, but it was a stout obstacle.

As cavalrymen they had little acquaintance with infantry weapons, their own speciality, the sabre, being distinctly unserviceable in the novel situation in which they now found themselves:

They kept pooping away at our squadrons on the left of the Barricade with rifles, and coming v. close under the smoke, so we began to wonder how to fix the bloody bayonets with which we had been issued two days previously!! However, we were relieved at 4.30 a.m. and marched back about two miles to get breakfast, *v.* hungry and sleepy. Just as the dinners were boiling De Lisle appeared, told us that the line had been broken between the Carabiniers and the London Scottish, and that we must counter-attack! This bloody prospect almost made us sick, however still with empty bellies we began plodding up the usual wire-enclosed ploughed fields on the left of Messines, being pooped at by *very* high and wild rifle fire, till we found the troops on our left halted and those on our right coming out of Messines, and the whole line fell back about ½ a mile under *v.* heavy rifle and Maxim fire.

It was a very trying day for the men, they were d———d hungry, cold, and kept seeing wounded men come hopping back, bleeding and howling, and swearing the Gs. had broken through (which they very nearly did).

The line held, just, but Messines and its Ridge had been taken, and would remain in German hands for the next two and a half years.

The fighting was at its fiercest, however, in the vicinity of Ypres itself. The Germans had entered the town on 13 October, extracted money with menaces but had not stayed; the next day the British occupied it, and now the Germans wanted it back. The harder they pressed, the more determined the Allies became to thwart them.

The British 7th Division, under Major-General Thomas Capper, not long arrived from England, found itself immediately involved in the defence of Ypres along the axis of what would soon become the notorious Menin road. Major F. S. Garwood, Royal Engineers, commanding 7th Signal Company, kept a day-by-day account of the Division's baptism of fire:

Saturday 31 October: A very fierce attack on the Gheluvelt part of the position. Shelling exceedingly heavy all day. The GOC [General Officer Commanding] went early to his new day headquarters, where it was only possible to maintain communication by Motor-Cyclist Despatch riders. Our part of the line appeared to be holding well, when at 1.30 p.m. alarming messages began to come in from the north of Gheluvelt: that part of the line was falling back. In accordance with orders received, in the absence of General Capper, General Jackson CRA [the Artillery Commander of the Division] withdrew the 7th Div. HQ some 3 kilometres back to Hellfire Corner, where we took up our quarters in a little estaminet. Large numbers of wounded were coming in to Ypres down the Menin road, along which there passed a steady stream of vehicles, consisting of our heavy batteries and our first line transport. Beside the little estaminet were the recent graves of five French officers who had been killed by shells.

At dusk two German officers (one wounded in the jaw) were brought in as prisoners. One officer pretended that he had been told that we shot all our prisoners, which shows what lies the Germans spread among their troops. It appears that two fresh Corps have been launched against us, the Kaiser being determined that Ypres must be captured at all costs. News came that the British had advanced with great gallantry, as it was growing dark, and had driven the Germans out of the woods at the point of the bayonet, recapturing most of their lost trenches.

We spent a very uncomfortable night. I slept on the hard floor of the back room with my head on a sergeant's boots.

For Captain Harry Dillon, days merged into a confused blur as the desperate fighting continued. 'I am glad you have kept my letters,' he wrote, when he finally managed a word to his family on 4 November, 'as it is impossible to keep a diary, and if alive I should like to look through them later and write up the gaps. We have not had our clothes off or washed or a regular sleep since the 21st. Just fighting like hell, then lie down and sleep to wake up and fight again or find rations have been issued, or to hurry off elsewhere.'

'Elsewhere' now meant the vicinity of that same Menin road, where the 2nd Oxford and Bucks were involved in the kind of bayonet fighting in the woods referred to by Major Garwood. Dillon's account continued:

As soon as it was light the Germans opened with all guns, lots of men were buried in their trenches but were got out and into others, and remarkably little damage was done; but at about 3 p.m. to my horror I saw X [*sic*, a reference to the next battalion] retiring. This was the absolute devil as it meant I had to get out and rush along and report. They told me to retire and try to stop the Germans getting past a certain road. From then on it was awful; as soon as we left the trenches they opened on us with every gun and rifle, we got back however, neither of my officers was hit and I got the new position and collected about 150 men. Things looked real nasty as the Germans by this time were pouring through the gap and filling the wood we were in.

Under the circumstances I thought that to do something unexpected might upset their apple-cart, so fixed bayonets and went straight in; we soon came across them and had the finest fight that ever was fought. I make no pretence at liking the ordinary battle, and anybody who says they do is a liar; but this was quite different. We first came on some fifty of the grey swine, went straight in and annihilated them. We were very quickly into the next lot and in a few minutes we were shooting, bayonetting and annihilating everything we came across. To cut a long story short, we drove the whole crowd back and by 2 a.m. were back in our trenches again. Five holes in my coat as a souvenir, but only twenty-three of my company left. This fight has done me more good than I can say. Another forty came in later.

Sixty-three survivors out of the 136 with which he had begun the action meant a loss of over fifty per cent, but such figures make even more depressing reading when, as Dillon pointed out in his account, his company's normal full strength should have been 240.

'The 18th consecutive day of this terrific struggle,' wrote Major Garwood on 5 November. 'The infantry have had no rest and nobody to relieve them in the trenches. All day they have been under incessant and accurate shell fire and the Infantry of the Division have lost nearly all their officers and 75% of their men. The Signal Company has had extraordinary good fortune as we have only lost two men killed. But eighteen horses have been killed and one cable wagon and two light spring wagons have been lost.' But there was positive news as well:

A captured order states that on 30 October the German Emperor informed Three Army Corps that Ypres must be taken at all costs. Ypres has not been taken and it does not now look as if it will be.

The German effort was not yet finished – there was a determined attack by the Prussian Guards on 11 November, during which they broke through north of the Menin road and at one time had little between them and Ypres except a line of British guns. 'Everybody in a panic, running away, leaving rifles, equipment, everything,' noted Sergeant T. M. Cubbon, but despite this his regiment held: '15th Hussars charged those who broke through and drove them back.' This was the last high point of the German effort; the crisis passed, though there were certain desultory engagements over the following days and the battle would not be officially closed down until 22 November.

Now it was a case of digging in and waiting for the next season. Such

Entrenchment: Men of the 2nd Scots Guards digging trenches, Armentières area, late 1914. (Q 57380)

trenches as they had were sketchy, often badly sited, and almost everywhere waterlogged. Flanders fields had proved no better than those of the Aisne. In fact, they were a great deal worse. 'It's a filthy district this,' wrote Captain Fleming discouragingly to his fellow officer, who was shortly due to join the regiment, 'huge flat ploughed fields, very relaxing, and the mud!!! No possibility of exercise and we are all getting as fat as butter. It's deadly dull sitting in the trenches and it's all my eye about their comfort. At least any that we have been in are perfectly loathsome.' His overall view was pithily put: 'Console yourself with the reflection that it may be bloody in Britain but it's positively *fucking* in France.' He concluded:

> Well, old lad, don't hurry to come out, you can have my share of the glory for 1 Turkish bath, 1 game of squash and 1 good slosh after an old Jack Puss with my Bassets.

There had been much talk of the war being over by Christmas but it was now increasingly obvious that much more time would be required – and many more men. Ever since August under the inspiration of Lord Kitchener a vast new volunteer army had been in the making in Britain. How necessary this force would be for the winning of the war was eloquently acknowledged by another Cavalry officer, Captain E. W. S. Balfour, Adjutant of the 5th Dragoon Guards, in a letter of 3 December:

> There is not much left of the old Army and the new Campaign is going to be fought and won by a great half-trained National Army – where you've got to take what you can get and not laugh at people for being a certain class or making fools of themselves. But if the old Army is going to be worth its salt and remain the backbone of the show, it's got without jealousy and in humbleness to allow itself to be absorbed into a less efficient whole, and have amateurs put over them and see daily laughable mistakes and old lessons relearnt in bitterness and go on helping without superior bearing. Anyone who doesn't recognize the above is not either rising to the occasion or anything but a self-satisfied self-seeker. We've all got to simply sacrifice anything for an *esprit d'armée*. The end of the war will depend on it.

Killed in Action at First Ypres

Lieutenant Neville Woodroffe, 1st Battalion Irish Guards – seen here in a pre-war photograph – went to France in August 1914 and fought throughout the opening campaigns. He failed to survive the war's first hundred days, being killed in action on 6 November. An account of his death by a fellow officer stated: 'He was killed leading his men against the German trenches. Of the 35 men that went with him none returned. Only 2 days before he had been specially mentioned for bravery in action. He had held a position until long after the rest of the Battalion had retired.' A number of his letters – all to his mother – have survived. Although some of them appear to have been written in great haste, they give a clear-sighted and vivid view of the nature of the fighting on the Western Front in the first months of the war.

The following is from a letter written during the Mons Retreat:

> September 3rd. We have been trekking hard all these last days. Heat and dust terrible. We were in action the day before yesterday. We got in a wood with only the Coldstream and were surrounded by Germans. The wood was very thick and the enemy was no less than 100 yards off. We lost considerably including nine officers three of whom only can be accounted for.

In a later letter, undated but probably written on 13 September, he gave further details of this action – including a brief reference to casualties through what is now known as 'friendly fire'; the letter is also notable for its list of casualties, some of them from famous Anglo-Irish families.

> The Coldstream and us were together but the wood was so thick that I fear many shot one's own men [sic]. We lost the following officers then:– Lt-Col Hon. George Morris our CO, Major Crichton 2nd in command, Lord Desmond Fitzgerald, adjutant, shot in the ankle, Capt. Tisdall, Lord Innesker, Lord Castleross, Blacker Douglas, Hon. Aubrey Herbert MP who volunteered as interpreter to our battalion. I think the first two were killed but the others I believe are not very seriously wounded.

Lieutenant Neville Woodroffe. (HU 63245)

The Brigade of Guards have lost heavily as regards officers, and besides that the very best of fellows, many of whom ranked as one's very best friends. Lockwood was shot yesterday while he was standing up telling some wounded Germans to convey in their language to another party of Germans that if they held the white flag up they were to throw down their arms. John Manners, whom you know by name, shot himself, when he saw that the alternative was to surrender to superior numbers of Germans. He only had about five men with him. Harcourt Vernon is wounded.

The Germans are very fond of wood fighting and detail snipers to get up trees where they are not seen and pick off the officers, others lie on the ground and if caught pretend they are dead. The wood fighting is intense but they are terrified of the English fire and typical British infantry advance over open ground. We pushed through the wood, dug trenches and held the position in the trenches for six days under heavy artillery fire the whole time. Shrapnel and high explosives have a terrible effect on one. A shell burst killing the man next to me and wounding others.

The next two letters date from the stalemate weeks of the Battle of the Aisne. The village referred to in the first letter is Soupir, on the northern bank of the Aisne to the east of Soissons. This letter is especially interesting for two reasons: it shows that the traditional means of opting out of fighting through a 'Self-Inflicted Wound' did not take long to reappear; it also suggests that what was shortly to become virtually commonplace after entrenchment – the advance over open ground against strongly held positions – could seem militarily unacceptable ('sure massacre') to the professional soldiers of 1914:

30 Sept. We continue to hold this position the other side of the Aisne and have been entrenched now for over sixteen days. One is beginning to feel the reaction after all our previous marching and we are longing to be on the march again. This is really the first time that we have been in the same position for more than one day. It is in some way a rest after our previous experience but we are shelled all day long and have occasional fusillades at night.

There is a wonderful Château in the village, very large, new and vulgar. It has now been turned into a hospital. It has lovely gardens, but they have been practically destroyed by guns, and horses being allowed to wander and mess all the lawns and flower beds. But war is war and the owner must consider himself very lucky the whole thing is not in ruins. It seems odd to see the wounded lying in the most wonderful beds and sheets and others on the very finest carpets you could find. It seems a favourite and old trick to shoot one's finger off when one is cleaning one's rifle. Two men were admitted to

hospital having blown off their fingers cleaning their rifles.

We seem to be going to hold this position indefinitely as it means sure massacre to advance over open ground in face of a most deadly fire from rifles and Maxims at such a short range.

This is a terrible war and I don't suspect there is an idle British soldier in France. I wonder when it will end; one hears so much. There has been more fighting and more loss of life crowded into seven weeks than there was in the whole of South Africa. It is awful what the Brigade of Guards have lost and being like one big regiment one knows everyone and feels it all the more.

7 October. Things look very much the same, and it is comparatively monotonous after our previous adventure. We had a small patrol out in front of our trenches yesterday and it was awful to see the massacre and refuse which a wood to our left disclosed. Dead Germans and a few of the Wiltshire regiment which had been there fully a fortnight ago and in terrible conditions. Legs stuck in boots lay out in the open and corpses shattered from shell fire lay at short intervals. Kits and rifles, ammunition, helmets, tools etc. all lay in heaps. The stink was awful. We buried what we could, but most one could not touch. However, enough!

His last message, on a plain postcard, is dated 3 November:

I am afraid I have not had time to write a letter though I have heaps to tell you. The last two days have been ghastly. The Germans broke through the line. We have lost ten officers in the last two days and yesterday the battalion was less than 200 men, though I expect some stragglers will turn up. All the officers in my company were lost except myself. All in No 3 Coy and all bar one in 4. We have had no rest at all. Everyone is very shaken. I do hope we are put in reserve to reform for a few days. I will give you a full account later. The whole Brigade has suffered heavily. Thanks for letter. Love to all. Neville.

A Nurse at First Ypres

Within a few days of the outbreak of war Jentie Paterson, Scottish by birth and a Nursing Sister by profession (trained at Guy's Hospital, London), joined a contingent of nurses prepared to respond to the national emergency by undertaking foreign service. She and her companions, all members of the Queen Alexandra's Imperial Military Nursing Service Reserve, arrived in France on 24 August and over the following weeks served in hospitals in a number of places including Rouen, Nantes, Versailles and Boulogne. The onset of the First Battle of Ypres, however, required nurses nearer the point of action and on 5 November she and a number of others were ordered to a Casualty Clearing Station at Hazebrouck, a railhead town near Armentières. Ten days after her arrival Sister Paterson wrote a long letter (of which the following is an abbreviated version) to a friend on a committee organizing comforts for the troops.

No 5 Clearing Station,
Expeditionary Force,
16 Nov. 1914.

My dear Martha,

I received your p.c. of 20th–10–14 away up here today; it went to Versailles forwarded to Boulogne and then on here. I hear you say where is here? Well, we see the flashes of the guns and hear the roar day and night. We are the furthest-up lot of sisters except those on the trains which have penetrated to within a mile or two of the lines. Last week one such train was under fire while they were moving in the wounded and they are the first sisters to be specially commended – we are dying for our turn next. This is the first time that these hospitals have ever had sisters attached and the added responsibility for the Colonel, as the Germans are treating we women so abominably, was not readily acceptable. He told us frankly when we arrived he was greatly against us coming for reason stated and also because we would have to rough it but now he says he does not know what he would do without us. We hope we shall keep in the fire front till we reach Berlin. But I do wish it was all over. We were

asked to come by the chief Matron and had to say we were going voluntarily and realised the risks in case our home people would jib. We carry very little baggage. Sometimes we feed and dress [the wounds of] 200–300 in a day. Sometimes we keep them a night if there is not an ambulance train in to take them off; then we get faces, hands and feet washed and at least change their socks most of which we cut off. They are moulded to their limbs generally having been on 5, 6, 7 weeks.

You hear a whistle, then up dash ambulances one after the other, next the doors of my ward swing open (I have at present a huge hall, belonging to a Monastery) and in tumbles a dusty weary crew followed or preceded by stretcher cases. We seat them at long tables at the end, give them a bottle of stout each and cigarettes, see if any require immediate dressing, then order a piping hot meal, soup and stew and chunks of bread. Our Colonel feeds them awfully well, then we generally let them sleep while we attend to 'stretcher' cases. It is hard work but when you see the convoy go out you are repaid.

Soap here is a luxury and dear. Many thanks for the socks, they will be forwarded here with my other parcels. Please thank the ladies of your Committee and tell them how I distributed the last lot. Now the men travel in comparative luxury, motor ambulances, lovely ambulance trains, at first carts without springs and cattle trucks on straw, such a difference since August and a regular staff of sisters, Drs. and Orderlies on every train.

Orderlies [i.e. Royal Army Medical Corps men] to my mind are all very well but they can *never* take the place of women nurses. To begin with they lack *education*, perception and conscience. A man can be a Dr. and order treatment but he has not the patience nor detail to carry out the nursing part and the Orderlies being of a different social status to us, his ideas of cleanliness differ and he never, not even the best, grasps 'Surgical Cleanliness'. I would rather work with the most 'fatheaded' woman probationer under me than a nursing orderly. They mean well and are kind to the patients *but*, oh, there are 100 buts!

This is a most central point. We are just at the

road-side and we see all kinds and conditions pass. 'Terriers' [i.e. soldiers of Territorial battalions] on their way to the front get a cheer; they are generally singing. French *Cuirassiers*, French Artillery, French Cycle Corps – in fact all specimens down to German prisoners (how glad they are to hear a word of their own language) – are gazed upon by yours truly. The French Regiments are more artistically dressed, but doubtless make more conspicuous targets. The Dragoons, who wear 'gold' (brass) helmets with huge tails of horse hair down their necks (to protect them from sabre cuts) and who look like our 'Life Guards', have during the War the brass veiled in a chamois or a blue cover which makes you think of 'the family teapot' put away for the summer!! The infantry and artillery uniforms are also picturesque – Infantry dull red trousers and cap and long blue coats looped back at the sides but they lack the smartness of our 'putteed' legs. No, I still love the British Tommie even at his grubbiest and then poor soul he often gives us more than he thinks. One kilt the other day was white with lice. He had been in the trenches for weeks. If they think they are 'alive' and heaps are,

they always beg us not to remove their shirts but to send an orderly and the most severely wounded apologises before he allows us to remove his socks and explains the condition of his feet. Poor souls, we assure them not to worry; they've done their share of the work and now it is our turn.

We lost one man today. Poor chap, leg black, operation, died on the table. Another (as if to cheer us up) who seemed more desperate had mortified up to the level of right kidney. He had 17 incisions in his abdominal walls and is going to pull through; that is another reason we are here. Such cases could not live without operation at once and they require careful nursing afterwards. Of course we have no beds, only stretchers, no air cushions, no sheets, so you use all your skill and ingenuity. I had a man last week who was almost pulseless for hours, today he is eating tinned chicken and travels to the base, tomorrow, with a healthy stump! It is marvellous what can be accomplished amidst the din and dirt and dust of a convoy, and a good hot meal and sleep goes a long way.

Midnight: the windows tremble and the guns are still going hard. . . .

An early photograph of a Casualty Clearing Station, at Oultersteene near Bailleul; one of the 'serious' wards. (Q 436)

'Will they never come?' Lieutenant Rowland Owen, already much quoted and seen here in a pre-war photograph (HU 63246), enjoyed a brief celebrity in late 1914 thanks to a letter written in November while he lay wounded in a hospital in Boulogne. A keen rugby footballer who had played for Yorkshire, he was also captain of the Huddersfield Old Boys Club, to the secretary of which he wrote: 'This year was going to be our great year. Well, so it is if we send as many men to the field of battle as we send to the field of play.' Published in the local press, Owen's comments inspired a cartoon in a national weekly which became the basis of the recruiting poster shown opposite. (Q 81329)

Owen was killed at Hill 60 in April 1915. In its commemoration of his death, the *Huddersfield Chronicle* stated: 'There can be no doubt that that cartoon and Lieutenant Owen's words, crystallised into the question "Will they never come?", gave a great fillip to recruitment at the end of last year.'

Will they never come?

PART TWO

DEADLOCK
November 1914 – March 1918

On our front we appear to have lost thousands, killed, wounded or captured and what have we to show for it all? One trench! What a waste of life. Not only life, but young life.

Bombardier J. W. Palmer
26th Brigade, Royal Field Artillery
9 May 1915

The Boche makes a lot of noise with his infernal instruments but it is extraordinary what little damage he does . . . indeed, the thing seems a deadlock here. Neither side seems able to advance over the broken, crater-covered, shell-shattered ground.

Captain Geoffrey Donaldson
27th Battalion, Royal Warwickshire Regiment
5 June 1916

Scene of desolation in the Ypres Salient, with a derelict Mark IV tank; photograph taken 15 February 1918. (Q 10711)

INTRODUCTION TO PART TWO

In an important letter to Sir John French dated 2 January 1915, Lord Kitchener, Secretary of State for War, referred to the German lines in France as 'a fortress that cannot be carried by assault and also that cannot be completely invested'. He went on to suggest that this implied a need to consider the possibility of operations elsewhere, thus launching an argument that was to dominate British strategical thinking for most of the war, as to whether ultimate victory could or could not be achieved without breaking down Germany's resistance on the centre stage of the Western Front. Since such initiatives as were subsequently devised – Gallipoli, Salonika, Palestine – took place away to the east, the proponents of the two causes came to be known as Westerners and Easterners. Later, in 1917, Italy would emerge as another favoured area in Easterners' eyes. Overall the Westerners got their way, though the issue became one of increasingly fierce debate every time a new 'push' produced what seemed to be the inescapable consequence of the deadlock war: small gains combined with huge losses.

There was no question at any time, however, of closing down the Western Front. The enemy had to be contained, and the invader had to be ejected from French and Belgian soil as soon as possible. Meanwhile, if the German lines constituted a fortress, then the Allies would have to make theirs a fortress too. Each side, as it were, would have to lay siege to the other. The Germans were better equipped for this eventuality than their enemies. They had expected to attack heavily defended strong points – such as the Belgian fortresses (in the commonly accepted

sense of the word) which had lain in the path of their advance in 1914 – and so they had taken with them appropriate weaponry, such as mortars, demolition charges, and mining and tunnelling equipment. By contrast, the British, in the words of their official historian, were 'quite unprepared and had to improvise everything. Hand-grenades were made of jam tins, and mortars of field-gun cartridge cases. The Mills grenade, which became the service missile, was not sent for trial until March 1915, and the Stokes mortar not until November 1915. Little did any General Staff expect the strange situation of the two sides being dug in only a few hundred yards apart, in places as little as 30 yards.'*

This is the context of Part Two, the central and the longest part of the book. It contains sections on most of the great battles which took place between 1915 and 1917, but they are not dealt with equally or in the same way. There is thus no single major essay on such famous battles as the Somme or Third Ypres; instead there are a number of sections dealing with various aspects of them, whereas smaller, often neglected, actions such as Loos or Messines are given separate and detailed treatment. Compressing the battle sections has allowed space for numerous other subjects: for example, patrols and raids, troop entertainments, fatalism, military executions and the treatment (in some cases the mistreatment) of prisoners. There are also sections on individuals, from private soldier to junior general.

*Edmonds *Short History*, p. 82.

First Winter, and the Christmas Truce

Already by the end of the First Battle of Ypres, the nature of the new siege-type warfare which was to continue for over three years was becoming apparent. Lieutenant J. A. Liddell, machine-gun officer of the 2nd Battalion Argyll and Sutherland Highlanders, wrote to his father on 26 November 1914:

> It's a war with no glamour or glory such as one expects in a huge world-wide show like this. Modern weapons are too deadly, and the whole art of war, and all tactics as laid down in our books, has been quite altered. No advancing across the open by short rushes. Now it's all digging new lines of trenches by night until one is a couple of hundred yards from the enemy. Then a bombardment with enormous shells for a couple of days, until trenches and men's nerves are smashed to ribbons, and a surprise rush in the middle of the night.

Liddell took an equally pessimistic view in a letter to a friend ('My dear old Flum') written on 29 December:

> You don't know how boring and nerve-racking this trench business is, and how long off the end of the war seems. It would appear that it has to go on until the Germans are quite exhausted, which might take some little time.
>
> Well, Flum, this is a dreadful war, and now they've started using grenades and bombs with great frequency, it's a little worse than before. Some of the lines are only 25 yards apart, and are all full of water and mud. It's awfully cold and wet too, and I'm sure that none of the 10,000,000 or so combatants would mind if peace were declared tomorrow.

There was no such prospect, however – all the bright hopes of the previous summer that the war would be over by Christmas being now, almost literally, dead in the water.

Improvisation and survival were the keynotes of the first winter season in trenches. Defences were everywhere inadequate and were not improved by weeks of cold, wet and, frequently, snowy weather. The German lines were in an equally rudimentary and dismal state. Watercourses overran and fields turned to slime, which was then tramped upon by the boots of thousands of men and the hoofs of hundreds of horses, or scoured by the wheels of innumerable limbers and gun-carriages. 'I have come to the conclusion that this damned place is a sort of second Venice,' Dougan Chater, a subaltern of the 2nd Gordon Highlanders, told his family on 13 January 1915. 'When you find a piece of dry land you think there must be some mistake. I was up to my waist in water two or three days ago – I tried taking off my shoes and socks but struck a few empty meat-tins and desisted!'

In such circumstances any kind of refuge that offered cover and a dry footing was drafted into use, even the most humble. 'The last three days

**Winter in the trenches.
Officers of the XI Hussars
in trenches at Zillebeke,
February 1915, when
according to the
Regimental History 'the
weather was bitterly
cold'.** (Q 51171)

**The Machine-Gun Section
of the XI Hussars, same
location, January–
February 1915.** (Q 51194)

before coming back into billets,' Chater continued, 'I have been living in a pig-sty! It was really quite palatial – we cleaned it out, put fresh straw in and found some corrugated iron for a roof. Luckily there had not been any pigs in it for some time.'

Pig-sties might be turned to good use, but many larger buildings in the forward zone were simply destroyed, with no right of protest from their inhabitants. Lieutenant J. D. Wyatt, 2nd Battalion, Yorkshire Regiment, noted in his diary (7 December 1914) the unhappy consequences of such acts, a military necessity now that the firing lines had congealed:

> A lot of houses are being demolished by our Engineers to clear the 'field of fire' for our guns. It is heartbreaking to see old women trundling a barrow away with the few things she can save in it. Then our fellows go and blow her house up. War is awful for civilians. Far worse for them than for us. May England never be the seat of conflict!

The local people suffered almost as acutely behind the lines, where countless buildings were commandeered as rest billets for the troops. Many of these were cold and squalid and did nothing to improve a morale which in the case of units which had suffered heavily in the recent fighting was often at rock bottom. Robert Scott Macfie, Colour-Quartermaster-Sergeant of a Territorial battalion, the 10th King's Liverpool Regiment – generally known as the Liverpool Scottish – wrote to his sister on 24 December 1914:

> This is Xmas Eve, and we are all very homesick. The men are in an empty barn, cold and draughty, and have scarcely recovered from our spell in the trenches. I am in a wretched cottage close to the barn door. The kitchen is my store, and a shell must have passed through it for it is very deep in debris. I sleep with three others on two beds – the first time for months – in a tiny bedroom across the passage. It is also in disorder and filthy, and one can judge the haste in which the inhabitants must have fled by the fact that the cheap wardrobe is still full of their clothes. Other soldiers have been billeted here and we found, when we came, a bucket of burning anthracite on the bedroom floor. We have been able to dry our soaked clothes and even to beat off some of the baked clay, but we are tired and dispirited. 94 of the company we brought out from England remain, and it is evident that we have almost ceased to exist as a regiment. The men are singing in the barn to keep up their spirits in the dark, the little town has just received the attention of the Germans who sent six shells over it half an hour ago, and we are waiting to march off to an even less comfortable residence in which to spend Xmas, viz. 'dugouts' – holes in the ground, cheaply roofed and furnished with straw.
>
> We went into the trenches cold and wet, for there was heavy rain and a snowstorm as we marched there from the muddy farm. When we came out we were colder, wetter and ever so much muddier. The next morning I found that all the exposed parts of my skin were thickly coated with hard mud (my clothes of course were worse). After trying in vain to brush, rub or pick it off, I went to a cottage near the creamery, borrowed a basin, took off every stitch of my clothing in the garden, and during a heavy snowstorm scrubbed myself from head to foot at the pump. It is quite the most heroic thing I have ever done!

I wish we could be photographed coming back from the trenches. I fancy we must resemble Siberian exiles rather than soldiers. We wear anything we like. We are not the least like a regiment in England, spotlessly clean, all dressed precisely alike, and every man erect, and every button in its place. We have woollen headgear, comforters that wave in the wind, gloves of various colours. We carry buckets and enamelled cups and mugs are tied to our belts with string. Our legs are covered indifferently by spats, puttees, or hosetops from home. We do not walk erect or step out with a soldierlike stride. We slouch along at the rate you would walk down Bold Street if you were half an hour too early for your train. We hang our heads, march at irregular intervals in twos, threes and fours, and often a man falls gradually back, unable to keep up. Many are lame, and we would make a terribly depressing picture. Fortunately we move at night and nobody sees us.

Macfie's opinion of the dispiriting powers of mud was widely shared. When Sergeant William Edgington, Royal Horse Artillery, who had been through the Mons Retreat and all the early battles, came to sum up the first winter in his diary he commented: 'The one great memory during this time is rain and mud, mud, mud up to the knees.' But there was a positive side too, as his battery had been out of the line and thus able to concentrate on recuperation and making good:

23 Nov. to 14 Jan. Remained in reserve and spent the time in reorganising, cleaning and overhauling and making men and horses comfortable. During this time we built cookhouses, made a library for the men, erected a bath house (hot and cold), an eating shed for the troops (*à la buffet*) and got all steel work bright. In fact settled down to more or less peacetime conditions.

Macfie's expectation, as expressed above, that his company would be in the line for Christmas was, in the event, not realized. Continuing his letter in more cheerful mood, he wrote:

XMAS DAY: We are not in 'dugouts' after all, but billeted in barns and workshops in an odd straggling village, almost every house in which, as seems usual here, is an inn or a café. I have a very cold place to sleep in, but it was rather pleasant when I opened the big barn door this morning to see a typical Christmas scene – clear sharp air, and a white hoar-frost dazzling everywhere.

Had he and his men been at the front, they might have witnessed or even shared in the remarkable Christmas truce which was taking place over substantial stretches of the British line, and sporadically, if only in the form of a mutually accepted ceasefire, in the areas held by the French and Belgians. Inspired by a widespread mood of 'live and let live' in the weeks following the bloodletting of the opening campaign and also by a natural inclination to relax at the festive season, the impulse to truce, to take a brief holiday from war, was undoubtedly assisted by the sudden onset of Macfie's 'typical' Christmas weather. Arriving generally on the 24th, it froze the mud, rimed the jagged edges of ruined buildings and the barbed wire, turned the trees into Christmas ones, and reduced the impact of the dismal cocktail of smells – from chloride of lime, dead sheep, and corpses (following recent flurries of fighting) out between the trenches – which by now had become the accepted, if hated, concomitant of trench life. Christmas Day itself was to become a beautiful day everywhere, though out in the open fields the sun took some time to break through the morning haze. This account of 25 December 1914 is from a diary by a soldier (name unknown) of the Queen's Westminster Rifles:

> Friday 25 Xmas Day: Freezing and a bit misty. We started walking about behind the trench and after a bit we got out the front and then we saw Germans doing the same thing, we waved and they did until at last we got so close that five of us went out to meet five of them and started exchanging keepsakes, buttons etc. Went back for dinner and had Maconachie and Xmas pudding and potted duck. After went for a walk along to our left towards the Rifle Brigade and on to the Lille Road. Here I found about 200 English drawn up across it and twenty yards further down about 300 Germans looking at each other, in the end they all mixed up and started exchanging fags and buttons. I got some fags, a cap badge, a button and some cigars. It seemed the weirdest thing in the world that you should be talking to the men you were trying to shoot the day before and to crown all a German officer got a camera and took our photos in a group. All tonight there wasn't a shot fired.

Lieutenant J. A. Liddell's 2nd Argyll and Sutherland Highlanders were among the units which were drawn into this Christmas fraternization between the lines, as Liddell reported in his letter of 29 December:

> On that day everyone spontaneously left their trenches and had a meeting halfway between the trenches. Germans gave us cigars, and we gave them chocolate and tobacco. They seemed very pleased to see us! Some had lived in England for years, and were very bucked at airing their English again.

Among the fraternizing battalions on Christmas Day were units of the Meerut Division of the Indian Army (the Indians were the first Empire troops in action on the Western Front). Captain P. Mortimer, attached to the Division as a Requisitioning Officer, observed the proceedings and described them in a diary entry written on Boxing Day:

> The enemy came out of their trenches yesterday (being Christmas Day) simultaneously with our fellows – who met the Germans on neutral ground between the two trenches and exchanged the compliments of the season – presents, smokes and drinks – some of our fellows going into the German lines and some of the Germans strolling into ours – the whole affair was particularly friendly and not a shot was fired in our Brigade throughout the day. The enemy apparently initiated the move by shouting across to our fellows and then popping their heads out of their trenches and finally getting out of them altogether. V. Fine and frosty in the morning but raining hard at night again.

Mortimer's last comment is significant in that it shows how brief was the seasonal truce provided by the weather, in a winter which rightly won a reputation among the fighting troops for being cursed with above average rainfall. But the fraternizing mood itself lingered, continuing in some areas until February and beyond. Thus as late as 19 March Captain F. E. Packe, 1st Battalion Welch Regiment, back in France after being

Friday, January 8, 1915.

The Daily Mirror

CERTIFIED CIRCULATION LARGER THAN ANY OTHER DAILY NEWSPAPER IN THE WORLD

WHY DELAY? THE DAILY MIRROR OVERSEAS WEEKLY EDITION contains all the Latest and Best War Pictures and News, and is therefore the Best Weekly Newspaper for your friends abroad. You can obtain it from your Newsagent for 3d. per copy.
Subscription rates (prepaid), post free, to Canada for six months 10-; elsewhere abroad 13'.
Address—Manager, "Overseas Daily Mirror," 23-29, Bouverie Street, London, E.C.

AN HISTORIC GROUP: BRITISH AND GERMAN SOLDIERS PHOTOGRAPHED TOGETHER.

Foes became friends on Christmas Day, when the British and Germans arranged an unofficial truce. The men left the trenches to exchange cigars and cigarettes, and were even photographed together. This is the historic picture, and shows the soldiers of the opposing Armies standing side by side.

wounded, could write of the part of the line to which he was sent that it was

> an absurdly quiet spot, it was one of those places where they fraternized with Germans at Xmas and a certain amount of the truce has gone on apparently, anyhow there was very little firing by day and never really heavy by night and I only had one man hit in two nights – not badly – and he was the only casualty in the regiment! We never had a single shell the whole time I was there.

Yet should anyone have surmised that if no shots were fired the war might somehow go away, such thoughts were pure illusion. Nine days previously the British had launched the first of a number of determined but unsuccessful attacks on the German lines to be made in 1915, each one of which would produce heavy losses. In the pauses between such attacks the routines of trench warfare would get into their stride. Perhaps the shrewdest comment to emerge from this winter period occurred in the diary of Captain J. W. Barnett, Regimental Medical Officer of the 34th Sikh Pioneers. 'I think we will win through,' he wrote on 21 December 1914, 'but our casualties will be appalling.'

The Christmas Truce of 1914, as publicized in the British press, January 1915. The photograph also shows evidence of the frosty weather, as described by CQMS Scott Macfie, which gave the episode a suitably seasonal decor.

The Trenches

'The trenches': the phrase was to be so regularly used, and came to represent so important a reality, that over the next four years it was inevitably a matter of great curiosity among people who had not seen them or served in them. '*What is life like in the trenches?*' – how often the question must have been put, in letters to the front, or face to face to soldiers on leave. Inevitably, there were those who simply avoided writing or talking about the subject, but by contrast there were many others who were happy and eager to explain. Thus Lieutenant John Staniforth, 7th Battalion, Leinster Regiment, could write to his family in May 1916, 'I wish you could come out here just for a flying visit and see what things are like.' That being impossible, he compensated by a piece of particularly vivid description. He invited his readers to imagine an approach to the front at night, by train to the railhead and then onwards by bus:

> Then the bus would come to a few blackened shells that was once a village, and you would be told it was unsafe to drive any further, and you'd have to get down and walk. Before long you'd top a little rise, and then stand and catch your breath with the whole Front spread out before your feet. Imagine a vast semi-circle of lights: a cross between the lights of the Embankment and the lights of the Fleet far out at sea; only instead of fixed yellow lamps they are powerful white flares, sailing up every minute and burning for twenty or thirty seconds, and then fizzling out like a rocket – each one visible at ten miles distant, and each lighting up every man, tree and bush within half-a-mile. Besides these you will see a slim shaft swinging round and round among the stars, hunting an invisible aeroplane; and every instant flashes in the sky like the opening of a furnace-door and there is a clap of thunder from the unseen 'heavies'. The whole makes a magnificent panorama on a clear night.

Underneath this sky, a firework display by night, often blank and empty by day – though there might well be the sudden smoke of a shell explosion, or, more frequently than after dark, the twistings and turnings of an aeroplane evading anti-aircraft fire or caught in a dog-fight – lay the labyrinth of the trenches. Communication trenches led forward to the reserve, support and firing trenches, saps pushed out into No Man's Land, and for the new arrival this whole area could be a place of chaos and confusion, as Second Lieutenant Tom Allen, 1st Irish Guards, explained to his family after arriving in the Loos–Lens area in early 1915:

> Getting along a trench is not as easy as you think. For one thing it is not straight for more than four yards (it is 'traversed' to prevent enfilade and shell fire having much effect). Then there are all sorts of odd off-turns, to officers' dugouts, or other lines of trenches: at other places there are steps down and other unknown steps up where a piece of parapet has been blown in, or some

walls of a traverse have collapsed. In these mazes where we have fought each other so often and each side has held the ground in turn, you can never be quite sure whether a trench won't lead you straight to the German lines. In more than one place in our present line we actually do have communication trenches connecting our and their lines.

If Allen saw the trenches as a zone of mazes, Staniforth, guiding his readers in imagination to his Signals Officers' dugout, saw it as

a world of moles, burrowing always deeper and deeper to get away from the high explosives: an underground city with avenues, lanes, streets, crescents, alleys and cross-roads, all named and labelled and connected by telegraph and telephone. 'No. 3 Posen Alley' was my last address, and you reach it via 'Piccadilly', 'Victoria Station', and 'Sackville Street'. After you've wandered for perhaps two hours you'll see a hole at your feet with a mass of wires of all sizes and colours running along the ground and disappearing into it. Go down twenty or thirty steps, down mud steps, and you come into a low, long cave, lit by candles stuck in bottles and a swinging hurricane lamp.

Also happy to describe the trench world in precise detail was Lieutenant Philip Brown, a subaltern in the Durham Light Infantry. He wrote the following account for his mother in October 1915:

I wonder if I can give you an idea of what the life is like. We have our turns of duty and off duty. If I am off in the middle of the night my day begins with 'Stand To' at dawn. I wake up, and listen for a minute to the sentries talking and mice scuttling. Everything is grey and damp in the autumn mist.

A rare view of the front by night; the photograph shows a German star shell bursting over the trenches, Ploegsteert, Belgium, March 1916.
(Q 445)

Trench tableau: an officer emerging from a dug-out with the unlikely but typical name 'Savoy Grill'. (Q 17329)

A few stray shots, but little more. I tramp down each narrow lane between the high banks of sandbags and past my men in a little row of three or four in each bay, standing with bayonets fixed and generally yawning. The order 'Stand Down' comes, the day sentry sits down and looks up into his periscope, and the others stretch themselves, and move off to get rations, to light fires, to clean rifles. One party pushes a trolley with a load of rum bottles down to a ruined farm to get water. Soon there is a smell of frying bacon, and I go round to examine rifles before breakfast. After breakfast some men are set to clean the wooden boards in the footway, others are working at a dugout, others sleep (they get most of their sleep in the day). Next I crawl down the trench where my batman was wounded, and decide that it must be deepened. This covers me with mud from the waist down, as I crawl all the way. Lunch (or dinner, for it is our chief meal), and then sleep. Tea, and 'Stand To'. The trenches begin to look gloomy now, with a dripping of rain, and darkness coming on. Mice scuttle over the path as I go my rounds, and a rat hops over a sand-bag on the top of the parapet. Work begins again at 'Stand Down'. There are more sentries, a party for water, a working party improving the parapet and wire, and so on. We are just going to enjoy a dinner–supper of soup and sardines on toast. Then I go on night duty, visiting sentries and the listening posts, firing an occasional flare out into the darkness and receiving all kinds of information, much of it highly imaginative. One man hears a dog 'whinnying', as he calls it, in front, another can see a man signalling up in a tree, and a third is certain that some one is shooting from behind our line.

An engaging 'Tommy's eye-view' of the world of the trenches survives in a letter to his mother by Private Kenneth Garry of the Honourable Artillery Company (despite its name, an infantry unit) dating from late 1915. He was in the vicinity of Plugstreet Wood, Belgium, an area with a reputation for being relatively peaceful, even 'cushy', though this did not necessarily mean an easy time for the run-of-the-mill ordinary soldier:

A day in the trenches may be said to start with 'stand to' in the morning at daybreak. On the day in question, which was Wednesday 15 December, it was raining a nasty drizzle, and we turned out in the macintosh capes provided, then stumbled round the 'duck-walks' to a particular 'bay' of the firing trench which we helped to guard. There we stand and stamp our feet to keep them warm and also to keep us awake.

Eventually the word was passed from the next traverse to 'stand on', upon which all except a previously selected man are at liberty to get their breakfast. The 'stand on' came about 7 o'clock, and I went down a communication trench and across some fields to a pump where, being exceptionally lucky in this particular set of trenches, we can draw water. This is carried in two-gallon petrol tins. If the pump was not there and the particular trenches we were in did not happen to be quiet ones, a fatigue would have to go at night with the men's water bottles to the nearest water cart. On arrival back I found that my chum Maisey had got the primus going, and a mess tin of water boiling for breakfast. We made some café-au-lait, from the tin, which is the most useful drink, (with cocoa and milk) as nothing else is needed, as in the case of tea, to complete the drink. This drunk, we were informed by our corporal that we were to go on fatigue at 9.30 in gumboots, and equipment, no rifles. It being now 8.30, we began to wonder whether we should get bacon in time. This is cooked by the regimental cook over a small brazier, and owing to scarcity and dampness of fuel, is never to time. We enquired and found we might manage with luck to get some, so we set to on bread and jam in the meantime, also changing into our gumboots. By some good chance, we drew our ration of bacon and ate it just in time before the corporal in charge came down the trench collecting the fatigue.

We were taken along to the dump which is merely a place where soil having been excavated for sandbags, spades, picks, barbed wire, spare duck-walks and other trench material is kept. Here we drew (which is an Army term meaning 'given') shovels and were taken on by the officer to the part where we were to work. This was a portion of a communication trench, where the sides were giving way. It was our business to lift the sandbags out of the bottom and dig out the loose earth and mud. The actual sides and parapets would have to be done by a night fatigue. It was drizzling on and off most of the time and we had to keep working to keep warm. We knocked off at 12.20 and got back to the dugout just before 1 o'clock.

We crawled in and lay down for a rest when the sergeant came round, and informed me I should have to be on guard at 1 o'clock. So in the few minutes that were left, I put on my great coat, and over it, my equipment again and my

Members of Private Kenneth Garry's battalion the Honourable Artillery Company, photographed in the line at Sanctuary Wood, Ypres area, June 1915. (Q 49376)

A sergeant demonstrating a simple mirror trench periscope, as described by Private Garry. The generally jovial mood suggests that the photograph was taken in a very quiet sector. (Q 2876)

cape. Then it being time, I went round to the firing bay and got my rifle out of the covered rack there, and duly relieved the sentry.

It is of course unhealthy to look over the parapet during the day, but by employing a periscope, the German trenches can be seen. The best of all is the penny glass in a metal clip to fix on a bayonet or stick. The Hun takes a fiendish delight in spotting periscopes, it gives him great delight to see bits of glass fly into the air as the result of a well directed shot. And it is always that expensive periscope that your dear old aunt sent you that gets caught. So I sat down on the platform with my back to the enemy and fixing the periscope on my bayonet, held it up at such an angle as to see best.

There was nothing to be seen, only a line of earth and sandbags with occasional pieces of timber lying about, the whole looking like a mound of earth thrown up by workmen excavating a drain. When you get tired of sitting you can get up and have a peep between the sandbags, and if extra bored you can fire a shot. But a man can be in the trenches a year and need never have a shot, for he would probably not have seen a Hun.

At night, lookout is kept by constantly peeping over the parapet, but when a shell is fired you must keep down. There is more opportunity for firing now, as provided you have noted during the day the position of, say, a cooker or a sniper's post you can safely fire. Besides, firing an occasional shot helps to keep one awake and passes the time away.

At four o'clock I came off after being relieved, which in the trenches consists of the new guard walking along the duck-board to the traverse. The old guard probably recognises him, and says 'You so-and-so'. The answer is usually a grunt as the newcomer is just out of bed. Then there are no more words spoken, but the one on the parapet gets down, puts his rifle in the rack and walks off, while the new one gets his rifle out in turn and mounts on to the platform.

Another sleep till a quarter to six, then some more coffee brewing to assist our efforts to keep warm. I was called on again at six, and at half past 'stand to' came round, which completed a very quiet day in the trenches.

If some of the foregoing accounts have a certain breeziness, it is because they were intended as much to reassure as to describe. Garry, in fact, was to know much harder experience and, as a Second Lieutenant in the 13th Battalion Northumberland Fusiliers, to join the long list of fatalities in 1917. For many the world of the trenches was not a subject for cheerful entertainment even at the best of times – hence this dismissive summing-up by an artillery officer, Captain Ronald Schweder, in a letter to his wife dated 15 May 1916:

Charming life this is. Both sides bury themselves in mudholes and peep at each other through slits in the earth. Occasionally one side or the other has a bombardment which consists of blowing off £10,000 worth of ammunition and killing no men. Then they retire to their holes to lick their sores like two dogs after a fight.

Nor was Lieutenant John Staniforth always in the buoyant mood in which he wrote the lively account with which this chapter began. Thus on 10 August 1916 he could write, wearily:

It's all just heat, flies, and monotony. I'd give worlds for green fields and blue water, instead of stony white chalk, blinding in the sun-dazzle and scorching to touch.

For Second Lieutenant Eric Heaton, posted to the 16th Battalion of the Middlesex Regiment (also known as the Public Schools Battalion) in February 1916, his early experience of trenches produced no first-time euphoria. He wrote this in a letter to his father dated 2 March:

One sees things from a very different standpoint out here, the seeming useless-ness of it, day after day in the trenches with great exposure, and very little really happening. Of course occasional bombardments and it is wonderful what men can put up with. The weather the last time we were up was frightful – intense cold, snow and fog. There is little sleep for the Officer, there is the continual round of duty, continually on the watch for any signs of an attack. I think we were all very delighted to get out into billets.

TEXT-BOOK TRENCHES

From the personal notes of Second Lieutenant Eric Heaton, 16th Battalion Middlesex Regiment. (HU 63247)

'It is necessary to have more than one line of trenches. First line of trenches known as Fire trenches. Second line Support trenches. The latter should be 30 to 100 yards in rear varying according to the nature of the ground and connected by communication trenches.

'Trench digging *now done by Infantry* – not by Engineers. Trenches must often be dug at top speed. Ordinary Relief – 4 hours. Length of relief however depends on (i) Nature of Work (ii) Total time it will take (iii) Climate (iv) Condition of men. Spacing of men – by day – open trenchwork 2 paces apart. By night in order to avoid noise 3 paces apart.

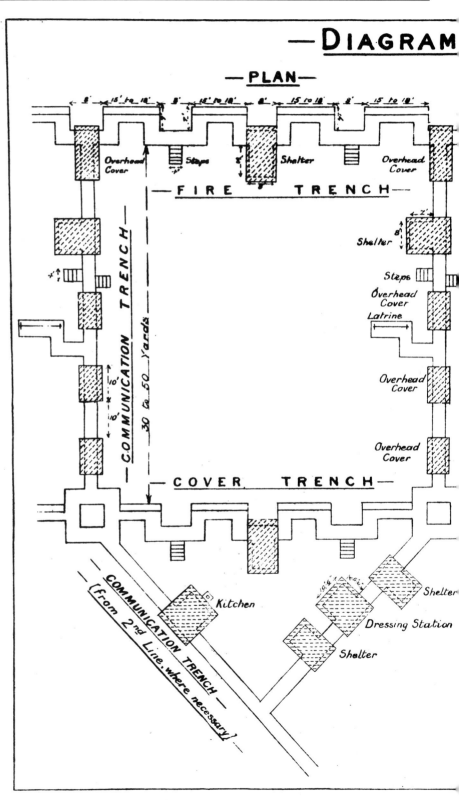

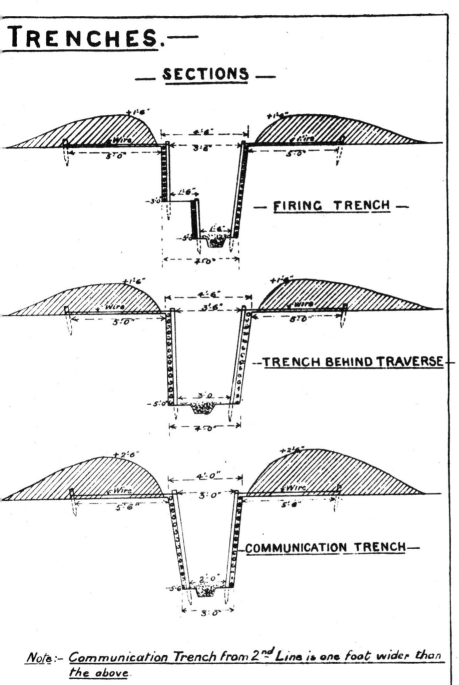

TRENCHES.—
— SECTIONS —

— FIRING TRENCH —

—TRENCH BEHIND TRAVERSE—

—COMMUNICATION TRENCH—

Note:— Communication Trench from 2nd Line is one foot wider than the above.

Note:— Dimensions both before and after revetting are shown above. The latter must in any case be adhered to.

'Communication Trenches: These connect fire trenches, support trenches and positions in rear. Three kinds:— (i) Straight (ii) Zig-zag (iii) Wavy.

'Latrines: Should be dug as soon as possible. Must be kept clean — care must be taken that no excreta is trodden into trench — cause of disease.

'Kitchens: Should be placed in cover trench and kept as clean as possible.'

The Guns

Artillery in action, with gun-crew stripped to the waist; 8-inch Mark V howitzer, 135th Siege Battery, Royal Garrison Artillery near Henin-sur-Cojeul, 27 May 1917.
(Q 2263)

The area of the trenches was not exclusively the possession of the Infantry; as has already been implied, the Artillery was also a vital part of it. The guns of Royal Horse Artillery (mobile light guns), the Royal Field Artillery (medium guns) and the Royal Garrison Artillery (heavy guns) were the siege cannon of the Western Front war; they, rather than the rifle or, deadly as it was, the machine-gun, were to be responsible for the great majority of its casualties.

To the infantryman, whose weapons were carried on his person, the sight of the weapons of the artilleryman in action could seem awesome, as is evident from this description by the infantry officer Lieutenant John Staniforth, 7th Leinsters – newly arrived in France and having seen for the first time a gun-crew at work:

> It was a lovely picture; the gunners stripped and sweating, each crew working like a machine, the swing and smack of the breech-block as clean and sweet as a kiss, and then a six-foot stream of crimson from the muzzle, a thunderclap of sound, and away tore the shell over the hills to Boche trenches 5000 yards away.

Significantly, Staniforth was writing, not in high summer, but in winter – December 1915. Feeding the guns could turn a man into a mass of sweat even in the bitterest weather; it was a tough, physically demanding slog. The guns too could show the effect of a sustained bombardment. 'Since my last letter,' wrote Bombardier Richard Downing, D Battery 65th Brigade RFA, in an undated letter of 1916, 'we have fired until our gun has been red hot.' He added: 'I can tell you the Germans must have had Hell.' This was one of the artilleryman's prime satisfactions. 'I like nothing better', one anonymous gunner wrote in early 1917, 'than giving Germans "iron rations".'

The importance of the artillery in the new kind of war was not lost on the thoughtful infantryman, as is clear from the respectful reaction of Captain Eric Gore-Browne of the Post Office Rifles to the experience of observing – or rather hearing – big guns in action:

> They are so concealed that from a few yards away you would not know of their existence, then a sudden burst of flame and the roar of the departing shell and a noise that goes right through your ears while the air for twenty yards around seems to collect in a heavy mass and bang you in the chest. It was very interesting indeed and sometimes I think I should like to have been a gunner. There is more romance about the other branches, but it is the one that wins battles in the end, I think.

It was doubtless the impersonality of the artillery's contact with the enemy that made Gore-Browne see the world of the big gun as being deficient in romance. Artillerymen generally fired from a distance 'over the hill' at positions or forces they could not see; if they could see they could be seen and would therefore be highly vulnerable. Mathematics and map references were as much part of their armoury as shells. Not for them the heroic attack across No Man's Land, or the charge with the bayonet. In social terms they were one down from the infantry – but then the highest social rung in this war was still occupied by the cavalry, who, unless dismounted to fight as infantry, were in the end to play little more than the role of understudy-in-waiting from the time of entrenchment onwards.

There were, however, some artillerymen who were present in the vicinity of the front lines and who might be required at times to go out beyond the friendly wire into No Man's Land. Those firing the guns needed precise information in order to pinpoint their targets, so there always had to be a responsible artillery representative, usually a junior officer, at a suitable forward observation point (usually called an OP – or O-Pip – or sometimes an OS after the variant Observation Station), from which the enemy could be watched and his movements noted. Information from such points was passed by telephone, so another vital artilleryman at the front was the signaller, whose job was to superintend the wire, pay it out as required and keep it in constant repair. In any over-the-top advance artillerymen always took part, with their reels of telephone cable, so that information could be fed back to the battery-lines.

Observation balloons and aircraft were also used for artillery spotting,

A German 21-cm howitzer firing. A 'gun' fired with a long low trajectory; a 'howitzer' fired its shells with a high curving arc like a lob at tennis. Howitzers were particularly effective against entrenched positions. (Q 42436)

but the OP was the standard basic device of gunnery intelligence. Often remarkable ingenuity was used to devise OPs which offered a useful viewpoint while seeming to present an innocent face to the enemy. One device was to convert the trunk of a shell-damaged tree by gouging out its interior and inserting a ladder; another was to rig up an OP in a ruined house or factory or – in the mining area around Lens and Loos – pithead. The diary of Battery Sergeant-Major Douglas Pegler, B Battery, 106th Brigade, RFA, describes a notable example, established in a half-destroyed building on Hill 63, near Ploegsteert in Belgium, which became known as the 'Barrel House':

> 9 May [1916]: In place of the chimney stack that had been destroyed by shell fire we have erected a 36 gallon beer barrel on the roof, through which we – standing on a ladder with head and shoulders inside the barrel – are able to observe. There is a horizontal slit for the eyes.
>
> 14 May: From 'Barrel House' one can see any amount of things Boche, men, horses, transport, ammunition wagons and horses, and pot shots with guns are the order of the day.

Such OPs could not be guaranteed a long life, and the Barrel House suffered the fate of many such resourceful inventions. On 10 June the

A faked tree of a type used by both sides for Artillery Observation Posts. This one, at Hill 63 near Ploegsteert, was constructed by the 1st Anzac Corps; photograph taken 2 December 1917.
(E(AUS) 3861)

Germans got three direct hits on it; on the 13th they destroyed the barrel completely.

When in the summer of 1915 Bombardier Downing's Battery found their position under effective enemy fire they extracted a brisk revenge:

> On Sunday the Germans put six direct hits into our Obs Station, which has caused us to make another. Well! We paid them back by popping some into theirs. I was gun-layer and managed to pop in 7 direct hits out of 10, and was complimented for my laying. Chairs etc were simply seen to be blown through the roof.

Not all guns were monsters in fixed positions; there was still a use for the dash and *élan* of the gun crew coming into action at speed. Bombardier J. W. Palmer, himself a signaller of the Royal Field Artillery, recorded the following dramatic scene during the Battle of Loos in September 1915:

> Then we witnessed a really stirring sight, one that we had not seen since the Mons days. Galloping horses bringing the guns up the Hulluch Road from Vermelles. Drivers bent over their horses necks, whips out urging them on. It was one of the most thrilling sights I have yet seen out here. Then with a quick manoeuvre they swung round and, without the least hesitation, dropped into action and opened fire.

Rain and mud. Rain and its inevitable consequence, mud, were constant bugbears on the Western Front. The photograph opposite, of two officers of the 8th Battalion of the Worcestershire Regiment at Héburterne, Somme region, August 1915, shows that trenches could be flooded to knee level even in high summer. (Q 90925)

The photograph above captures another hazard of the Front: horses or mules stuck in the mud. Captioned 'Australian mule-drawn vehicles in a muddy area. Potijze Farm, 19th October 1917', it shows typical ground conditions in the Ypres Salient during the Third Battle of Ypres (often known as the Battle of Passchendaele) (E(AUS) 963)

'Rest' — and Rest

'I think we were all very delighted to get out into billets,' wrote Second Lieutenant Eric Heaton on 2 March 1916 after a trying time in the trenches [see p. 55]. However, being withdrawn from the line might bring relief, but there was no guarantee that it would bring the relaxation and recuperation for which men craved after a spell in the front line. As an earlier letter of Heaton's made clear, the word 'rest' suffered from a distinct ambiguity:

> The term Rest Billets does in no way mean rest. It simply means not living in the trenches, but it entails taking up fatigue and working parties to the firing line with stores and stuff.
>
> Friday night was one of the worst nights I have had for some time. I was detailed to take 20 men up to the front line with stores and to work for 8 hours. It was a pitch dark night and rained heavily and with great difficulty I found my way along the trenches which seems an endless maze and it is not easy to keep touch with all your men. However I got there all right and back in the morning. I go up again tonight on the same thing.

Complaints at what infantrymen saw as the misuse of their precious rest periods occur frequently in letters and diaries, virtually from the beginning of entrenchment. Hence this diary note of 12 January 1915 by Lieutenant J. D. Wyatt, 2nd Battalion, Yorkshire Regiment:

> On fatigue for the RE. I think it's shameful the way men are put on fatigues when out of the trenches. Rest! A lot of rest they get! It doesn't give them a chance to get dry even. However, such is war.

A similar outburst occurs in the diary of Battery Sergeant-Major Douglas Pegler, Royal Field Artillery, under the date 31 March 1916; an entry which shows that gunners also were required for fatigue duties:

> We are going into action again – Hurroo! One gets far more rest in Action than at rest. Rest camps would be all right if they would only let you rest but they won't.

Endless fatigues over Easter 1915 produced the following unhappy response from Private Harold Anderton, 13th London Regiment; this is from a letter to his mother dated 4 April:

> Special seasons always make my thoughts revert to England and all she holds dear to me. I don't think I have ever spent Easter away from home. I certainly never expected to spend one in such strange surroundings as my present ones.
>
> We have an easy time during the day, but at night plod that weary road to the trenches time and time again, with fodder for our comrades, and with letters, wood, coal and barbed wire, corrugated iron and diverse other articles necessary for their consolation, comfort or safety. Comparatively it's a safe and easy time, but as an Easter holiday it's the most miserable I've experienced.

Fatigues could be often far more than mere drudgery; on lively and active sectors they could entail considerable risk. A Corporal of the Royal Field Artillery, J. W. Gower, wrote the following in his diary during a so-called rest period in March 1915:

> We go to the trenches with wire entanglements to help the Engineers, for we are expecting another attack shortly. Taking these things up is very dangerous work as we are exposed to the German lines. They keep popping away all the time. We go up at night but their star shells enable them to discern us, so we have to lie down when these go up. We have generally lost a good few men when this has to be done.

Private Alec Reader, 1/15th London Regiment, had a somewhat similar experience a year later, with the difference that by this time the role of the Infantrymen was not to help the Engineers but to do the work required themselves. He began his account – to his 'Dear Ma' – on 31 March:

> The Batt. is on a rest and will not go in the trenches for a day or two yet. Tonight I am on a working party and we are going in front of the trenches to erect barbed wire entanglements. We are in a fairly quiet part of the line, so I shall be all right and will let you know what I think of it tomorrow.
>
> Fools Day 11 a.m. – Last night's affair was a wash-out. We were taken up the line in lorries and dumped in a ruined village. There we drew picks and shovels and marched up to reserve trenches for digging. We started up at 7 p.m. and got back 3 a.m. Reveille at 7.30 this morning. The soil last night was

Billet accommodation for the other ranks of front-line battalions took many forms: in country areas, barns and outbuildings of all kinds; in built-up areas, any kind of unused industrial or abandoned housing. This photograph, taken on 16 January 1916, shows soldiers preparing for the day outside billets at Vermelles, in the industrial zone associated with the Battle of Loos. (Q 29051)

A fatigue party carrying duckboards over a support line trench at night. Cambrai sector, 12 January 1917. (Q 6420)

awful – it was composed of sticky clay and flints and the only way to get it up was to pick it up and then take it in your hands and throw it over the parapet. A spade was useless as the earth stuck to it and would not budge.

Yet such fatigues were not universal and there is no doubt that in the appropriate circumstances the fact of being out of trenches, particularly after a stressful time, could provide a sense of pure elation. Thus Captain Eric Gore-Browne, Post Office Rifles, writing to his wife on 4 August 1915:

> We halted in a stubble field and our travelling cookers (excellent institutions) produced hot tea. Dawn was breaking here and it was rather a wonderful sight in the half light, the corn stooks, dim figures everywhere of men and horses, and the twinkling of pipes and cigarettes like endless glow-worms.

Real rest, however, was only possible when men were able to make their escape from the fighting zone. Many developed an almost sentimental affection for towns or cities behind the lines which, because they showed few or none of the signs of war, allowed a blissful forgetfulness of the squalors and tensions to which they would all too soon have to return. Lieutenant L. S. Lloyd, 18th Hussars, in a diary note dated 8 January 1916, praised Béthune as 'quite the best town we had struck', selecting for honourable mention its 'good shops, clean billets, and an excellent little pastry shop for tea'. Perhaps the last-named establishment was the one previously visited by Captain Gore-Browne, on an occasion in

LA GUERRE DANS LE NORD

BÉTHUNE — Les Autobus de Londres

553

September 1915 when he and his friends managed between them twelve gâteaux and two pots of tea.

Amiens, behind the Somme front, was another favourite refuge, remaining out of range of German guns until their great advance in 1918. J. D. Wyatt, now a Captain serving with the Gloucestershire Regiment, described in loving detail how he spent a Sunday there in March 1917:

> I went to the 10.30 a.m. service at the Cathedral and heard some lovely music. It is a wonderful change to spend a day in civilisation again, with decent meals, trains etc., and all the everyday adjuncts of civilisation that one misses so much out here. We had lunch at the famous Godbert Restaurant whose boiled fillet of plaice with lobster, oyster and mushroom sauce took a prize at the Paris Cookery Exhibition. Anyway it was wonderfully good. In the afternoon we went to the Pictures and afterwards had tea at the *Chat Bleu*.

An outing to Amiens had also given special delight to Captain Ronald Schweder, RFA, as he indicated in a letter to his wife dated 9 April 1916:

> The country behind the line looks so peaceful and pleasant that one couldn't think of a war being carried on within a few miles. We landed in Amiens about 11 a.m. I could have shaken hands with anyone. It seemed so nice to see people bustling about and trams going. I stepped off the bus just by a lovely-looking sweet shop, so in I leapt at once, and sent you an egg full of chocolate which I hope will arrive safely.

Some weeks earlier Schweder had had occasion to go to Abbeville,

Béthune, a favourite place of escape from the trenches, with its cafés, patisseries and air of comparative normality. Note, however, that in this wartime postcard the name has been obliterated by the Censor, while the presence of 'Les Autobus de Londres' indicates that the front was a mere bus-ride away. (HU 63248)

Major Ronald Schweder, Royal Field Artillery. An Old Etonian who, unusually, had joined the ranks when he volunteered in 1914. He was no great lover of war, of which he wrote in a letter in early 1916: 'What a pastime war is! Invented by idiots to make life unbearable for ordinary mortals.'
(Doc 117)

travelling by rail. He had begun his journey on one of the filthy, clapped-out trains much hated by the Tommies which trundled with agonizing slowness between the base areas and the front, but at Noyelles he changed to the Paris-Boulogne Express with dining-car and *wagon-lit*. 'It was really an excitement getting on such a train once more,' he wrote. 'I gazed out of the windows and tried not to see my boots and spurs so that I could imagine I was a civilian.' (Boots and spurs seem sometimes to have worried Captain Schweder; on a later occasion when with his battery during perfect summer weather, he complained that they continually caught his eye on a day more suitable for flannels and tennis.)

Apart from home leave, perhaps the most satisfying respite from the front was provided by official orders that came from above, instructing the recipient to report to such and such an establishment behind the lines for a specialized training course. Such courses provided a legitimate reason for being away from the trench zone of which many were delighted to avail themselves. Hence Second Lieutenant E. F. Chapman, 20th Battalion Royal Fusiliers, could write to his sister on 8 September 1916 – with a sense of relief and contentment after having been involved in the fighting on the Somme – from a coastal resort famous in *fin de siècle* France:

I expect Mother will have let you know by this time that I am down at Le Touquet on a machine-gun course. It lasts a week – I shouldn't mind if it would last for the duration! I assure you that it is most decidedly better than the line! You can eat and drink whenever you please. You can wash every day, and take off your clothes at night. You get as much sleep as you want. You smell flowers and the sea instead of dead bodies. And you are not shelled. What more do you want?

First Battles

In the long catalogue of British attempts to break the deadlock on the Western Front the Battle of Neuve Chapelle holds pride of place. It was the first of its kind. Lasting only three days, from 10 to 12 March 1915, it was a small affair compared with the great confrontations that came later, but it set a pattern that was to become more or less standard for many months: an attack launched with high hopes and great courage ending in disappointment and frustration. Yet this was no callow exercise in the throwing away of lives.

Indeed, for an opening move in a new style of war it was an extremely sophisticated one. Aerial photography provided intelligence, timetables were compiled for the artillery, a light railway was constructed to help bring up supplies. At zero hour an attacking force from Haig's First Army, which had been concentrated with much speed and efficiency, went into action after only the briefest of preliminary bombardments against a sector of the German line which – British intentions not having been signalled in advance, as happened too often later – was relatively lightly held. As a result an effect was achieved which, during the many months of trench warfare, was only to be repeated at Loos (September 1915) and Cambrai (November 1917): a genuine initial breakthrough. The attack ultimately failed because of inadequate exploitation, but then the battle plan, although carefully devised, took the action only so far; when it came to response to events, a combination of inexperience, hesitation and the 'fog of war' snatched defeat from the jaws of what almost promised to be a notable victory. Additionally, the fact that the advance was on so restricted a front, while an advantage at first, became a liability later, as reserve troops jammed with forward ones in a virtual bottleneck. Moreover, the Germans wasted no time in reinforcing their line, with the result that targets there for the grasping were rapidly transformed into strong points of fierce resistance.

How the battle seemed to an officer who witnessed both the first success and the subsequent confusion can be seen from the account by Lieutenant J. D. Wyatt, 2nd Battalion, Yorkshire Regiment – an account written sometime later, since he became a casualty on the final day, being wounded badly enough to be sent home to 'Blighty'. The opening bombardment began at 7.30 a.m. At 8.05 the first attack went in. Wyatt's turn was next:

> 10 March. At about 8.45 we were told the front German trench had been carried and soon after the Brigade began to move off. We went off down the road and then struck across the fields towards our old original trenches in front of Neuve Chapelle. We got to the old trenches about 10 o'clock and really one couldn't make out what was going on. On the right the prisoners were coming in in streams, but we were not allowed to advance. It seemed we were to work by the right and the right was temporarily held up. And there we

remained with nothing in front of us till 2 p.m., four precious hours lost, never to be regained. At 2 p.m. we advanced and meeting with but feeble resistance to our front but losing somewhat from enfilade fire from our right flank, went on till dusk. Then we were told to dig ourselves in and there we stayed. There was little in front of us *then*, but it was no good. The CO had orders to go no further. So we started making a trench. At 18 inches we came to water so had to content ourselves with making a breastwork.

11 March. We held on to our position all day. The troops on our right were counter-attacked but not we fortunately, as we were rather thin. As the day went on, it was evident the Germans were getting up both men and guns. We were very sick that we hadn't been allowed to push on the previous night and also about yesterday's delay of 4 hours. We lost a few men that day by sniping from our right flank.

12 March. That night the Germans counter-attacked heavily on the right and got up a lot of guns. During the day we got our first taste of shelling. I gather one shell burst close to me and that ended my interest in the battle. I vaguely remember lying at the bottom of a shallow trench and then, when it grew dark, being told by someone to go and find the Doctor. I remember wandering for hours and stumbling into holes and once found myself in a trench occupied by the Border Regt. At last I got to a dressing-station of some sort. There I was given a Sal-Volatile and put on a Motor Ambulance and taken into Estaires. I spent what little remained of the night there.

In addition to the main attack, there were subsidiary attacks to the north and south, but these achieved little. The 1st Battalion King's Liverpool Regiment, for example, suffered a fate which many other battalions would experience in Western Front battles, that of being stopped by barbed wire entanglements through which there was no passable breach. Its leading men were shot down mercilessly at the wire as they tried to force a way through it, and after losing heavily the battalion was forced to withdraw to its trenches. All this was witnessed by a young Territorial officer of a supporting battalion, Second Lieutenant Gordon Bartlett, 1/5th King's Liverpool Regiment, for whom this was his first taste of real action. The adrenalin was clearly still flowing when he wrote to his family on 13 March:

For three days and nights none of us got a wink of sleep, our nerves strung to the highest pitch waiting to charge every minute. We were in the trenches acting as a covering force to our 'regular' comrades, who attacked the German lines on Thursday morning; the 1st King's Liverpool's in that charge lost 200 men and officers, among the latter Archdeacon Madden's son. Other regiments suffered heavily too, yet by their pluck our brave lads achieved their aim. Critics say Mons and Ypres were nothing to it. An inferno of artillery and rifle fire for hours. Our own trench was blown to pieces in parts, we had many wounded, and ten killed, how any of us lived through it is a marvel. We were all praised by the 'Regular Army' officers for our courage and the way we helped to bring in the wounded, some of us being specially mentioned for decorations. I did my share in bringing in and succouring wounded to the utmost, and earned my Captain's praise. It is impossible to describe the scene, dead piled up in front, men crawling in with limbs blown off, and other

horrible wounds. The Germans suffered just as heavily, though. Shall never forget these last few days, never. Every man who took part in it deserves the VC.

All that was left of a Battalion of Gordon Highlanders after Neuve Chapelle 1915: about 180 men. (Q 90288)

The determination and bravery described by Bartlett was acknowledged elsewhere, notably by the French. If nothing else, Neuve Chapelle achieved an important breakthrough in persuading Britain's senior partner that she meant serious business on the Western Front. This would be underlined soon afterwards by two other efforts in the same sector, at Aubers Ridge (9 May) and Festubert (15–27 May), both of which added substantially to the casualty roll but with little or nothing to show in terms of ground gained.

A little over a month after Neuve Chapelle, a minor victory was achieved some thirty miles to the north. On the southern rim of the Ypres Salient – that dangerous zone which was to be defended over the years by the British with the doggedness displayed by the French at Verdun – Hill 60 was a point of vantage bound to become a bone of bitter contention. A man-made eminence sixty metres above sea-level (hence its name) created by spoil thrown up during the building of a railway cutting, it loomed menacingly above the flat Flanders plain. From it the towers of Ypres, which were still largely intact at this stage, were clearly visible, barely two miles off. In an area where mining under enemy lines was largely impossible owing to the high water-table, Hill 60 was an obvious challenge to the tunnelling units of both sides. By 7 April the British had enough mines ready to launch a surprise attack. Major William (Bill) Murray was an officer of the 27th Brigade RFA whose battery took part in the operation. In a letter to his sister written on the following day, he attempted to invoke the scene by comparisons with landmarks near to the family home in Cumberland:

> I will try and describe to you our fight here yesterday. Imagine to yourself a hill about the size of the one Moorthwaite farm stands on and our trenches all along the nearside of Moorthwaite lock. The sappers and miners have tunnelled into the hill opposite in every direction and filled it up with dynamite, also imagine the hill to be full of Germans, and then imagine that hill rising straight up into the sky and bursting to pieces and you will get some notion of what took place last night at 9 p.m. As soon as the hill subsided again every gun opened and the infantry rushed it and took six German trenches. Of course the Germans started too and by the time it was dark all the fury of all the nations was let loose. Imagine hundreds of guns all firing as fast as they could, and the same number of shells bursting, and making just as much noise as the guns, and in addition the whole of the infantry with their Maxims firing as hard as they could. What a night, and then at daybreak they counter-attacked and drove out the KOSB but the 'Jocks' as they are called were not going to be turned out. They went in with the bayonet and I don't think the Germans will forget that attack. I don't think they will get us out now but I expect we shall have another night of it tonight.

Murray's prophecy was correct, for the Germans were not going to give up easily – indeed they won the hill back one month later on 5 May. In the fierce hand-to-hand fighting which the geography of the place made almost mandatory, there were many fatalities, among them the young officer whose appeal to the sporting crowds of Britain had given him a brief celebrity some months earlier, Lieutenant Rowland Owen [see p. 38]. He was killed in action there on 18 April.

On 22 April, to the north-east of Ypres in the vicinity of Langemarck, the enemy launched a major military initiative, one indeed that was substantially to change the mood of the whole war. It was noted as follows in the diary of the Captain J. W. Barnett of the Indian Medical Service:

> 22 April. Cannonade on Ypres very violent. Hear that Germans used gas and wiped out the French – 50 guns lost but Canadians saved the day.
> 25 April. Saw gassed men – blue faces choking and gasping. How we hate the Germans.

That first use of gas was to give Germany an evil name in British eyes, and when barely two weeks later a U-boat sank the liner *Lusitania* off

southern Ireland, her reputation for chivalry in war, already reduced by tales of atrocities in 1914, fell virtually to zero. The British would speedily reply in kind, but there is no doubt that the moral high ground was conceded by Germany to the Allied powers by what happened on that 22 April 1915.

Writing two weeks later from a hospital in Yorkshire to which he had been sent with a severe foot wound that would lead to amputation, Lance-Corporal Jim Keddie, a Scottish soldier serving in a Canadian battalion, described to his mother what he saw that day:

> We went up on the 20th to take up reserve trenches north of Ypres, we had practically nothing to do for the first two days then it was on the afternoon of my birthday that we noticed volumes of dense yellow smoke rising up and coming towards the British trenches. My Coy was not in the firing line and we did not get the full impact of the gas, but what we got was enough for me, it makes your eyes smart and run, I became violently sick, but it passed off fairly soon. By this time the din was something awful where we were, we were under a crossfire of rifles and shells, we had to lie flat in the trenches. The next thing I noticed was a horde of Turcos making for our trenches, some were armed, some were unarmed. The poor devils were absolutely paralysed with fear.

Keddie's so-called 'Turcos' were French Colonial troops of the 45th (Algerian) Division, which with the French 87th (Territorial) Division was holding the line at the point of the German attack. In the event both

Photograph entitled 'The morass near Hill 60'; the view in 1916 showing the result of the fierce fighting of the previous year. (Q 37366)

An image of the 'gas' war, which began with the Second Battle of Ypres in 1915. *The Gas Mask* **by the War Artist Eric Kennington.** (Art 668)

divisions broke and ran, leaving a gap of approximately four miles in the Allied defences and a more or less open approach to Ypres. However, the Germans had played their card more as an experiment than as part of a serious push and failed to make the best of their advantage, advancing only slowly and in some areas being deterred by their own gas. As Captain Barnett correctly acknowledged, the Canadians saved the day, their 1st Division, of which Keddie was a member, improvising a new forward defence line and even launching counter-attacks.

These were the first moves in what was to become known as the Second Battle of Ypres, a battle which was to be a particularly brutal and savage one, fought in anger and without compassion or quarter. Among its many casualties was William Edgington, who had been in the war from the first, had been through the Mons Retreat and taken his part in many subsequent actions. He had been doubly promoted since First

Ypres, becoming a Sergeant-Major in December and a Second Lieutenant, moving from the Royal Horse to the Royal Field Artillery, early in April. He was clearly delighted at his swift elevation, but this thoughtful, highly professional soldier would not long survive his rise to officer status. The following are extracts from the final entries in his diary:

Wed Thurs Friday Sat Sun Monday 1 May Battle still going on. Hear all kinds of reports, both good and bad. Talk of falling back. I fully believe we have had a critical time which is not ended yet. The Huns do not appear to be short of Amm^n by the way their shells are flying. I took my guns back about 2 miles, just out of Ypres, NE Corner. No sleep now. Shells come from all directions N– S– and East and also from the sky. We are evidently going to fall back after holding this line for 6 months. Hard lines.

Tuesday 2 May Our casualty list must be growing alarmingly. One continual stream of wounded being carried back along the roads, the dead being buried where they fall. When will it end?

Lieutenant William Edgington, 2nd Lieutenant 62 Battery, RFA. Killed in Action 8 May 1915; photographed when serving as a Sergeant of the Royal Horse Artillery in Poona, India. (HU 63249)

Edgington was evidently too heavily engaged over the following days to write any more in his diary. A memorial card printed for his family supplies the information that he was 'killed in action at Ypres, between 3.30 and 4 p.m. on the afternoon on May 8th, 1915, aged 36 years'. Underneath is printed a phrase that would become a favourite text on many future war-graves: 'Until the day break and the shadows flee away.' His body was not found when the war cemeteries were constructed after the war and his name is among the 54,000 on the Menin Gate at Ypres.

'When will it end?' Probably Edgington's final question referred to the whole war, but in terms of the action then in progress, it would last for thirty-three days, closing down finally on 25 May. It was not in fact one continuous slog, rather a sequence of sub-battles with brief respites in between as the fighting surged and subsided in various parts of the Salient. Each of these would eventually be assigned its official name. The Battle of Frezenberg Ridge, which took place between 8 and 13 May, consisted of a series of vigorous attacks by the Germans on British positions which as the crow flies were little more than three miles from Ypres itself. Among the units who took the brunt of the enemy's last attack was the so-called 'Cavalry Force' – i.e. cavalry regiments fighting as infantry, one of which was the North Somerset Yeomanry, a unit of the 3rd Cavalry Division. Private Cecil Sheppard of the NSY wrote the following unsparing account to his sister some days later:

For 3 hours they sent over shells at the rate of at least 120 per minute. The noise was deafening and the range was perfect. Our trenches either side of us were blown in and sorry to say shells dropped in the trenches and killed and wounded many of our men.

After the 3 hours there was a lull of 5 minutes and the Germans attacked. It was a relief for us to have something we could reply to and I tell you we practically stood on the parapet in our excitement and mowed them down. It was really great and in front of the NSY part of the trenches they were sent back. The attack lasted about ½ hour and our fellows were so incensed that any wounded man seen to move was immediately riddled with bullets and it

Corporal Cecil Sheppard, 1st North Somerset Yeomanry, survivor of the fierce Battle of the Frezenburg Ridge, 8–13 May 1915. (HU 63250)

really was a pitiful sight to see the ground strewn with German dead lying in all positions.

After a lull of about ½ hour they started the bombardment again, worse if anything than before, incensed as they probably were by the failure of the attack. They kept it up this time from 6.30 a.m. to 6 p.m. practically 12 hours with shells as before about 100 to the minute. How any of us escaped God in heaven only knows. So fortunate was our Troop that only 2 of the 20 were wounded and one killed but in the other troops a much sadder tale has to be told. Some had 3 left, some a few more. As to the officers we lost 10 out of 14 including the Colonel, Adjutant, 2nd in Command, 2 Squadron leaders and the Major of the Maxim gun. One shell pitched in a trench killing 9 – 3 officers and 6 men, while one man in the middle of them was buried but escaped unhurt. Our 2 Maxim guns were blown to atoms and altogether the casualty list numbered about 120. The Regts on either side of us suffered as many or more, the Royal Horse Guards coming out with only 80 left and the Leicester Yeomanry with I believe only 40. Such was the scene through which thank God I was allowed to come unscathed, but I can tell you the nerve-racking was terrific, one man in our trench breaking down and having to be taken away. Men were of course blown to bits and one man in the next trench had an arm and leg off. We were to stay in 3 nights but after such a bombardment (the heaviest of the war) we were relieved at 1 a.m. on Friday morning.

I hope you won't tire of reading this account but I cannot lay too much stress on the fact of someone who must have been watching over me to save me from the shells and shot. The only other thing the Germans could have used against us would have been the Gases but the wind was against them so they could not be used, but of our Division of 2700 we had 2000 casualties so you can see it was very terrible. I have chosen you my dear to send the account to and will you please read it to my mater and explain to her that I cannot write to both of you so please let her know all about it as soon as you can. Shall be glad to hear from you as often as possible as you will recognize that the time we are going through is a very worrying one. Don't forget to give your thanks that I am up to now quite well.

With all my love and kisses

Cecil

Sheppard's figures were, as it turned out, overstated, the 3rd Cavalry Division's actual toll being 226 killed, 827 wounded, 178 missing. Yet as the official history states, 'the cavalry lost very heavily', one index of this being the fact that no less than one brigadier and seven commanding officers became casualties, three of the latter – not including Sheppard's own CO, Lieutenant-Colonel G. C. Glyn – losing their lives.[*] Perhaps the worst omen was that actions such as the one described seem to confirm the arrival on the scene of a new brutality, with scant pity shown for the wounded. In the words of one prominent historian, '"Second Ypres" was, for its size, one of the most murderous battles of the war.'[†]

[*] *Military Operations. France and Belgium. 1915*, Macmillan 1928, Vol I, pp. 334–5.
[†] Cyril Falls, *The First World War* Longmans, 1960, p. 93.

The Battle of Loos

In July 1915 C. A. Ashley, a volunteer infantryman under training in Yorkshire, returned from a brief weekend leave to find that he had been transferred to the Royal Engineers and was under orders to leave for Chatham the following morning. Several of his colleagues had received similar instructions. At Chatham, together with men drawn from other infantry units, they were put in bell-tents on the barrack square, given khaki if they had not been issued with it already, promoted to the rank of corporal, and informed that they were to go to France as soon as possible and that there would be no time for embarkation leave. A week after arriving at Chatham they marched out of barracks and entrained for Southampton; crossing to Le Havre they made their way by one of the usual slow-moving trains to the town where the British had their GHQ, St Omer.

Searching for common ground, the members of this ad hoc party had discovered that the only thing they had in common was a knowledge of chemistry. They gathered that there would shortly be an attack and speculated that their function might be to test the water as the army advanced. But this new unit, now officially known as Special Company 186 Royal Engineers (a second one, numbered 187, was created at the same time, and there would be two others, 188 and 189, by August), had been constituted for another, more aggressive purpose. 'We learned', wrote Ashley – in an account necessarily produced much later on account of the confidential nature of the work in hand – 'that our part in the attack would be to let off poison gas.' General Haig had decided that when it came to the next major offensive he would surprise the enemy with his own weapon; in short, the Germans would be getting their own back. Ashley's account continues:

> Cylinders of gas were to be placed in trenches in front of the infantry, and the gas was to be let off through iron pipes to be attached to the cylinders and placed over the parapets. We practised with cylinders and pipes, and thought that perhaps this was a job for plumbers, but were gratified to hear that chemists were needed to give confidence to the infantry. On August 22 we gave a demonstration, letting off a small quantity of chlorine gas for the benefit of Sir Douglas Haig. He was accompanied by his corps and divisional generals and a few French generals with magnificent uniforms.
>
> In preparation for the attack we were all split up into sections and marched to various points. Clem and I found ourselves in the cellar of a house in Vermelles. We were all armed with revolvers and brassards [i.e. armbands] of pink, green and white. Then we were given watches, which were to be synchronised later – mine stopped during the night and never worked again – and a printed sheet of instructions. Gas and smoke were to be let off alternately over a forty-minutes period, with thick smoke only during the last two minutes so that the infantry could follow immediately behind it.

The offensive in question, which would be named after the small mining village of Loos which was a prime object of the attack and was taken in the first few hours, was to be launched across an area of open land between La Bassée to the north and the industrial city of Lens to the south. (If Ypres represented the extreme left of the British sector of the Western Front, this area was the extreme right.) Originally planned for 15 September, it began in the early morning of the 25th. It was fought in parallel with a French attack; indeed it was the French who had mandated where the British thrust should be – against the wishes of the British commanders, who were opposed to the move in principle and who considered that if an attack had to be made this was not the best place to make it. For reasons of Allied solidarity, it went ahead.

One curiosity of the battle is that the armies did not have the terrain over which it was fought to themselves; curiously, local business was continuing very much as usual. Second Lieutenant Cyril Rawlins, a transport officer in the Welch Regiment, wrote this description of the battleground in a letter dated 28 September.

> We are right in the middle of the French coalfield, dead flat, featureless country: dozens of big gaunt mines and huge black slag-heaps: little sordid dirty villages, and roads made of black mud a foot deep: the mines are working just as if nothing were going on, and little pit locos and trains of tubs are crawling about, with melancholy shrieking whistles.

Before the attack 150 tons of gas in more than 5000 cylinders were carried up to the front. It was no easy task transporting the long, heavy cylinders through the twisting communication trenches, the more so as this was done under cover of night. Secrecy was paramount: in all orders and communications the word 'gas' was avoided in favour of the innocuous term 'accessory'. The whole operation was brought to the starting point without any breach of security.

On the night of 24–25 September Sapper G. J. Matkin, of P Cable Section, IV Corps, who as a member of the Royal Engineers was aware of the gas attack to come, noted events in his diary:

> Supper in Mazingarbe, all the boys marching for the trenches were singing and cheery. 187 Field Company distributed along front trenches for the purpose of manipulating gas cylinders. Returned to billet 9 p.m., slept till 11 p.m., on duty 11 p.m. to 8 a.m.
>
> Message says: 'Operation order 110 holds good. The hour of zero for tomorrow will be communicated later. Weather favourable. GHQ'
>
> Reports from all Bdes coming in about midnight saying gas apparatus all ready and wind favourable, viz W to SW and varying from 1 to 5 mls per hour.
>
> Saturday 25th. Message saying cavalry have arrived and are in readiness just near Noeux les Mines. Messages coming through every hour from meteorological observers in trenches notifying direction of wind and velocity.
>
> Zero notified at 3.30 a.m. as being for 5.30 a.m., all Brigades informed.

In the trenches Corporal Ashley and his comrades were poised to carry out the task which had brought them to the forefront of the action:

> We put on our gas helmets, which consisted of a hood of grey flannel soaked in chemicals (the photographers' 'hypo') that we put over our heads and tucked into our tunics. Visibility through a piece of mica let into the helmet was soon limited by condensation and although the morning was cold we were soon uncomfortably hot. I removed my equipment and revolver to give me greater freedom, and put them on the parapet.
>
> To attach a pipe to twelve cylinders in succession and then turn the tap on and off in a period of 38 minutes does not sound a significant task, for the gas took less than two minutes to flow out of each cylinder and we had two pipes. However, working as hard as we could, and without intermission while smoke was being sent over, we managed to empty only ten cylinders, which we later discovered was more than the average. The difficulty was caused by the release of pressure making the nuts so cold that they would not fit easily on to the new cylinders. (This had been thought of too late, in subsequent attacks rubber connections were provided.) One man, we were told, was so frustrated that he carried his cylinders some distance forward and then tried to burst them by firing at them.

Sapper Matkin's account continues:

> Raining slightly, wind SSW 2 mls per hour when our signal for commencing gas went up. A steady stream of white cloudy smoke gradually streamed out

Troops advancing to the attack through gas: a remarkable private photograph taken by a member of the London Rifle Brigade on the opening day of the Battle of Loos, 25 September 1915. (HU 63277B)

Overleaf: Part of the Loos Battlefield. One frame from an eleven-section panorama, captioned: 'Taken from: NW of Lens. Direction: Loos, Pont-à-Vendin, etc., includes Hill 70'. Undated, possibly early 1916. (Q 42152)

and passed very slowly towards German lines. At the same time our artillery poured concentrated fire towards rear of German 2nd line trenches. Terrific bombardment. German shells could be seen bursting this side of our gas-bank-cloud, making vivid bursts of fire. A weird spectacle to see the brown and black smoke bursting in the white cloudy gas. Rocket went up at 6.30 to intimate gas was to cease. Guns still banging it into them. Gas clouds taking long time to disperse, infantry waiting for it to clear before they attack.

Watching events from a well-protected Observation Point from which he could pass information rapidly to his general's command post was an artillery officer in the 6th London Brigade RFA, Captain Hadrian Bayley. His division, the 47th, was involved in the seizure of Loos. This is from a letter he wrote the same day:

> The drama has started. 40 minutes the poison is allowed and at 5.30 our infantry are to charge over the no man's land. There they are. Up the ladders and over the parapets they stream. Was there ever such a moment? More and more they stream. Line after line disappears into the smoke. One or two men go down – one or two are crawling back wounded. Ever the lines go forwards into the fog. If they are defeated they would stream back. The German fire grows gradually, the fog lifts and they have captured the first line trench. Through the murk I could trace our men to their objective and before 8.30 in the morning I telephoned down our attack was completely successful.

Overall, however, good news was rare on the first day at Loos. The gas was only spasmodically effective; in one part of the front, the most northerly, the wind was blowing the wrong way, but nevertheless the gas was released – the divisional commander having ordered that the pro-gramme must be carried out, whatever the conditions – contributing to what the official history would call 'a day of tragedy, unmitigated by any gleam of success'.* Bombardier J. W. Palmer, 26th Brigade RFA, noted in his diary some of the effects of gas on his comrades:

> The field of battle to our front presented a shambles. There appeared to be bodies everywhere. When I saw the effects of the gas on our lads I realised what they had suffered when the Germans first used it. Then we were totally unprepared for it but here at least we had the masks. I heard later that the masks were quite serviceable but during the charge which was nearly 800 yards in places, they were unable to get their breath. Some were unable to see and many in panic just pulled the masks off. By the afternooon the faces of our lads who lay in the open changed colour and presented a gruesome spectacle. Their faces and hands gradually assumed a blue and green colour and their buttons and metal fittings on their uniform were all discoloured. Many lay there with their legs drawn up and clutching their throats.

Another feature of Loos that would recur was the frustration of the hopes of the Cavalry to play the decisive role that had traditionally been theirs in battle. Although primed and poised for the charge, they waited vainly for the order to advance. The paucity of their contribution to the

---

*Military Operations. France and Belgium. 1915, p. 251.

battle can be deduced from these terse entries in the diary of Lieutenant L. S. Lloyd of the 18th Hussars:

> 25th. Heard about midday that British attack had gone well – 1st and 2nd line Hun trenches captured – 'Ready to move at any Moment' state.
>
> 26th. Spent all this day in readiness to 'Go through the Gap'. Heard heavy gunfire – Huns counter attacking.

The battle dragged on well into October, but in essence the result was decided on the first day. The losses continued. The French for their part suffered even more heavily than the British; one of their divisions reached the crest of that much coveted strong point, Vimy Ridge, but had to withdraw. It would be another eighteen months before Vimy was wrested from German hands.

For the British the best prize was Loos itself, famous for its so-called 'Pylons', also called 'Tower Bridge', twin lattice-girder minehead towers which the Germans had used for observation and which British guns had failed to destroy. They had seemed indestructible and dominant to the troops in the trenches opposite. Now that the British had seized them the Germans wasted little time in bringing them down.

A battle such as Loos, of course, consisted of far more than what was taking place at the front, demanding among other things a prodigious effort in terms of supply – of everything from shot and shell to food and drink. This is evident from a letter written to his mother by the transport officer Second Lieutenant Cyril Rawlins on Tuesday 4 October – a letter which also shows how utterly confusing and daunting such a battle could seem to its participants while in progress:

> Tenth day of battle: I cannot write much: everything is chaos: riding, riding, all day, all night: for five days I have had no rest and snatched sleep where and when I could anywhere; I am grimy and unshaven, plastered with mud: day and night, rations, water, ammunition, machine-guns, bombs; always the crash and thunder of the guns; the night sky lit up by the flashes, the dawn murky with the smoke of shells. Rattling, jolting, galloping limbers, streams of wounded, roaring of shells, mud everywhere. The very roof of Hell!!

One consequence that took some time to become apparent was that Loos was the end of the road for the BEF's first Commander-in-Chief. French's reputation had not been high before the battle and after it he was even more vulnerable. Earlier in the year he had dismissed General Sir Horace Smith-Dorrien, who had been out in France since August 1914; now it was his turn to go, while for Smith-Dorrien's fellow Corps Commander of the early campaigns, Sir Douglas Haig, came the elevation to supreme command for which he had long craved.

TRAINING FOR THE FRONT

Behind the fighting zone were numerous camps and other establishments providing training and courses of all kinds for both new arrivals and hardened warriors. The largest and most notorious training camp of all was the so called 'Bullring' at Etaples, featured here, where the regime was so severe that many men were glad to leave it to get to the front. (HU 33342)

Inset: A major aim of all such training was the inculcation of the offensive spirit. The photograph shows New Zealanders practising the ultimate in offensive warfare, the attack with the bayonet. (E(AUS) 298)

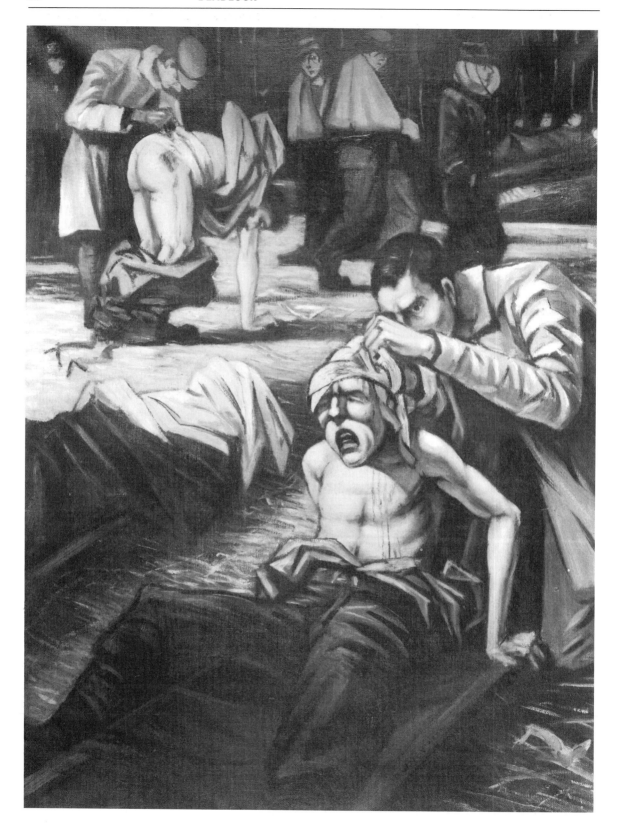

Wounds, 'Blighty ones', Fatalities

There could be a good side to being wounded. Responsibility was taken away, you became someone else's problem. Captain H. C. Meysey-Thompson, wounded on 20 September 1917 and put on board a hospital train, described his reactions in his diary:

> A beautiful autumn day and I rather enjoy the journey down. The sensation of travelling as a parcel – put into the train and taken out at appropriate times – is very soothing.

Bombardier J. W. Palmer, wounded at Loos and in hospital in Versailles, was also aware of his good fortune, but only by contrast with another soldier who had drawn the shortest of straws:

> One poor fellow has both arms missing and is blind. How lucky I must consider myself.

Palmer had seen a worst case short of death – perhaps a case worse than death. The Western Front produced a large crop of men who would survive it in a pitiable state, deprived of the opportunity of leading any normal or meaningful life. Others who had huge problems to surmount but who were encouraged to make the best of things were the amputees. Amputation of limbs took place in the First World War on a far greater scale than in the Second, regularly being seen as a first rather than a final option. In the case of Private Fred Norman, it is clear from a letter written at his request from France that the medical authorities in the hospital to which he was despatched for treatment in May 1915 believed that amputation of his leg was necessary because his life was at risk, presumably from gangrene. That action having been taken, it was urged upon both the soldier and his wife that this should not be seen as the end of the world. 'On the contrary,' wrote Captain Towse to Mrs Norman, 'when once he has become accustomed to the loss, he can do just as much and be just as useful as he ever was, but of course a few things are debarred him.' One thing that was debarred him was the continuance of his military career, a matter of prime importance to a regular soldier who had served almost nine years with his regiment when he left the Army in February 1916, 'being', according to the formula on his discharge certificate, 'no longer physically fit for War Service (Para 292 King's Regulations)'.

Another soldier whose career ended in similar fashion, after over thirteen years with the Royal Field Artillery, was Acting Bombardier B. C. Jones. He described his wounding and its consequences in the diary he had kept since landing in France in August 1914. He had survived Neuve Chapelle and Loos but his number was on a German missile in December 1915:

> Tuesday 7 Dec I take over duty at the Batty position, Germans shelled swamp just behind batty (about 50 yds), about ½ past 2 Germans commenced

Opposite: An official war artist's unsentimental record of one inevitable consequence of war: C.R.W. Nevinson's *The Doctor*. (Art 725)

A photograph preserved with Bombardier B.C. Jones's diary. Jones is seated on the extreme left of the group, photographed either at Brighton or, more probably, at the hospital at Roehampton in South London where wounded soldiers were fitted with artificial limbs. (HU 63251)

shelling near the battery. One shell (4.2) hit the dugout of our telephone pit. I remembered no more until I woke up in Béthune Casualty Clearing Station No 33, where I find I have been severely wounded. Left hand blown off, left arm ripped up 12 inches. Scalp wound 6 inches, wound on over side of knee (left) 5 inches.

Wednesday 8 Dec In hospital.

Thursday 9 Dec Operation on upper arm for gangrene (successful).

Friday 10 Dec Feeling very bad.

Saturday 11 Dec Feeling the same.

Sunday 12 Dec I remain here for 8 days then removed to St Omer Nº 10 Casualty Clearing Station on La Bassée Canal by hospital barge, very comfortable. After remaining here at St Omer for a few days (7) I am removed by train to Etaples (24th General Hospital) on the 29 December. I am sent to England on the Hospl Ship *Dieppe*, then by train to Nottingham, remain in bed until about the end of February. I am eventually transferred to Brighton where I am operated on and re-amputated on the 3rd June 1916 awaiting Roehampton for Artificial limb.

Jones's diary contains only two further entries. At the bottom of the page concluding his account as above, he wrote

GOD SAVE THE KING

At the top of the following page he noted the signing of the Armistice on 11 November 1918.

His discharge from the Army took place with effect from 11 September 1916.

The best wound of all was what was known as a 'Blighty', or 'a Blighty one': the kind of wound that guaranteed a man a ticket for the home country, but left him basically sound in wind and limb, with the prospect of being able in due course to continue with life, liberty and the pursuit of happiness – particularly happiness. Battery Sergeant-Major Douglas Pegler noted in his diary in February 1917, in obvious disappointment, that he had nearly got a 'Blighty'. He noted also that his fellow Sergeant, Kelly, had found himself in similar straits. 'He is now', wrote Pegler, 'reviling his luck in fluent Dublinese.'

Major Ronald Schweder reported in March 1917 the case of a soldier's delight at receiving an undoubted 'Blighty'. 'I saw a fellow get a lovely wound in the head with a bit of shrapnel. He was so pleased, he made me laugh.'

Captain John Staniforth finally achieved a 'Blighty' in May 1918 after two and a half years in the field. He had been through much and fought valiantly; when the 'Blighty' was vouchsafed, he accepted his dismissal from active service without the slightest reluctance. He told his parents:

MO just arrived. And he tells me he is going

TO SEND ME

OVERSEAS

TO

BLIGHTY

IN A DAY

OR

2

! ! !

Nuff said. Goodbye-ee

For some soldiers about to go into action, what sustained them was the belief that they would come through with that much prized ticket for home. On balance, it was a fair option, and it was arguably the best option. To come through unscathed would mean you would be there for the next battle. To be killed? There was precious little future in that. To acquire a wound that could be patched up quickly so that you would be back in the trenches in no time? There might not be much future in that either. To emerge with a 'Blighty one' which signified that you had done your duty and could therefore stage an honourable, conscience-free withdrawal? That was the most satisfactory outcome of all – and with any luck the war might be over by the time you were restored to full health.

Thoughts of such ways of escape were not confined to soldiers. In a letter to Captain C. L. Overton, a Company Commander in a Territorial Infantry Battalion, written during the great battles of early 1918, the girl whom he would eventually marry urged him: 'Do get a nice Blighty, and quickly.'

Death was so commonplace on the Western Front that it ceased to seem remarkable. Lieutenant A. G. May, an officer of the Machine-Gun Corps, commented:

Somehow one gets used to seeing the dead. I remember the first of our dead I

saw and all I could think of was that he looked peaceful and feel sorry for his folks. After a while I think one becomes thick skinned or case hardened to seeing our own dead, maybe this is not reasonable but it would be bad to be emotional about it.

Such would appear to have been the general wisdom, but there were innumerable exceptions to the rule, particularly with regard to losses within a group of close friends. Harold Brooks, who served as a telegraphist in the Royal Engineers (Territorial Army), through the winter of 1915–16, described such an event in his diary – an occasion made worse by the fact that one of the two men killed had a brother in the same unit:

29th February. We have been plunged into gloom by the deaths of Harry Hawkins and Joe Hanna, which occurred today whilst out with a working party. The day's work had been finished and the wagon had started on the return journey. A shell pitched about five yards from the back of the lorry and splinter cut right through the floor, some slashed the side, and others went through the roof. Harry and Joe were on the tail board and caught the full force of the explosion. Joe pitched forward, killed instantly, but Harry lingered, apparently, for about an hour at the dressing-station, happily, as far as anyone could judge, free from pain. Alf Coles and Trehearne both received slight wounds which were dressed on the spot. How it was that nobody else was hurt is a miracle, as all the working party was packed into the lorry.

They were buried at the Military Cemetery on the Poperinghe–Beningshelst road, nearly opposite the Château Elizabeth. Life is cheap here, but as circumstances permit, the dead are given such honour as active service will allow. In the case of this funeral all men who were not actually on working parties or in action in the trenches were in attendance. Feeling was rather tense as we all gathered together before the parade. Everyone felt the blow very keenly, but none could comprehend the anguish of Alf Hawkins, it must have been a terrible ordeal for him. I, with Bill Banton, Poole, and George Martin, acted as bearers to Joe. God grant that we do not have to go through such a ceremony again – it is terrible.

'If your number's on it . . .': Religion and Fatalism

Lieutenant John Staniforth, officer of a southern Irish battalion, the 7th Leinsters, noted with amusement the strange behaviour of an NCO when taking part in a bombing raid against enemy trenches. '"In the nameof theFatherandoftheSonandoftheHolyGhost," said Corporal Chievers, crossing himself wildly, and cast the bomb into space.'

Yet Corporal Chievers was not only taking his deep-rooted Irish Catholicism to war, he was also acting in accordance with the accepted religious tenets of both sides. The ordinary German soldier bore on his belt the legend 'GOTT MIT UNS' 'God with us'; (which claim, with its use of the word '*uns*', was convincing proof for some Tommies that the Germans *were* indeed 'Huns' in fact and not just in current phraseology). Similarly the British were ever ready to evoke, or assume, God's support for their cause. Thus Second Lieutenant Cyril Rawlins could write in the early, hopeful phase of the Battle of Loos, 'We have smashed the German line, captured prisoners and guns, and we're *going ahead*!! Surely the God of Battles must smile on us at last.' By this rule of thumb, the final outcome of Loos should have indicated a smile withdrawn.

One Sunday in September 1914 on the Aisne Major Lionel Tennyson, 2nd Battalion, The Rifle Brigade, was on duty in the front line. Near at hand he could hear the hymn-singing of the British at their routine church parade. At a slightly greater distance he could hear the hymn-singing of the Germans at theirs. His diary contains no overt comment on the event, but the circumstances, of both sides invoking the reassurance and protection of the same God, speak for themselves.

The key question in most men's minds was not, however, the righteousness of the cause for which they were fighting – that was largely taken for granted – but the matter of their and their comrades' survival. Inevitably the circumstances of a form of war in which men were under constant threat from an enemy within earshot concentrated men's thoughts on this subject, so that from the beginning the search was on for some sort of credo or philosophy to help them to cope.

For many, conventional religion could supply all the answers. Without necessarily considering themselves especially worthy, they attributed their prospects of coming through to divine benevolence. 'Of course I know', wrote the Canadian Andrew Munro from France in June 1917, 'that our lives are in the hands of One who alone looks after us. We cannot help realizing it in a place such as this is.' There were many, too, who believed that their safety would be assured by the power of prayer. Second Lieutenant Tom Allen of the Irish Guards, writing in 1915, concluded on the strength of letters he had censored that 'there cannot be many villages in Ireland where prayers are not being said for the I.G. One man writing was quite convinced that "prayer turns bullets".' With an equally firm belief in the power of prayer, Major F. J. Rice, a command-

An unanswerable problem illustrated. A crucifix preserved amid the ruins, in the aptly named village of Misery, March 1917. (CO 1099)

A crucifix destroyed at Bellenglise, 9 October 1918. (Q 9353)

ing officer in the Royal Field Artillery, could write on Armistice day 1918:

> The great day has arrived and the family is none the worse for the war. It is very wonderful, and I am most deeply thankful for the way we have all been protected through it. All the prayers of our relations for us have been answered and I trust we shall never forget these great mercies.

In a different context S. H. Raggett, a former infantryman and officer writing in 1919, recalled sensing the presence of the divine hand when in 1915 he saw the town of Festubert devastated by bombardment:

> Everywhere the ruins of war. Nothing stood except one thing – a cross with the crucified Christ nailed to it *alone* remained. I saw that cross and wondered. Everything mutilated, and yet the cross still stood. It seemed to be a message of Hope. 'He that believes in me shall *never* die.' I realised then that we could *never* lose the war. I realised later that we should have won it earlier had we thought less of *ourselves*, and more of God. There is much we don't understand, but we *shall* understand – some day.

Yet such comments begged too many questions: in Raggett's case, why was it that in one place a crucifix survived, while in another it was shattered like any other object in the way of shot or shell; in Rice's case, how was it that some equally virtuous and believing families lost all their sons; in the case of the Irish Guards, why was it that they acquired as formidable a casualty list as any other unit; in Munro's case, why was it that some men came through, while others, equally deserving, did not? This last question was especially troubling, and even more problematical was the undoubted fact that frequently good men were knocked out while others, less worthy, were spared. As Captain Harry Yoxall observed in August 1917 after his battalion had suffered the loss of some fine officers and men in the opening attack of the Third Battle of Ypres: 'All the best seem to go.'

For many, perhaps the majority, conventional religion could not resolve problems like these to their satisfaction, and there grew up a widespread, simply expressed fatalism, of which the essential belief was that if you were to live you were to live, if you were to die you were to die. In other words, if somewhere there was a bullet or shell with your number on it, there was nothing you could do about it; till then just soldier on. Thus Captain F. E. Packe could write to his family about his brother – also an officer in France – and himself in March 1915:

> Try not to worry too much about our both being out, if we are meant to come back we shall and if not one can wish for nothing better.

The 'fatalistic' point was made even more precisely by Lieutenant John Staniforth after six months at the front:

> I'm a great believer in my star. If I were going to be killed I'd have been killed long ago. Walking about the trenches all day long hand-in-hand with death, you can't help become a fatalist.

Yet Staniforth was a convinced Christian who spent his later life as a clergyman of the Church of England. It would seem that trench fatalism was far more than simply a means of shrugging the shoulders at issues too large to grasp; it was a genuine cult for the occasion, or, looked at another way, a pagan heresy given temporary legitimacy and acceptance by the awesomeness of the prevailing conditions. One soldier who acknowledged the strong grip of this impromptu creed while not subscribing to it himself was Private, later Second Lieutenant, A. R. Williams, himself a convinced believer and a son of the manse; he wrote in September 1916:

> The degree of spiritual progress reached by the average man is a cold fatalism which is astonishingly and altogether undeniably widespread. It must give some satisfaction or it would not be so conspicuously common.

One officer who was evidently not fated to survive was the Irish Guards subaltern, Tom Allen. He had a near-miss from a bullet when going up to the trenches for the first time in February 1915 and another a few days later. On the second occasion he was counting enemy dead beyond the barbed wire following a German attack when a bullet whistled through his hair. He was rebuked in a rich brogue by one of his men: 'Get down, sorr; that was meant for you.'

Sadly Allen's number was on another enemy missile within a matter of days; he was killed, not by a bullet but by a shell, while looking through a periscope from a front-line trench, before the month was out.

Among those who survived, there were many who felt that they had somehow been granted a charmed life; plainly no missile had their number. When S. H. Raggett asked a fellow ex-soldier what had struck him most in the war, the latter replied: 'I was struck most by the bullets that missed me.'

As opposed to those who were sure they would survive whatever the odds, there were others who became utterly convinced that they would *not* do so – to the extent that in some cases men would suddenly become quite certain that they were about to be killed. Captain Oliver Woodward, 1st Australian Tunnelling Company, was confronted by such a case in the final days of the war – on the eve of the attack across the Sambre-Oise canal during which the poet Wilfred Owen was to lose his life. Woodward himself admitted to having been especially anxious at that time, in that rumours of a possible armistice were in the air, leading him to comment: 'We had weathered the storm and just when we seemed about to enter the harbour the cry of "breakers ahead" was sounded . . . The query which kept coming through one's mind was, "*Shall I be fated to come through safely?*"' (Author's italics.) For one of his company it appeared that the answer to this question was that he would not:

> Corporal Davies, one of my best NCOs, came to me and asked whether I would take care of his personal belongings and post them to his wife should anything happen to him. I was feeling rather despondent myself and Corporal Davies' outlook on the future did not help to cheer me up. I spoke firmly to him, told him not to be foolish, and imagine he was going west. We all stood that chance, and we had to keep cool and collected. He replied: 'Captain, nothing you can say will remove the conviction that I will be killed. Will you

please do me the favour I ask?' Merely to ease his mind I consented and took charge of his personal effects. Before daylight broke next morning, Corporal Davies had made the supreme sacrifice, and had gone west. He was killed by a shell while we were out waiting for zero. This incident left me dazed and greatly impressed. In temperament Corporal Davies was of the calm type, he was a soldier who was as fearless as any soldier can truly be in war, had never failed in carrying out his duties in a most efficient manner, and inspired the confidence of his men. There could be no suggestion of fear or panic causing him to act as he did in coming to me. He knew his call was coming. Why should this have been? I cannot even hazard a suggestion, but these are the facts.

Yet such a conviction could be belied by events. In November 1916 Second Lieutenant Edward Beddington-Behrens, an artillery officer in 126th Brigade RFA, wrote to his sister: 'Do you know, I feel that I am going to get killed in this war, this feeling has almost reached a dead certainty lately.' Yet he came through unscathed, to write in later life, indeed, that he had always been convinced that he would survive. So forebodings of this kind must be seen, surely, as little more than self-induced hunches – with the risk that a soldier's premonition might become self-fulfilling if it drove him to act negligently or deliberately to expose himself to enemy fire.

To come through an action untouched – i.e., to be fated to survive while one's comrades died around one – might seem a wonderful free gift, a clear bonus, but it could leave scars as well as bring relief. It is well known that some who have lived on while their comrades did not have carried a sense of guilt ever afterwards. Thus Major H. E. Trevor, a regular officer in the 2nd Battalion King's Own Yorkshire Light Infantry, wrote on 26 September 1914 regarding the Battle of Le Cateau fought one month earlier:

I can hardly tell you how much the loss of my four officers and most of my best NCOs upset me. I felt that I too ought to have been killed.

Similarly Second Lieutenant Cyril Rawlins could write in 1915 after looking at 'the faces and forms of [his] dead comrades' killed in an attack, 'I almost wished myself with them.'

In the end to the conundrum, 'Why him? Why not me?' there was no ultimately satisfactory answer. The standard reaction to this as to so many of the problems thrown up by the Western Front war was 'San Fairy Ann', well defined by Brophy and Partridge in The Long Trail as:

An extremely popular phrase, approximated into English from the French ça ne fait rien – It doesn't matter, it makes no difference, why worry? Fatalistic, cynical, applicable to all kinds of situations.

Yet there were substantial areas in which war fatalism could offer neither help nor satisfaction, and where organized religion could and did step in to considerable effect. The role of the Army chaplain, indeed, grew rather than diminished as the war went on, for it was the chaplains who took care of the rituals associated with death and burial and the chaplains who wrote thousands of letters of consolation to the families of killed 'other ranks' which in the majority of cases would otherwise have received only the cold notifications of the state. Moreover, when the ultimate punishment of execution was inflicted, it was the chaplain who invariably found himself assigned to be on hand to offer prayers and companionship during the condemned man's last hours.

Significantly, the most successful chaplains were not those who saw the war as an opportunity to proselytize or to obtain what were known as 'wind-up conversions', but those who realized that their best service to their men was to go out and suffer with them – and help in every *human* way they could. The following letter was written in April 1916 by Captain W. Bell, the Adjutant of the 4th Royal Fusiliers, to the mother of the Reverend E. N. Mellish, an Anglican chaplain who was to emerge from the war with both a Military and a Victoria Cross:

> I cannot let this opportunity pass of telling you what a splendid man your son Noel is. During the recent operations at St Eloi in which my Battn unfortunately lost heavily, he did the work of ten men in dressing and helping wounded men. He is a most modest and unassuming man, and would probably say 'he was only doing his little job', but I was there and I know the splendid work he did, many a man owes his life to your son, and we are proud of him.
>
> The men of the Battalion love him, and swear by 'our Padre'.

In the end it was the deed, rather than the word, that spoke to men in such extreme situations. At a time when conventional creeds could seem not to apply, religion could hold its place through the activities of its finest practitioners.

More, beneath all the doubts and uncertainties, there was unquestionably a basic, ingrained sense of Christian hope, a belief, for many a confidence even, that somehow all the blatant, terrible injustices of war would be put right beyond the grave. Thus Captain Eric Gore-Browne could find another note than one of grief and despair in a letter to his wife describing the carnage of the Battle of Loos in 1915:

> No painting or poem or writing will ever give you a picture of a battlefield either while it is actually on or afterwards. I am glad to have seen both. There is something very magnificent and unselfish about it, and death in many shapes and forms, some beautiful, some ugly, makes one feel less fearful about it all, and that there must be a hereafter where all these brave fellows are going to meet again and have their reward.

Executions at dawn: from the Diary of an Assistant Provost-Marshal

In December 1915 Captain T. H. Westmacott was appointed Assistant Provost-Marshal of the First Indian Cavalry Division. His duties included attendance at military executions, of which he witnessed three, the first for the purposes of instruction, the others as officer in charge. His diary includes full accounts of two of these grim events, only withholding the name of the soldier concerned. On the later occasion, he had to undertake the task dreaded by any officer commanding a firing squad, that of administering the *coup de grâce*.

There were 346 executions during the war, 322 of which took place on the Western Front. No Australians were executed – the Australian authorities refusing to exact the death penalty despite strong representations from the British Commander-in-Chief – but the figures include twenty-five Canadians and five New Zealanders. Only three officers were executed. Desertion was the most common offence, but there were also executions for cowardice, sleeping at or leaving a post of duty, disobedience, striking a superior officer, casting away arms and mutiny. Murder accounted for a number of others, as in one of the cases described by Westmacott, though this was not simply a civil offence in a military situation, but a response to extreme provocation from an unsympathetic superior.

14 April, 1916. I was staying with Bowring of the 51st Division, and we received orders to attend the execution of a deserter in the Cheshire Regiment. The man had deserted when his battalion was in the trenches and had been caught in Paris. He was sentenced to death, but the sentence was remitted, and he was sent back to his battalion. He did so well in the trenches that he was allowed leave to England. He deserted again, and after being arrested was sent back to his battalion in France, when he was again sentenced to death. This time he was shot. We got up at 3.30 a.m., and Bowring and I were driven to the HQ of the 5th Division, the car breaking down on the way. When we got to DHQ Coates, of the 15th Hussars, the APM had gone on with the firing party. We caught them up, and I found Coates, the firing party and a company of the Cheshires drawn up opposite a chair under a railway embankment. The condemned man spent the night in a house about half a mile away. He walked from there blindfolded with the doctor, the parson and the escort. He walked quite steadily on to parade, sat down in the chair, and told them not to tie him too tight. A white disc was pinned over his heart. He was the calmest man on the ground. The firing party was 15 paces distant. The officer commanding the firing party did everything by signal, only speaking the word 'Fire!' The firing party was twelve strong, six kneeling and six standing. Before the condemned man arrived, the firing party about turned after grounding arms, and the OC firing party and the APM mixed up the rifles and unloaded some of them.

On the word 'Fire!' the man's head fell back, and the firing party about turned at once. The doctor said the man was not quite dead, but before the

OC firing party could finish him with his revolver he was dead, having felt nothing. The company was then marched off. The body was wrapped in a blanket, and the APM saw it buried in a grave which had been dug close by, unmarked and unconsecrated.

26 June, 1916. A Sowar in the 29th Lancers shot the Wordi Major (native Adjutant) of the Regiment dead. He then threw away his rifle, tore off most of his clothes, and rushed off to the HQ of the Lucknow Brigade, where he happened to catch General Morton Gage, the Brigadier, in the street. He told the General a long story, but as the General was British service he could not understand a word. The man was a Delhi policeman, and a Jat, who enlisted for the period of the war. He is a sulky kind of fellow but there is no doubt that the Wordi Major, who was an absolute rotter, goaded the wretched fellow to desperation.

After this date we moved down to the neighbourhood of Doullens for the battle of the Somme. Until the 13th of July the man was in my charge and I had to drag him about with DHQ until that date, very hard luck on the man. He behaved very well the whole time and one day he said to me, 'Sahib, I am quite certain now that I shall not be shot, as you have kept me so long.'

19 July. Had a long ride of about 28 miles to Villers Chatel, north of Aubigny, Yadram, the murderer, riding with me under escort the whole way. On arrival, orders came in for his execution.

20 July. Rode over to the Lucknow Brigade HQ and to the 29th Lancers and arranged everything including the place of execution.

Sent Yadram to the Regiment under escort to have the sentence promulgated. Gibbon, the Divisional Chaplain, was a great nuisance, as he obtained leave from the Divisional Commander to visit Yadram during the night. As Yadram was a Jat and not a Christian we all considered it a great piece of impertinence on Gibbon's part.

21 July. Got up at 2.45 a.m. and went over to the 29th Lancers with Gordon, the General's ADC, and Winckworth, my assistant. The Regiment was drawn up dismounted in hollow square with the firing party and the chair in front. The firing party consisted of twenty men, five from each squadron. They grounded arms and faced about and moved 3 paces to the rear, while I mixed up the rifles and unloaded some of them. Then they marched back and picked up their arms. The prisoner was then brought up under escort blindfolded with a white disc pinned over his heart, and he sat down in the chair. As Sergeant Walsh, my provost sergeant was tying him to the chair, he shouted in Hindustani, 'Salaam, O Sahibs! and Salaam, all Hindus and Mahometans of this regiment! There is no justice in the British Sirkar. I did this deed because I was abused. Those of you who have been abused as I was go and do the same, but eat your own bullet and do not be shot as I shall be.'

Then the OC firing party gave the signal, and the party came to the present, and on the word 'Fire' they fired a volley. The regiment and the firing party then faced about and marched off. Five bullets had gone through the disc, but the man still breathed, and I had to shoot him through the heart with my revolver, a horrid job. The grave had already been dug at the firing point, and Yadram was put straight into it and the grave was filled in and levelled by a fatigue party from the regiment.

'Smile, boys, smile': Soldiers' Humour

On 26 March 1916, behind the lines of the Somme front, Second Lieutenant Kenneth Macardle listened fascinated to the sounds of merriment emanating from one of the bell-tents in which the men of his battalion, the 17th Manchesters, had been billeted after a spell in trenches. Conditions were appalling. 'It snows and rains,' he noted in his diary, 'and hails, freezes and thaws and blows with a truly Hunlike frightfulness.' Moreover, the tents were by no means out of the range of enemy shell fire. Yet these Tommies were clearly in excellent spirits. Impressed and moved, Macardle wrote the following eloquent tribute:

> The men are happy in an unwonted sense of security. And make the night noisy with their singing of songs only fit for a camp but clever and funny, composed by the brighter geniuses in the ranks and set to popular airs; so because that strain of certain danger, of a vigorous, ingenious, relentless Death searching them out persistently, is for the moment relieved by a hardly certain safety, fifteen men in a small bell-tent, in the most villainous weather devised by an incomprehensible providence to make us miserable, sing and laugh and are happy as though they had pitched their tent on the banks of the Thames.

In 1920, looking back on his war experiences from the vantage point of peace, former Lieutenant S. H. Raggett wrote:

> A man who could smile and laugh in the face of adversity and in the presence of death was a man of incalculable worth. The morale of the army was kept up by those men who smiled.

Songs and snatches, many of a rhythm to be sung on the march, were perhaps the most popular way of making the best of things because all could join in, but jokes and wheezes of all kinds came easily too, and not only for the men. Humour knew no rank. Thus Captain Ronald Schweder could write to his wife of a dugout mess which he and his fellow officers had taken over in March 1917:

> There are in this mess quite the rudest pictures I have ever seen. Ladies by the dozen with nothing on. Under one of them is the Bairnsfather saying cut from one of his pictures, 'If you know of a better 'ole, go to it.'

He added his own pay-off line:

> Rather an apt saying, but not quite possible out here.

Humour even infiltrated No Man's Land. When in August 1916 the officers of the 21st KRRC were instructing representatives of a greenhorn battalion in trench techniques, it was decided to involve them in a somewhat unusual demonstration of the British mastery of that grim zone beyond the wire. Captain H. Meysey-Thompson described the episode in his diary:

Tommy Humour — as caught by an official photographer. The ruins of Contalmaison Château, on the Somme battlefield, photographed in September 1917.
(Q 2792)

After dinner arranged a little entertainment for our guests (Sherwood Forester officers) in the form of a walk in No Man's Land to hang my old breeches in a tree as a signal of defiance of the Hun. A particularly agile Sherwood Forester shinned up a pollarded willow and disposed them most artistically in its topmost branches, where they looked very well.

Humour could also appear on the battlefield. After Messines Sapper Harold Brooks noticed a fresh German grave marked by a wooden cross on which had been pencilled, by way of sardonic variation on the well-known phrase, 'He died to strafe us all'. A more innocent, schoolboyish way of mocking the enemy was to make play with his convoluted grammar and word order. Thus Lieutenant John Staniforth, during a bombardment:

Today Brer Boche's motto seems to be, 'It is a fine morning. There is nothing in the trenches doing. Let us a little frightfulness into the town pump.'

Lavatorial arrangements were, of course, an obvious butt for humorous comment. After superintending certain humble but necessary construction routines while his battalion was in billets, Staniforth produced the following variation on the theme of a well-known recruiting poster:

Hand me the office harp:
'What did you do in the Great War, dad?'
'I dug latrines for others, my lad.'

From this it is no great leap to the following, from an officer's letter of early 1915:

Have you seen the new but very vulgar toilet paper? A picture of the Kaiser on

The everlasting hygiene war, depicted in 4th Division's 1914 Christmas card. (HU 63253)

The self-mocking war. The Headquarters staff of the 21st Divisional Artillery, in its 1915 Christmas card, shows itself engaged in a range of cheerfully pointless activities. (HU 63254)

The romantic war. One young officer's sensuous vision of our closest ally. (HU 63255)

each piece and written underneath the words: 'The Kaiser in his new Toilet role'.

This is a variant from a long-running seam, other subjects of such graphic wit being Hitler and even, more recently, Saddam Hussein.

Many officers besides Macardle were struck by the apparently invincible humour of the ordinary soldier. Thus Staniforth could write in May 1918, following what had been for the British arguably the worst, certainly the most touch-and-go, months since the first battles of 1914:

> I heard a new term for the shrapnel helmet today from that cynical humorist, Tommy Atkins. He now speaks of it sardonically as his 'battle bowler', or, in the language of the Ordnance Store, as 'Bowlers, battle, one'.

Throughout the war humour was the best way of coping with the often intolerable conditions of trench life. One of its almost unavoidable hazards was infestation by lice, leading to the curious fact that one of the regular sound-effects of the Western Front, along with the crump of shells and the sputter of rifle or machine-gun fire, was the crackling noise resulting from the running of lighted cigarettes or matches along the seams of shirts and trousers, the trench-louse's favourite habitation. Communal bathing combined with a complete change of clothing was the army's method of 'strafing' lice – or fleas, another predictable and equally undesirable trench companion – the vats of breweries being a favourite location for such hygienic exercises. It was this phenomenon which produced the comic Christmas card shown on page 101. The anti-louse campaign also inspired the following anonymous effort, described as 'Extract from a censored letter', dated 15 November 1914 and preserved over the years in an officer's private album; Keatings' powder, it should be noted, was a well-known, though evidently less than totally effective, contemporary remedy:

> I found a squadron of Ulhlans on my chest and a battery on my back. I launched the famous regiment of Keatings against them but it failed to gain success. The enemy renewed attack at dawn and as General Bitem I counter-attacked with a force under General Killum; but not until General Scratchum brought his men into action could the tide of battle be turned. So the battle rages on my chest; on my right flank there is nothing new.

Paradoxically, it could be argued that trench humour was, to a certain extent, deadly serious. As Captain Eric Gore-Browne put it in a letter of August 1915:

> One has to be absolutely all there all the time and hang on to one's humour like grim death – otherwise I think you are bound to crack.

A French Artist with the BEF

Jean-Emile Laboureur, a thirty-seven-year-old French artist and a great Anglophile, was mobilized as an interpreter in 1914. He was eventually attached to the 12th Division of the BEF. Attracted by the anti-heroic 'business as usual' attitude of the British, he produced several portfolios of drawings showing the off-beat, casual moments of military life, scrupulously avoiding all horrors or heroics or any concession to sentimentality.

The pictures shown here – drawn in what has been described as 'his own highly disciplined, sparsely linear style', which had been developed before the war and showed clear awareness of contemporary cubist developments, are from his *Petites Images de la Guerre sur Le Front Britannique* ('War Sketches from the British Front'), a sequence of prints dating from 1916. He worked with an engraving tool called a 'burin', using any scrap of metal he could find at ammunition depots. He was later attached to the Americans for whom he performed a similar service.

Not popular with the French censorship because of what seemed too frivolous an approach, his engravings can now be seen as a valuable record of aspects of the war largely ignored by official artists and photographers. One of his strengths is the recording of unexpected but significant detail, such as, in the background of the station scene, the steam (reminiscent of gun-smoke) of the trains (which are angled like guns); or the fact that the principal figure in the drawing of the camp before battle is carrying out the homely task of tying his tie – a necessary act but not one that would have seemed worthy of record by martial painters of the traditional kind.

Top right: *Les Adieux du Permissionaire*
(A Soldier's Farewell after Leave)

Right: *Le Campement avant la Bataille*
(The Camp before a Battle)

The 'No Man's Land' War: Patrols and Raids

In June 1918 Gunner Harold Coulter, a trench mortar specialist in the Royal Field Artillery, wrote an article for a school magazine in England to try to answer the question which he knew was worrying many civilians back home. They were fully aware of what was happening during what he called the 'great engagements' on the Western Front, but they were unclear as to how the soldiers occupied themselves in the intervals between. His answer was: 'Within that Line which is called the "front" there is a continuous harassment in some part or other, occasioned by raids into the enemy's lines and also enemy raids into our own lines.' Raids, he went on to explain, varied greatly in purpose and extent:

> Sometimes it may be a silent night raid for the sole purpose of catching one prisoner. At another time a raid may be carried out on a grand scale in day time, with the purpose of penetrating deeply into enemy trench systems to do the utmost damage possible in a specified time. This latter type, however, is not nearly as numerous as the former type.

The decision to instigate such 'minor enterprises' (to quote the title of an official booklet about them issued in 1916) came early in the war. It was on 5 February 1915 that the then Commander-in-Chief, Sir John French, issued a memorandum in which, in the words of the Official History, 'he called attention to the importance of constant activity and offensive methods, although standing on the defensive. Thus he gave official authority to what were known in the army as "raids", local attacks on a small scale to gain ground, take advantage of any tactical or numerical inferiority on the part of the enemy, and capture prisoners for "identification" purposes, *i.e.* to determine what units were on a particular front.'*

Raids came top in the pecking order of activities in the periods between battles. Before raids, however, there were patrols: forays out beyond the wire to spy on the enemy, assess his fighting potential, and generally assert pre-eminence in the space between the trenches – which from late 1914 onwards was acquiring its now long accepted name of No Man's Land.

Asserting such pre-eminence was often seen as a specialist activity. Some officers were better at it than others. One of the former class was Captain Reginald Gill, 28th Battalion, Australian Imperial Force, the first 'Digger' officer to win the Military Cross on the Western Front – for gallantry during the Battle of the Somme [see p. 119]. Before being drawn into that high-profile encounter, he had been involved in smaller-scale activities against the enemy during a period of routine trench warfare when serving as his battalion's scout officer. He explained his role in a letter to his brother dated 16 July 1916:

*History of the Great War: Military Operations 1915, Vol. I, pp. 31–2.

I had all the patrols to do at night between our lines and the Huns, not a very nice job as the flares are going up between the lines continuously throughout the night. We have had several exciting little encounters with hostile patrols, until in the end, just before we left that portion of the line we were completely masters of 'no man's land', the Germans being afraid to come outside their wire. As a matter of fact we patrolled up and down outside their wire, if anybody was seen by us they were immediately bombed. All this of course was leading up to one thing, a stunt we intended to carry out, and to carry it out properly 'No Man's Land' had to be ours.

Among those who were called on to patrol and master No Man's Land were some who took to this high-risk nocturnal activity as to the manner born: for others, however, it was a constant trial. 'I really believe that I am after all a coward for I don't like patrolling,' wrote Second Lieutenant H. E. Cooper, 1/5th Battalion, Royal Warwickshire Regiment, in a letter to his parents in June 1915, adding the discouraging statistic: 'The bn who alternate with us here have lost three officers (or rather two officers and an NCO) on this business in front of my trenches.' He then described a typical outing beyond the wire, with full reference to his own psychological reactions:

Let me try to picture what it is like. I am asked to take out an 'officer's patrol' of seven men; duties – get out to the position of the German listening post (we know it), wait for their patrol and 'scupper' it; also discover what work is being done in their trenches. I choose my favourite corporal (a gentleman, a commercial traveller for the Midland Educational in civilian life) and my six

Two men of the 12th East Yorkshires wearing snow suits leave their snow-covered trench on a daylight patrol, Arleux sector, 9 January 1918. (Q 10,624)

most intelligent and most courageous men. My sentries and those of the first platoon of the battalion on my right are told we are going out so that we shan't be fired on. Magazines are charged to the full, one round in the breech; bayonets are examined to see if they slip out of the scabbard noiselessly; my revolver is nicely oiled; all spare and superfluous parts of equipment is left behind. Everything is ready.

As soon as the dusk is sufficiently dark, we get out into the front of the trenches by climbing up on to the parapet and tumbling over as rapidly as possible so as not to be silhouetted against the last traces of the sunset. No man feels afraid for we have grown accustomed to this thing now, but every man knows that he has probably seen his last sunset, for this is the most dangerous thing in war. Out we walk through the barbed wire entanglement zone through which an approaching enemy must climb, but we have a zigzag path through the thirty yards or so of prickly unpleasantness; this path is only known to a few. The night has become horribly dark already, and the stillness of the night is broken only by the croaking of many frogs, the hoot of an owl and the boom of distant guns in the south. The adventure has commenced.

We lie down in the long grass and listen. Nothin' doin'. I arrange my men in pairs – one to go in front and one to either flank, the corporal and myself remaining in rear, but the whole party is quite close together, practically within whispering distance of one another. We all advance slowly and carefully, wriggling along through the long grass for a hundred yards or so, past the two lines of willow trees and across the stream, now practically dry. There we lie and wait and listen. One pair goes out another fifty yards or so, nearly to the German wire to see if there is anything about. Nothing is discernible, so they return, and for another hour we lie in absolute silence like spiders waiting for flies. It is a weary game and extremely trying to one's nerves, for every sense especially hearing and sight are strained to the utmost. Tiny noises are magnified a hundredfold – a rat nibbling at the growing corn or a rabbit scuttling along give us all the jumps until we learn to differentiate the different sounds. In the German trenches we hear the faint hum of conversation. Nothing is to be heard near us, but there is a very ominous sign – no shots are being fired from the trenches in front of us, no flares are being sent up and there is no working party out. This points to only one thing and that is that they also have a patrol out. There is no other conclusion.

Suddenly quite close to the corporal and myself there is a heavy rustling in the long grass on the right. Now, if never before, I know the meaning of – is it fear? My heart thumps so heavily that they surely must hear it, my face is covered with a cold perspiration, my revolver hammer goes back with a sharp click and my hand trembles. I have no inclination to run away – quite the reverse – but I have one solitary thought: I am going to kill a man. This I repeat over and over again, and the thought makes me miserable and at the same time joyful for I shall have accounted for *one* of the blackguards even if I go myself. Do they know we are here? How many are there? Are they armed with bombs like most German patrols? However, our queries remain unanswered, for quite abruptly they change their direction and make off to the right where to follow them would be only courting certain disaster.

So with great caution we come in and breathe again when we are safely inside the trench. I give instructions to the sentries to fire low down into the grass but it is very improbable that the German patrol will get anything but a fright.

Patrols were clearly tense and nerve-racking affairs, but there were times when the tension could be broken by a touch of good humour. The following is from the diary of the infantry officer, Lieutenant J. D. Wyatt, writing on 6 February 1915:

> A Bedford patrol went out and crawled very bravely close to the German barbed wire. They stayed a long time and listened and they were just about to crawl back when a voice from the German trenches said in perfect English, 'If you don't go away soon, we shall really have to shoot you.' They went.

A patrol might provide intelligence but it was essentially a clandestine operation: the enemy was not meant to know one had taken place. A raid was quite different: raids were meant to declare their hand – to hit and hurt the enemy and to gather information by seizing prisoners for inter-rogation.

Surprise was vital here too, but this was not always achieved, especially where a raiding policy had been intensively and regularly pursued. The consequence was that the Germans, far from being inclined

A party which had raided German trenches, date unknown, probably early 1916. (HU 63277C)

to sit passively in their trenches waiting to be attacked, might be up and waiting. Captain H. Meysey-Thompson wrote the following in his diary in July 1916, shortly after joining his battalion, the 21st Kings Royal Rifle Corps, at Plugstreet. A raid was mounted, led by a junior officer named Law:

> So many raids have taken place on the Division front by way of keeping the Hun occupied that he was quite prepared for what was coming and had a party waiting on the wire to meet the raiders. Law had a brisk scrap with them in No Man's Land, knocked some of them out, and brought all his party back; he had some casualties, however, an excellent boy in my platoon, named Bell, being killed, Law himself was badly cut about by wire and Gerald Buxton and CSM Gibson were helping the raid by letting off smoke bombs when one burst, burning them very badly about the face and hands.

Raiding as a policy inevitably had its critics. From a sceptical viewpoint, it could be seen as an activity of which the almost inevitable outcome was that in the course of maintaining harassment of the enemy, units had to suffer a steady trickle of fatalities and woundings in circumstances where even the most vigorous and successful efforts could have little more than a token effect on the overall situation. Private Robert Cude of the 7th Battalion, The Buffs [see p. 150], was particularly caustic; he noted in his diary in early 1918:

> An order comes through that the Corps require a German by the morning, so a stunt is arranged, and the result is that several decent chaps are sacrificed in a useless endeavour to carry out the General's orders. If it is successful sometimes the German will not speak or else he does not know any vital news or again he may give false news, so, to us, the achievement of the object is not worth the attendant loss of life. All we get, after losing half of our effectives, is the Corps General's thanks, perhaps, in person, then we can see the result – another ribbon added to a full tunic.

Yet Cude could acknowledge that at times the policy had its virtue, as in this entry written shortly afterwards, on the eve of the long-expected German attack on 21 March:

> We are sweating on the top line today, for prisoners caught in a raid last night state that all is ready and that it is timed to commence tonight.

This of course was the policy's specific defence, and there was also the argument that if units maintained an offensive stance at all times they would be far better qualified for a major attack than if they had simply sat peaceably in their trenches waiting for the next zero hour. There was a curious consequence to all this. Units whose reports regularly showed evidence of losses were looked on with special favour; they were obviously 'thrusting' battalions. The situation was neatly expressed by Lieutenant-Colonel Rowland Feilding of the Connaught Rangers in a letter of December 1916: 'A case of "trench feet" ... will provoke far more correspondence and censure than a heavy casualty list, which provokes none at all.'*

* *War Letters to a Wife*, London, Medici Society 1929, p. 140.

Attitudes to raids depended largely on their outcome. 'This raiding game is the most exciting form of warfare,' Captain Harry Yoxall wrote to his mother in February 1917, describing a raid mounted by his battalion, 18th King's Royal Rifle Corps, in the planning and execution of which he had played a significant part, 'and it's splendid when things turn out so successfully. Of course twelve prisoners doesn't seem very much, but it's a lot for trench warfare, especially as the raiding party was only thirty. For a small night raid it was a splendid result, and congratulations have poured in from all quarters.'

Yoxall went on to stress that success had not been simply a matter of bravado and good luck; this raid had been most meticulously prepared:

I don't know whether you realise the amount of labour which is put into these raids you read of so frequently in the papers. The orders for this one, which was quite a small affair, ran to eight type-written pages for instance: three times the orders were altered: and each time it meant hard and detailed work for all concerned. It has been interesting to see the plans take shape under the influence of the various brains which have worked on it – principally Graham Thomson, Smith and myself, though with suggestions from all quarters. And then last night came twenty minutes of intense excitement – and it was over.

It was less splendid when things went wrong, or where such success as was obtained was marred by the high toll in casualties. On 2 June 1916 a raid was carried out on the Somme front by a party from the 22nd Battalion The Manchester Regiment. From the diary account by one of the battalion's company commanders, Captain Charles May, it is clear there was some frustration in the air as the time for the 'stunt' approached:

We are a trifle sick about it, the Brigade having more or less taken it out of the CO's hands. It is a pity and a mistake. But, I suppose, it is one of the things we have to put up with for having a young and ambitious Brigadier who wants to run everything himself.

All this added to the normal concern of a unit at such a time. May recorded the progress of events:

2 June: The 'stunt' comes off tonight and the team has left, cheered by the battalion and full of hope with our good wishes behind them.

I wrote the above about 8 p.m. It is now 10 a.m. on the 3rd. Last night was one of the most anxious most of us have ever spent. The first word came about 12 midnight, after the most terrific bombardment. 'Most men returned, Lieutenants Oldham [the raid commander] and Cansino wounded.' The next was half an hour later. 'Sergeant Burchill killed, Oldham wounded, Street and Cansino and 14 men missing. Two prisoners.'

Nothing else. We could get no word through. It was horrid. The poor boys up there dying and we down here helpless to do anything. Poor lads. Burchill had no right to be there but he went out getting the wounded and was shot in the stomach doing it. Men say they would never have got in but for him. He was a gallant boy. So was Street. He was hit twice and got caught on the German wire. A sergeant tried to help him in but was twice wounded in the attempt. 'I'm done. Go back now, sergeant,' said old 'Stuggins' – and that's the last we heard of him. He had killed two Germans with his revolver a few minutes previously, but they got him in the end.

Oldham found the Boche wire uncut and he pulled it apart with his own hands. He was hit on the shoulder and the leg but stuck it till weakness compelled him to go back. He helped a worse wounded man along.

Sgt. Bradby was shot twice, bound up Burchill in No Man's Land, came into our line with all his men to report and then went out again with a patrol to search for the missing.

One of the missing returned this morning. He had been lost in No Man's Land. We are therefore six men and one officer (Cansino) unaccounted for. No one seems to know anything of poor Cansino.

Dransfield, one of my men, captured three Germans, shot one who tried to escape but brought in the other two. He also helped Oldham over the last bit in.

We have thirty men hit, two officers killed, one wounded and one missing. It is a heavy price, but no doubt it is the fortune of war. It has cast a shadow over us all.

3 June: We are in the line again. But it is a sad incoming.

Poor Street, Cansino and one other unidentified can be plainly seen tangled in a heap among the German wire right under their parapet.

The poor fellows are quite dead. It is evident now that Cansino, hearing Street was in difficulties, went to help him and was killed in the attempt. It is one more case of the Supreme Sacrifice. The boy did well.

It is pitiful to see them lying there but it is not possible for us to get them in, they lying too close to the enemy. No doubt he will save us the trouble tonight.

Poor Street was a married man with three children and Cansino was also married. It is a sad business.

The Somme: Hard Knocks, Hard Lessons

On 18 July 1916, less than three weeks into the Battle of the Somme, Major-General Archibald Paris, the Commanding Officer of the Royal Naval Division (which had fought at Gallipoli as naval personnel serving ashore but which now included normal Army units) wrote in a letter to a friend:

> The chief object is to kill and capture Boches which we are doing at a heavy cost. Of course we had hoped to be able to break through – at least some did, but I can't think there's much chance of that.
>
> It is all a question of killing a sufficient number of Boches – and if we can do it here, so much the better.

Paris's comment is a highly significant one, in that it is essentially a voice of the second stage of the great four-month encounter which, for the British, dominated 1916: the Battle of the Somme. In effect he was enunciating the doctrine of attrition, the basic philosophy of which was that if the belligerent powers killed each other's men in equal numbers, the Allies would in the end be bound to win. (This concept would move from supposition to certainty after the United States entered the war in 1917.) In brief, the argument was that huge losses could be accepted, so long as huge losses were inflicted. A breakthrough would be glorious if it came to pass – indeed Haig was ever hopeful of achieving one – but if this

One of the classic images of 1 July 1916; men of the Tyneside Irish Brigade marching into withering enemy fire as they came into enemy view at La Boisselle. The Brigade suffered many casualties even before it reached the British front line, two of its four battalions eventually losing, respectively, 620 and 539 officers and men. (Q 53)

Men of the 4th Battalion Worcestershire Regiment, 29th Division, reacting cheerfully to the presence of an Official Photographer while marching to the trenches on 28 June 1916, before the opening of the Battle of the Somme. (Q 716)

were not possible the long slog forward, inch by inch and yard by yard, would have to do instead. Meanwhile, kill Boches and pay the price.

It could be said that the second stage of the Somme lasted for 119 days, while the first stage lasted for just one. The Somme's famous opening day, Saturday 1 July 1916, was – by most accounts – a time of the highest optimism and hope; it was also the occasion of the largest casualty roll of any day in British military history. The details are now legendary: a mass attack, following a week of concentrated artillery fire on the German lines, of some eighty infantry battalions over a front of eighteen miles, the French attacking too (more successfully) further south; small gains, incredible losses – 57,000 British casualties overall, 19,240 of them fatal. The story has been told too often for it to require detailed description here, but the spirit of that day is so important to the understanding of the later Somme, and of later attitudes generally, that it should not be ignored.

The following account was written from hospital in mid-July by Lieutenant Will Mulholland, a volunteer officer of the New Army battalion, the 21st Manchesters. This was also known as the 6th (City) Battalion: i.e. it was one of the so-called 'Pals' battalions, of which many had been raised in the early months of the war through the efforts of local communities, particularly in Britain's industrial areas. The concept of comrades from civil life marching side by side to war was itself to be a notable casualty of 1 July, since 'pals' fell that day in their thousands, their demise bringing a profound sense of shock and grief to the communities which had sponsored them. The 21st Manchesters fared better than numerous other battalions, but they still suffered a casualty list of approximately 250, i.e. a third of their attacking strength.

Mulholland's battalion was in the attack by XV Corps, 7th Division, the target being enemy lines in the vicinity of the village of Mametz. Here the advance made some progress, Mametz itself being taken. Other notable units attacking in this area were the 8th and 9th Devons and the 2nd Gordon Highlanders. Another Manchester battalion, the 22nd (7th Pals), also took part. Mulholland's account is from a letter to a cousin in England:

> The day was going to be one of the sunniest that summer brings: the fields even up to the edges of the trenches were wonderfully rich with flowers. The larks were singing like mad, the louder the bombardment. Our guns had been going all week but about 6.30 they burst out into their loudest and most concentrated ROAR. I soon got the message that 7.30 was the hour. Strangely enough my spirits were beginning to rise once more. I felt jovial, hilarious and an absorbing excitement made me almost long for Z hour to be up and over – one of a victorious sweeping army.
>
> My company were not in the first line and had to follow the first battalions and consolidate the first three lines of Boche trenches – not so difficult and dangerous a job as some. Everything had been worked out mathematically beforehand. Zero came and three minutes after I swarmed up the ladder followed by a party which I conducted to their place of entry in the Boche lines.
>
> On the left the Gordons were going over as on parade.
>
> Occasionally a shell would burst and some poor fellow would be torn asunder. Men dropped out just as you read in books or see in pictures: in the midst of the great turmoil there was a strange silence somehow. The excitement of battle was still on me then – I wanted to push on and on.
>
> The Boche lines were smashed to nothingness by our artillery and I'm afraid I rather let go of the idea of sweeping up prisoners just then – one wanted to get on. Some of my poor chaps got hit – one close to me to whom I had just said, 'You come along by me – I'm very lucky.' Another's brains were blown out less than a yard off and at the same time a slight sting in my back told me a bullet had just grazed my tunic.
>
> Eventually we got to our destination where were the points we had to consolidate – but unfortunately there didn't seem many men left to do much digging. However one got something going. Soon after that a shell dropped in a trench and killed, I think, two (at least one) men just a pace behind me. Soon after that – bang, and I felt almost stunned, my shrapnel helmet was dented in right up to my forehead. But I won't go on – our troops were pushing on victoriously and by evening we all moved to Mametz – where we slept on the

'safety' side of a copse. The next day and the next were days of waiting, being moved about, thirst and complete exhaustion.

Shall I tell you of the horrors – deaths in every form – some calm and placid, some blasted and vaporized, some mutilated, one almost burnt to a cinder by me in a dugout. Thank God one could remember that those forms meant nothing to their owners; for them was sleep and oblivion or else adventure in some better state than this.

Mulholland himself was wounded on the third day of the battle by sniper fire just at the point when his battalion was being relieved.

The day had produced amazing bravery but also appalling suffering and shock, and it had not resulted in the major advance which had been confidently predicted. There was no question of giving up because of the scale of the setback, however; the push would continue – but the concept of the easy walk across No Man's Land on the assumption that the enemy had been virtually eliminated by artillery fire plainly needed radical rethinking.

That this was very swiftly perceived can be seen by the following letter written by an officer of long experience, Lord Loch, who was now serving as Brigadier-General General Staff (i.e. chief staff officer) of VI Corps.* VI Corps had not in fact taken part in the action of 1 July, but as an informed observer based in Third Army just to the north of the Somme front, Loch had been fully aware of what had been planned and had followed closely the march of events. He for one had not been entirely surprised that the battle-plan for 1 July had met with so little success. In a letter to his wife written the next day, he commented:

I said some days ago that I thought we were too ambitious and I fear it is in the longing to run ahead that has been our undoing. It is very much easier and surer to crawl than to run but our cavalry leaders wish to charge – I am now criticising which is wrong as I do not have the information to enable me to do so – [but] I have argued for a long time that our only chance in trench warfare is to move forward by very slow stages. In other words our first objectives must be limited and should be those which not only support each other but which can be seized and consolidated.

Our Army is wonderful considering the time it has been in being but it is untrained for anything except defensive warfare. There is a very great difference in the offensive and defensive types of warfare. The former requires a much higher state of military training. We will have to be very determined in our offensive tactics if we are to make any impression on the enemy this year. I think we will make him think, but I am doubtful as to whether we will really make him uncomfortable.

Loch would continue to comment incisively from the sidelines throughout the battle as the weeks of hard and bitter fighting went by. One of his most poignant, and significant, comments was written on 9 September:

The battle seems to go on with unabated fury. It is wonderful what the new army has done and is doing. But oh how we are paying for the want of

---

*Lord Loch is the subject of the section titled 'Arras: A Senior Staff Officer's View': see p. 159.

Morning in the Cattle Truck: Troops moving by train by H.S. Williamson, Corporal, King's Royal Rifle Corps (Water-colour, Art 1472)

The Route Nationale: Troops marching to the Front by H.S. Williamson (Pencil and water-colour, Art 1470)

A 'Crump'. A Shell exploding by H.S. Williamson (Water-colour on brown paper, Art 1473)

Above: **An Advance Post, Night** by John Nash, Official War Artist with the rank of Second Lieutenant from May 1918, previously Sergeant, 1st Battalion Artists' Rifles (Water-colour, Art 1158)

Right: **An Advance Post, Day** by John Nash (Oil, Art 1159)

Above left: **Ypres, Christmas 1917** by Gilbert Holiday (Coloured chalk and water-colour, Art 1464)

Left: **The Menin Road** by Ian Strang, Captain, Royal Engineers (Pencil and water-colour, Art 1640)

Above: **Thiepval;** part of the Somme battlefield as seen in the year after the battle, by Sir William Orpen, Official War Artist from 1917, with the rank of Major (Oil, Art 2377)

Far left: **Evening, after a Push** by Colin Gill, Official War Artist from 1918, previously in Royal Garrison Artillery from 1914, seconded to the Royal Engineers as a camouflage officer in 1916 (Oil, Art 1210)

Left: **Tanks in Action** by Edward Handley-Read, Captain Machine-Gun Corps, previously Artists' Rifles (Charcoal and water-colour, Art 196)

Left: **'Humanity' Stretcher-Bearer Post, 9th Field Ambulance** by Gilbert Rogers, Official War Artist, previously Lieutenant Royal Army Medical Corps (Oil, Art 3752)

Above: **British Red Cross
Society and Order of St
John Workers attending
Wounded on their arrival
at Boulogne,** by Haydn
Reynolds Mackey, Official War
Artist, previously Sergeant
Royal Army Medical Corps
(Oil, Art 3820)

Right: **The Entry of British
Troops into Cambrai,**
October 1918, by Lucien
Jonas, French artist; specially
commissioned for the Ministry
of Information, 1919 (Charcoal
and water-colour, Art 2278)

foresight and preparedness. Thousands of lives are lost through want of knowledge and training. I suppose it cannot be helped but it is awful to think of. The lives are the worst but the waste of money from the same cause is terrible. That will have its full effect after the war. I only hope that all this misery and sorrow will bring its lessons and that the world will be the better for it.

Whatever the lessons for the world after the war, the Somme had many lessons for the British Army in 1916. The old professional army had largely departed the stage in 1914; now in 1916 its successor citizens' army was learning its trade. It says much for that army that although dismayed by the first stage of the Somme fighting it was not defeated; it pulled itself together and went on fighting. It would not have been the powerful professional force it would become, especially in 1918, if it had not been trained and honed on the Somme.

Who won the Battle of the Somme? The Germans undoubtedly carried the opening round, but it could be argued that the British were the victors overall, even if the actual territorial gains of some seven miles in 120 days was less than the hoped-for gains of the first day. At the very least the new-style British army proved itself the equal of the German force with which it had been locked in combat.

An apt metaphor for the Somme occurs in the diary of Battery Sergeant-Major Douglas Pegler, RFA, whose B Battery, in 106th Brigade, 24th Division, joined the campaign in late July. From the start he was aware that what was happening in this battle was on a different scale from anything he had previously experienced. 'The cannonade of Loos', he wrote on 5 August, 'was nothing to what goes on here, and it never stops. Each Field Battery fires about three thousand rounds per day.' On 15 September – the day of a major British attack and of the first use of tanks in war – he saw at some point on the battlefield a grim spectacle which, as described by him that same day, fixes in the mind like the vision of some awesome sculpture symbolizing the Battle of the Somme:

> What ghastly sights there are to be seen here! Two men, a Prussian and a Coldstreamer, each transfixed with the other's bayonet remain standing, each dead body supporting the other. On each dead face can be seen the grin of triumph which he could not suppress when he saw his opening and took it, leaving himself open, killing and killed.

'All in a day's work': The Death of Captain Geoffrey Donaldson

A pre-war photograph of Geoffrey Donaldson.

When Captain Geoffrey Boles Donaldson went into battle on 19 July 1916 at Fromelles he knew that he had a very high chance of being wounded or killed. The day before he had explained the theory behind the action in a letter to his mother; there was, he wrote, 'urgent need of drastic measures on our front to hold back Hun reinforcements for the South and to do this certain troops had to be, well, more or less sacrificed.' He added: 'That is war, of course, and all in a day's work.'

In other words, the action at Fromelles, which lay in the La Bassée–Armentières sector near Neuve Chapelle, was to be a diversionary one, mounted with the aim of deterring the Germans from sending reinforcements to their beleaguered forces on the Somme. It was to be a sideshow, not part of the main drama, but that did not mean it was not to be fought with full vigour. Ground gained was less important than inflicting maximum harassment, and for this the price to be paid might well be a considerable one.

He wrote the above, however, believing that the attack had been cancelled, or at least temporarily shelved. Not surprisingly he expressed relief, not least because, as his letter went on to make clear, 'the whole thing had had to be organized in a few hours', the men of his battalion, the 2/7th Royal Warwicks, were 'very fatigued', his company was 'very weak in numbers' and they had had to 'move into new trenches to our right and had no time to reconnoitre the ground of our advance'.

The next day, however, the scheme was reinstated and that evening in full daylight Donaldson and his company duly advanced across No Man's Land. In the run-up to the action two officers of his company had collapsed from nerves and had had to be evacuated, which meant that Donaldson had to assume a more forward role than had originally been planned. The attack made substantial progress and he and a number of his men reached the German second line. However, the Germans fought back strenuously and within minutes he was dead – killed, it was believed, by a thrown grenade. It was the end of a life of brilliant promise. He was just twenty-three.

Donaldson, who had intended to become a botanist, had gone up to Caius College Cambridge from his public school, Oundle, in October 1912 and had taken first class honours in Part I of the Natural Science Tripos in June 1914. Instead of returning for his final year at university, however, he had volunteered, being commissioned in the Warwickshire Regiment in November. A month later he was promoted lieutenant and in March 1916 he became a captain. He went to France with his battalion in May of that year, being appointed commander of C Company.

The letters which he wrote regularly to his mother during his brief time at the front are full of detailed, informative descriptions of the routines of trench life, but there is evidence always of a thoughtful, independent mind. 'What impressed me most,' he wrote on 1 June after his first visit to the line, 'was the hopelessness of it all. I feel convinced that fighting will never end the war.' He was constantly aware of the presence of natural things amid the din and squalor. 'It is very extraordinary', he wrote on 5 June, 'to hear the larks singing at dawn, particularly over "No Man's Land", quite unperturbed by the whistling bullets and bursting shells.' A visit to Neuve Chapelle in early July brought out the delighted botanist in him. 'The grass grows high round the dilapidated gravestones and everywhere there is a profusion of garden and wild flowers, poppies, roses, larkspur, monkshood. I enclose a piece of Lysimachia from the churchyard. I only wish photographs could be taken here. The ruined Château with its fine clematis-covered gateposts and the Church and Calvary would make wonderful pictures. They impressed me more than most things I have seen.' As he settled into his new role, there was no hint of bravado; indeed, he did not disguise his anxiety at some of the more dangerous aspects of his work. This is from a letter of 23 June:

> The night before last I took out a patrol of four men about half way across No Man's Land. There is comparatively little risk attached to this work but it is of course a considerable strain on the nerves. Last night, I went out with Wakefield and a wiring party, that is to say with about six men improving our wire entanglements. I consider on the whole this is as nerve-racking a job as any, more so than patrol work. You must not think I shall go out like this every night. I have been out the last two nights as much to set an example and get the thing going as anything.

Reassurance, as in the last two sentences above, was always offered when possible. Yet when things were grim, he said so, without compunction. This passage is from his letter of 16 July, written three days before his death, describing a British gas attack:

> I can tell you that in that ½ hour before the attack started, I came nearer to 'having the wind up' or in other words losing my nerve than has ever been the case before. This was more especially the case as the RE officer responsible for letting off the gas on my frontage told me he had done several such stunts, but he thought the wind rather weak and did not like doing it in daylight as the Boche could shell more accurately. At 8.30 p.m. the show started. I had all the men in the trench out of dugouts and we all had our gas helmets on. It was like an appalling nightmare as you look like some horrible kind of demon or goblin in these masks. There were words of command along the line from the RE and then a loud hissing sound as the taps were turning on and the deadly greenish white vapour poured out of the jets and slowly blew in a great rolling cloud towards the opposite line of trenches.
>
> In the next bay to me, one idiot of a sapper turned the jet in the wrong direction, and filled our trenches with gas in slewing it round over the parapet.

A field postcard followed on the 17th, plus a brief 'note in haste' stating that the battalion was moving and that it might be a day or two before he could write again. Then on the 18th he sent the letter explaining the nature of the diversionary attack which, as he then thought, was no longer to take place. He wrote this from rest billets behind the line 'practically out of shell fire', stating that, 'now after a good night's rest and wash and an excellent breakfast, we are as right as rain'. He added:

> I don't think anything will affect my nerves now, so don't worry about me, dear, because I shall pull through all right and I am strong enough to stand any amount of fatigue. I expect we shall have some rest for a few days now.

Next day, however, the original plan having been revived, 2/7th Royal Warwickshire Regiment moved back into the line. The sacrifice referred to in his letter of 18 July was now to be required. The battalion's attack, to begin at 6 p.m., was a two-company one, with Donaldson and a Captain Bethel as company commanders.

In a letter of condolence sent to Mrs Donaldson on 26 July, the battalion's second-in-command wrote:

> I was in our front line trench and talked with your son several times during the seven hours' bombardment before the attack. Both he and Capt. Bethel were very cool, and encouraged the men by their example. As you may know, the 2/7th Battalion was the only one in the whole Division to get across into the German trenches and it was entirely owing to the cool and well-timed leading of Capt. Bethel and your son, and the splendid discipline of the men, that they were able to achieve such a glorious record for the Battalion. But alas it cost them their lives. The gap they have left amongst us can never be filled and the loss to you is, I know, terrible. I pray God that you may bear up under it. Your son died for his country, what more could he do.

Donaldson's death produced a flood of sympathetic letters, mourning the loss of a man so richly endowed. The Headmaster of his old school wrote:

> It is too hard to bear. This terrible sacrifice of all our best boys, and of all the best of the nation. It is too sad for words to think that your keen, capable, enthusiastic son, with all his capabilities for the future, should be thus sacrificed. How well I remember him, such a fine boy he was, so keen, so good.

Perhaps most moving of all was the letter from his Cambridge professor:

> Three of the five men whom my wife and I took to Provence in the summer of 1914 are now dead and also one of those who saw us off at Charing Cross. The war has been very hard on young botanists, but it makes one glad to think how splendidly they responded to the call.

The Australians at Pozières

The attack at Fromelles which ended the career of Geoffrey Donaldson was also the occasion of the first blooding of Australian forces on the Western Front. They had made a distinguished name for themselves at Gallipoli and would do the same in France, but Fromelles was not a propitious introduction. The Australian 5th Division was assigned to the operation and how it fared on that grim 19 July can be judged from the diary account of one its stretcher-bearers, Private Edward Penny.

> The charge took place about 6 p.m., and a horrible slaughter occurred. Our losses were estimated at 8,400 of which 1,300 were killed. The 8th Brigade entered the German trenches, No Man's Land being about 90–100 yards wide in front of them. They took about 120 prisoners, but it is doubtful if we could call it a success as the Germans forced us back again. This was a terrible affair, but the papers call it a small successful *raid* on German trenches. I was carrying wounded all night and most of next day, but there were hundreds left when we were relieved. Dead were lying in heaps blown to pieces.

An Australian soldier writing home, Somme 1916. (E (AUS) 30)

Fromelles was, however, merely an overture in comparison with the ordeal to come, at Pozières on the Somme.

From the old British front line at La Boiselle (centre point of the attack of 1 July) the countryside of Picardy lifts gently towards the vast open plateau which was the fighting-ground of the later stages of the Somme battle. North-west from Albert the Bapaume road, originally Roman, runs through a succession of tiny villages, of which Pozières is the first.

Pozières was to become a name scarcely less honoured in Australian history than that of Gallipoli's Anzac Cove or Lone Pine. In 1916 it was a strong German artillery position which had defied several attempts to forward the British advance when the Australians were put in to attack it on 23 July. Their 1st Division opened the encounter, with the 2nd Division taking over the spearhead role three days later, and the 4th on 5 August. The fighting would continue until early September; in the course of it – the Pozières of today is a total remake – the village was to crumble into a wilderness of brick-dust and shell-holes.

The Australian success was achieved only at great expense, as is clear from the following account written some weeks later by Captain Reginald Gill, 28th Battalion, 7th Brigade, 2nd Australian Division, who was to win the distinction of being the first Australian to be awarded a Military Cross on the Western Front, for his gallantry in this action:

> In one charge we lost 19 officers (14 killed and 5 wounded) and 670 men in about one hour, personally I was knocked down three times by the blast of shells and once buried and yet came out untouched, talk about luck or providence, our battalion came out with 67 rifles only. The trouble is, when a position is captured, trying to hold on to it during the work of consolidation; trenches are absolutely *obliterated* and it is a hard job to find where they have

been, one can only tell by a sense of direction and the distribution of the bodies. I pray you may never encounter a modern bombardment, it is simply hell let loose. The sights one sees are too dreadful to talk about, no chance of burial for the dead, they slowly rot on the ground, mangled and remangled by shells, and the flies come in swarms. Imagine trying to eat food under these conditions, also up to the knees in mud and water for 4 or 5 days at a time. I pray to God it will soon be over and this madness of slaughter come to an end.

Also in Captain Gill's battalion was Corporal Oswald Blows, who kept a detailed diary of his experiences throughout his two years on the Western Front. 'Well, dear diary,' he wrote, somewhat quaintly, under the heading 29 July 1916, 'I have to write now that which I would had never have occurred, and also my thankful deliverance from a living Hell.' For him a high point of horror in what he had just witnessed was the moment when the attacking troops had tried to rush the German line in a night attack:

Arrangements were for our artillery to open up at midnight, and bombard until 12.16 a.m., then our Infantry was to rush the first trench, while the barrage lifted and bombarded the second line for 6 minutes, then the barrage was to lengthen and us to take the second trench and push on as far as possible. At 12.00 our artillery was silent, and us near the Huns' barbed wire, which we had been told was all destroyed. A few minutes past 12 the Huns began to shrapnel us, and machine-guns were turned on and bombs thrown. A few guns only behind us opened fire, and when our men went forward to the wire they were mown down by enemy machine-guns, and when the wire was reached it was almost intact. Our guns opened up at 12.15, and some played on the barbed wire and amongst our own men, and what with this, the enemy's artillery from the front and from each side, the bombs and machine-guns, men dropped in dozens, many on the wire. It was impossible to get through.

Soon, however, Blows was able to record a turning of the tables, with the Australians calling the tune and the Germans in disarray:

7 August: At dawn on the 5th inst the Germans counter-attacked in front of 27th Bn who were reinforced by us. The Huns advanced in a mob, and an officer behind with a revolver. The enemy wavered before our machine-gun and rifle fire, but dared not turn back on account of their officer. The officer was immediately sniped by one of our fellows, and when he fell, the Germans threw down their rifles, and putting their hands up ran to our trenches shouting 'Mercy Comrade!' Then our artillery caught many of them, but about 200 came in in one bunch and many other smaller parties. One was a Sergeant-Major with an Iron Cross – he said he was the only Sergeant-Major left amongst his mob (167th Prussian Reserve), and he had only had the cross presented to him the day before he was captured – that was the weekly issue day, no doubt.

They made another attack on the nights of 5th and 6th, but were beaten off.

Australians often attracted wry looks and comments from their British comrades-in-arms for their contempt for normal military rules and their

Pozières, An Australian Episode, **by Adrian Hill, 1916.** (Art 322)

far from occasional air of arrogance, but their performance on the Somme brought them genuine admiration. Indeed, they were to win, with the Canadians, the reputation of being the most thrusting assault troops of the later stages of the war. A young British infantry subaltern, John Gaussen, Royal Warwickshire Regiment, paid them this almost fulsome tribute in a letter written within days of their opening attack on Pozières. Riding into Albert he had passed many Australians on the way. 'I give you warning', he told his family, 'that I am going to digress about them.'

They are a glorious set of men – absolutely the last word in physique and general bearing. They don't care a cent for anything – their infantry especially. In all frightful shelling they were splendid, though seeing that humanity cannot endure it, they were considerably upset. As for their stretcher-bearers – they were marvellous, walking about on the shell-swept road doing up the wounded as if they didn't realise that every moment was likely to be their last.

On one occasion they were being shelled to Hell in their new won trenches, and at last couldn't stand it any longer. They were beat, they were buried (I was buried three times) and dug out – they were crying like children – but they wouldn't go back out of the trenches, and they certainly wouldn't stop in them – so they, being fed up, went over and took the next Hun line!

Unhappy Warriors

Private Alec Reader, Post Office Rifles, killed in action on the Somme. 'I have undergone various emotions caused by war', he wrote to his mother in May 1916, 'have seen most things that happen in war and don't think much of it. War is a rotten game'. (HU 63257)

While there is no reason to doubt that comradeship and group loyalty gave many soldiers a courage and confidence they might not have otherwise possessed, there were unquestionably others who lived lonely and dispiriting lives in the antheap world of the Western Front. Even the act of entering that world might be a destabilizing experience, particularly for an ordinary soldier arriving not with a unit but on his own or with a handful of others – especially since his lowly rank meant he could claim no consideration or advice or a time to acclimatize. The following account is from a diary by an artilleryman, Gunner W. R. Acklam, a grammar school boy and, after Leeds University, a grammar school master, who was posted to the front in the autumn of 1916 during the Battle of the Somme:

> Sun 8 October: Nasty, rainy morning. Set off [from Albert] to find our brigade. After a lot of wandering about through deep mud, we found the wagon lines where they gave us a guide to HQ. He seemed to get lost and led us through all sorts of places with shells bursting round. My heart was in my mouth and so tired I could hardly walk. Came to a communication trench where a sergeant allotted us to our batteries. I went to B Battery. We had a bit of bully [beef] in the open with shells bursting all round and then I had to fill sandbags in a dugout where I felt a lot safer. Then horses came up with ammunition and I had to ride one back. It was awful, dead horses, etc. We galloped as fast as we could part of the way. Then my horse got loaded up and I had to walk to the wagon line where I slept in a forage tent with a big gun firing all the time. Feeling rotten.

Acklam adapted well enough after his unpropitious start and became a competent signaller (though despite his seniority and education he never achieved any promotion). By contrast, Private Alec Reader, Post Office Rifles, seemed to grow more and more despondent as time went by. During an early visit to the line in April 1916 he was proud of his ability to hold his position as a sentry during a severe bombardment – 'I was told that I had stood it very well,' he told his mother – but later he became increasingly apprehensive at the prospect of going over the top into battle. What added to the pressure was that he was only eighteen, which fact offered him a marvellous opportunity to escape from the front, should he feel able to avail himself of it. He wrote on 8 July:

> An Army order has been issued to the effect that 'Men between 18 and 19 are to be sent back [to Britain], but any who choose can volunteer to stay with their Battn.' The temptation to get out of this ghastly business is far greater than you can possibly conceive, but of course there's only one decent thing for me to do, that is to stay here, but OH! it's going to be very hard.

As it happened, however, his father was also in uniform and Reader senior decided to take advantage of a regulation which allowed a father to apply for his son to be posted to his own unit. On 14 July Alec wrote to his mother:

> I wish you wouldn't talk all that bosh about bravery. This ought to show you what a 'brave' boy I am: I am very glad that Dad has asked for me, as I am horribly fed up with this game. I could never have applied myself, but am only too pleased to shelve the responsibility.

Unfortunately the wheels of Army administration moved at so slow a speed that no final decision had been taken before the attack at High Wood on 15 September in which Alec Reader was killed.

Harry Stephen enlisted in early 1916 in the 16th Battalion Australian Infantry and was full of enthusiasm during his training in Britain. He was sent to France in December and by January 1917 he was in the trenches. On 14 February he wrote a letter to a brother and sister in England which painted a grim picture of trench life:

Second Lieutenant Innes Meo, 11th Battalion Royal Sussex Regiment, as a Prisoner of War, 1918. A talented and sensitive artist, he found it difficult to cope with the pressures of Western Front life. (HU 63258)

> Your welcome letter just received and was pleased to hear you are both well. I am also, but tired, I have just come out of the first line trench, a veritable hell after being 4 days and 5 nights without sleep and mixing with dead Germans and Australians in the same trench. We went in to reinforce the 13th and had to help them hold on as it was an important position and the Hun wants it back and he can't get it. By Heaven talk about cold, it's no name for it, it was terrible in the trench and all our water and food was in a frozen state. We are out now for a rest and then go back again. The Germans are about 70 yards away in some places, you can hear them talking, so of course you have to keep eyes and ears open all the time.
>
> I will do my best to take good care of my old frame but it's a tough track, I wish to God it was over, anyhow we have got to belt him first and by all that's good when you see your dead comrades around it steels you to courage and makes you feel that you must hit him and hit him hard. All are in good heart and ready for anything, so now I must soon shut up, wishing soon to be among you all and then we will have a good old time and then away to Dear Old Sunny Australia and Home Sweet Home, that's the time when the heart will be full.

Stephen was also to be killed in action, in the attack at Bullecourt in April 1917 during the opening phase of the Arras battle.

One officer who loathed the life at the front and spent his time there in almost total depression was Second Lieutenant Innes Meo. He had joined the Artists' Rifles in 1915 as an ordinary soldier, but after being sent to France he was put forward for a commission, emerging as a subaltern in the 11th Battalion Royal Sussex Regiment in time to serve on the Somme during the later stages of the battle. He scribbled his thoughts in a series of tiny diaries, from which it was clear that he was quite out of his depth in the military world and that his nerve was being steadily broken. His condition deteriorated so much that he was sent back to England to recuperate. The following extracts cover his last days in France before his departure:

> Sept 24 Sund. I shall probably get the sack as my nerves are no good.

Sept 25 Mond. My 30th birthday, an awful day. Still in these trenches. In the afternoon I was called to see the doctor. It seems possible if I live I may be invalided home. This night I was sent on an ammunition job. Conducting a party of 50 bombers to stores. It was hell! I was already tired and ill. This night we prepared a scheme to draw enemy fire. Oh it was hell!

Sept 28 Thurs. 1 p.m. A terrible bombardment was started, it is simply awful to hear, as I write the guns are crashing, roaring and the din is like a collision of hundreds of bad thunderstorms. God knows what mothers are losing their sons now.

Sept 30 Sat. *At last* reported at 134 Field Ambulance. Sent to CCS [Casualty Clearing Station] at Guezancourt. Examined, and am now going on, but staying the night. Officer in next bed with awful shell-shock, also airman with broken nerves. God, what sights.

Despite his relief at leaving the front, Meo was anxious to affirm that he had made some contribution while he was there. He wrote on 1 October:

Have spent 8 days under fire in trenches all the time and did my duties fully. Sep 22 I personally visited 3 listening posts between 2 and 6 a.m.

At last the hoped-for day arrived, though it was not a day of unalloyed satisfaction:

Oct 8 Sun 14 General Hospital. Still here, feeling ill and depressed.

I hear I am off to England at 4.30 p.m. Thank God I am about to leave this miserable country. I hope to God I never return.

Have been tortured all the morning by dreadful thoughts. How I wish I had a girl to care for me, waiting in England for me.

In fact, Meo did return to France and saw action once again – more in the way of victim than participant. He was taken prisoner in March 1918 during the great German attack and spent the rest of the war as a prisoner in Germany. It seems likely that this was his happiest time as a soldier.

'Stellenbosched': Nightmare of a Brigadier-General

On 28 August 1916, Brigadier-General F. M. Carleton DSO wrote to his wife:

> Darling Gwenny.
> I am going I am afraid to give you the shock of your life. I have, I fear, been stellenbosched. At any rate I have been deprived of the command of my Brigade, and ordered to report myself here.

'Here' was Amiens, where Carleton was writing from some obscure hotel. By contrast, the numerous letters he had written to his wife over the preceding weeks had carried the heading '98th Infantry Brigade, B.E.F.'. As GOC of an infantry brigade in a division – the 33rd – actively engaged in the Battle of the Somme, Carleton had been occupying a position of considerable responsibility and pride. Suddenly to be deprived of his command and sent to kick his heels in a city miles behind the fighting zone was the worst thing that could have happened to him short of actually being cashiered from the Army. The term he used in his letter would have left his wife in no doubt as to the depth of his dismay. Stellenbosch had been the site of a base camp during the South African War, a war in which Carleton had fought with distinction; for a senior officer to be sent there meant that he had been sacked, removed for not being up to the job, disgraced. In the majority of such cases this meant the virtual end of a soldier's career.

Carleton had no doubt in his mind that he had been unjustly treated. His letter continued:

> The men had been fighting for nearly six weeks and had suffered enormous casualties. They were done to a turn. We were ordered to do something which was a physical impossibility. We did our best and failed, human endurance having reached its limits. I have been sacrificed to the ambitions of an unscrupulous general but thank God have nothing to reproach myself with. During these last months I have learnt to rely more than ever in my life before on an Almighty who has given to me a peace of mind I did not formerly think possible and I feel that for nearly a year past I have served my God and country without fear of exposing myself to danger in the certain knowledge that I have done my duty.

His final sentence made clear how deep was his sense of shock.

> I want no sympathy nor do I want to see anyone, for at the moment I am almost done to all the world.

Frederick Montgomerie Carleton, aged forty-nine, had served in India, Burma, Egypt and Sierra Leone as well as South Africa, had retired from the Army in 1908, had returned to the colours in 1914, and from December 1915 to June 1916 had been commanding officer of the 1/4th

Frederick Montgomerie Carleton. Photograph taken at a studio in Amiens in the summer of 1916 shortly after his promotion to the rank of Temporary Brigadier-General. (DOC 429)

King's Own (Royal Lancaster) Regiment with the rank of Lieutenant-Colonel. On 18 June he had been promoted Temporary Brigadier-General in command of 184th Infantry Brigade, which had then been re-formed as 98th Infantry Brigade. He had been delighted at becoming a general, if only of the lowliest rank, and had set about his new duties determined to do well.

His immediate superior was the commander of his division, Major-General H. J. S. Landon; he it was who relieved Carleton of his post, the instrument of removal being the confidential memorandum reproduced opposite. This was addressed to XV Corps, commanded by Landon's own immediate superior, Lieutenant-General H. S. Horne. Horne was himself answerable to General Sir Henry Rawlinson, in command of 4th Army, who answered directly to the Commander-in-Chief.

Carleton's dismissal took place at a time of much tension and difficulty on the Western Front, when every pressure was being exerted to produce significant results. The problems facing the high command at this time were not only military ones; political questions were being asked as to why the weeks of action on the Somme appeared to be offering so few territorial gains despite the immense outlay in casualties. Carleton was, in his own view, doing his utmost given the battle-worn state of the battalions under his command, but he was plainly not producing good enough news to satisfy his various superiors. He was thus to become one of a surprisingly large number of Western Front generals who found themselves sent home during the First World War.* Unlike most others in this category, however, Carleton fought back, refusing to accept his fate.

He immediately requested an interview with the Commander-in-Chief but before any decision on this could be arrived at he was invalided home – the shock had affected his health – and sent to recuperate at a hospital in Eaton Square, London. Within days, however, he was at work writing and compiling a long and detailed petition which by 12 September was ready to be despatched to the Chief of the General Staff at BEF headquarters in France.

The nub of Landon's case against Carleton was in the second paragraph of the confidential memorandum:

> Present conditions are difficult and require characteristics in a Brigade commander which are not provided by Gen. Carleton, i.e. quick, practical methods of command, and a cheerful outlook which will communicate itself to the troops.

He set out to refute the case against him in all particulars.

From his dossier it seems clear that tensions between himself and his divisional commander had been building for some time. A clash with one of Landon's senior staff officers at Bécordel in July cannot have helped his cause, even though it seems clear that the task he was instructed to undertake on that occasion had been quite beyond his brigade's capabili-

---

*Haig once stated that he had dismissed more than 100 Brigadier-Generals. See Tim Travers, *The Killing ground*, Allen & Unwin, 1989, p. 13.

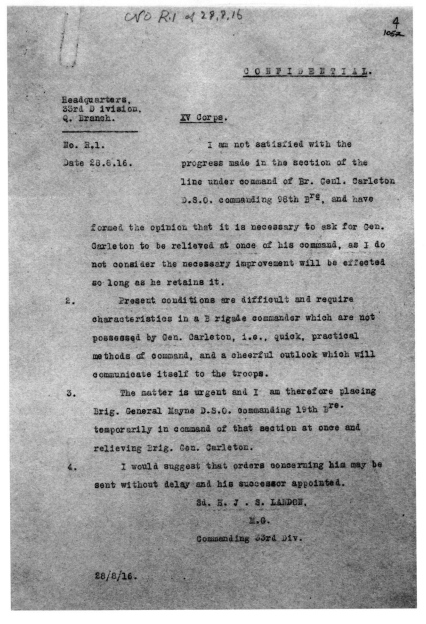

CNO R.1 of 28.8.16

4
105z

C O N F I D E N T I A L.

Headquarters,
33rd Division,
Q. Branch.

XV Corps.

No. R.1.
Date 28.8.16.

I am not satisfied with the
progress made in the section of the
line under command of Br. Genl. Carleton
D.S.O. commanding 98th Bᵈᵉ, and have

formed the opinion that it is necessary to ask for Gen.
Carleton to be relieved at once of his command, as I do
not consider the necessary improvement will be effected
so long as he retains it.

2.   Present conditions are difficult and require
characteristics in a Brigade commander which are not
possessed by Gen. Carleton, i.e., quick, practical
methods of command, and a cheerful outlook which will
communicate itself to the troops.

3.   The matter is urgent and I am therefore placing
Brig. General Mayne D.S.O. commanding 19th Bᵈᵉ.
temporarily in command of that section at once and
relieving Brig. Gen. Carleton.

4.   I would suggest that orders concerning him may be
sent without delay and his successor appointed.

Sd. H. J. S. LANDON,
M.G.
Commanding 33rd Div.

28/8/16.

The document of dismissal which brought about Carleton's instant departure from his post as a Brigade Commander during the Battle of the Somme and which provoked him to mount a determined defence of his actions and his honour. (HU 63260)

ties. Then on 18 August there had been a failed action in the vicinity in High Wood which had been followed by much explanation and argument. Again Carleton felt he had right on his side, but the need of the time was for success, not for cogent reasons why success had not been obtained. Landon's position was clearly not enviable if he were able to pass on only negative reports to the powers above, since this inevitably reflected badly on his own performance.

The chief item in Carleton's dossier was a detailed five-page report headed 'Diary of Events Covering Period 24th and 28th August'.

Reduced to essentials, what had happened, as seen through Carleton's eyes, was as follows:

On the 24th the 100th Infantry Brigade, plus one battalion, the 1st Middlesex, which had been borrowed from Carleton's 98th Brigade, launched an attack which left the forward British line near the still uncaptured High Wood – it would not fall until September – in a very confused state. As the attack had developed it had divided into two parts leaving a wide gap. When on the 25th Carleton took over the line he asked the Brigadier Commanding 100th Brigade if he knew the extent of the gap. 'He told me', wrote Carleton, 'that he had no idea.' Next morning Carleton arranged working parties for the coming night, sending precise instructions to all appropriate units for the construction of a new trench line across the gap. The officers who would be in charge of the working parties were selected and instructed to reconnoitre the positions where the work take place. So far so good, but heavy shelling throughout the day made the required reconnaissance virtually impossible, nor did the situation improve at night, the working parties being much hampered by incessant shelling. The result of all this was that by next morning little more had been achieved than the laying of a tape along the line where the new trenches were to be constructed. This had been done by Captain Morshead, OC 212th Field Company, Royal Engineers, who had been charged with superintending the work together with Carleton's Brigade Major (i.e. chief staff officer], Captain Watson.

On the 27th Carleton's problems multiplied. The 1st Middlesex, now returned to his command, had been three days in the front trenches under constant shell fire, had been in action and had suffered many casualties. Commenting on this in his account Carleton stated: 'I felt it was incumbent on me to relieve them. The relief I knew would hamper the work, but I did not see how this could be avoided.' In addition he had to mount a small attack on the enemy at a point called Wood Lane Trench, which meant that effectively he had only one fresh battalion on which to call for working parties that night. 'It is true', he acknowledged, 'that on this date two battalions of the 19th Infantry Brigade had been placed at my disposal. [However] both of these had come straight from the battle line, one battalion arriving late that night. The GOC 19th Infantry Brigade paid me a visit on this day, and pointed out how exhausted the men were after the hardships they had recently endured, and he begged me not to employ either battalion till next day. I told him I would do my best to meet his wishes.' But, as he soon realized, such assurances were not always possible to sustain. Despite his promise to the GOC of 19th Brigade he ordered one of the battalions assigned to him, the 20th Fusiliers, to undertake the necessary work.

The next day was the crucial one. Carleton was up early to see what had been achieved. His diary of events continues:

28th Aug. At 4.30 a.m. this morning, feeling very anxious about the progress of the work, I proceeded to the front trenches to the right of my line. While there these trenches were heavily shelled by the enemy, and I found it difficult to appreciate the situation. I ascertained, however, from inquiry that not much work had been accomplished the night before. This was partly due to the fact that the tape laid by Capt. Morshead had been destroyed by enemy fire, and not a trace of it remained. The working parties also appear to have arrived very late or not at all. In the case of the 20th Fusiliers, though this battalion had previously occupied the line, they appear to have been unable to find their way, and did not put in an appearance at all.

He gave urgent instructions to the COs of the units in this area and hurried back to base.

On my return to Brigade Headquarters, or shortly after, I found Genl. Landon. The Major-General seemed much exercised in his mind at the slow progress made. He repeatedly stated that the Corps was pressing for the completion of the work, and he informed me then, for the first time, that an attack was contemplated for the next day, and that it was essential the work of consolidation should be completed before. I replied that this was the first occasion I had heard of any date being fixed for the completion of these trenches. I told him however that had I known, I did not, taking all the circumstances into consideration, think it could possibly have been accomplished by this date. I however said I would send out instructions for the work to be proceeded with at all costs, and I immediately drafted and sent out the required order.

Carleton's order, included in his dossier, could not have been more uncompromising. It was, or so he must have assumed, precisely what was wanted by both Landon and XV Corps Headquarters. It emphasized the dissatisfaction of the Major-General Commanding 33rd Division at the progress made in closing the gap in question and continued:

He has instructed me to say that it is of paramount importance that the work should be completed without delay, no matter what the cost or how heavy the casualties, and Officers Commanding Battalions will be held personally responsible that this is carried out unremittingly by day and night from this time on by parties detailed for the purpose.

No excuse for failure to comply with this order will be accepted.

Landon departed and Carleton set about the business of the day. His attempt to satisfy his superior officer's demands, however, was not to prove successful. His account concludes:

At 2.30 p.m. that day, after having been in occupation of the line only 60 hours, I received instructions to hand over Command to Brigadier-General Mayne.

By 3 p.m. Mayne had taken over and Carleton was on his way to 33rd Division headquarters for further instructions. Within hours he was on his way to Amiens.

Carleton's 'Diary of Events' was intended to show that in terms of the circumstances which had led to his dismissal he had acted with full professional determination.

He also felt anxious to rebut any assumption that he might be lacking in personal bravery. His covering letter contained this paragraph:

I believe there is not a man in my old Brigade who will not support me when I say that I have shared to the full the perils and dangers of my men and have had as many escapes from death as most have undergone. I will quote only one in which my Staff Officer (Lieutenant Calder) was killed and Lieut. Burrell had his arm blown off and succumbed to his injuries the same night. Both those officers were walking by my side on the 19th July going round the front line, when this occurred. My staff could give many incidents in which I have narrowly escaped death while performing similar duties.

The memorandum of dismissal had contained a second accusation, namely that he 'lacked a cheerful outlook which will communicate itself to the troops'. In respect of this charge, he decided to attempt to refute it by means of extracts from letters to his wife. Thus he offered as part of his dossier a page of breezy quotations including this upbeat quotation from a letter of 18 July 1916, written during heavy fighting on the Somme: 'Keep your spirits up and be certain that I am as happy as it is possible for mortal man to be. No one could be otherwise in my position.'

As already stated, Carleton sent his petition to France on 12 September. Clearly it was impressive enough to be given the most careful consideration. On 16 September Major-General W. G. Peyton, Military Secretary to the Commander-in-Chief wrote in reply:

> I am to inform you that the Commander-in-Chief is prepared to consider your re-appointment to the command of an Infantry Brigade in the field when your services are again placed at his disposal.

Peyton added a second, personal note in his own hand:

> My dear Carleton,
> No report has gone home about you, so as soon as you are passed fit you will be returned to us and reappointed to a Brigade, but give yourself a sufficiently long rest or you will probably break down again.
>
> Yours as ever etc

On 10 October Carleton was appointed a full Brigadier-General. However, the brigade of which he was subsequently given command was not serving on the Western Front, but in Salonika, one of the 'sideshow' fronts of the war, offering at this time little prospect of serious action, and therefore limited opportunity for the recovery of his military reputation. On 20 October he left England to take up his new command, but Peyton had been perceptive in commenting on the need for him to look after his physical condition. In Salonika more soldiers died from disease than from fighting and Carleton was more vulnerable than most. His health soon began to break down, he was shortly transferred to Egypt and in August 1917 he was invalided home, this time permanently. From October 1917 to March 1918 he served at Woolwich, but he was suffering chronic pain and it was clear that his military career was effectively over. He survived the war by less than four years, dying following a heart attack in May 1922. He is on record as having stated that the Battle of the Somme was an event almost beyond human endurance and that it had taken ten years from his life.

First Tanks

Corporal Dudley White went to France in 1916 as a member of the Heavy Section, Machine-Gun Corps. This was in fact a cover-name chosen for security reasons; the Heavy Section's function was to operate tanks, which were first used in war during the Battle of the Somme.

Earlier in 1916 as this new weapon was being tested, its prime begetter, Colonel Ernest Swinton, had argued that tanks should not be used until a large force could attack over suitable ground; in this he was supported by the French, who were also working on the development of armoured vehicles. Sir Douglas Haig, however, took the view that even a handful of these revolutionary machines might procure the breakthrough which the Somme offensive had so far singularly failed to provide. He decided to use them in the attack that was being planned for 15

A 'C' Company Mark 1 Tank – C.19 'Clan Leslie' – photographed in Chimpanzee Valley, 15 September 1915, the day tanks first went into action. Corporal White, quoted here, was in 'D' Company. (Q 5574)

September. This was in spite of the fact that although the Heavy Section was to consist of six companies, only two were ready for action – C and D; Corporal White was a member of D Company.

The name 'tanks' had been chosen as a bluff, so that nobody would question the purpose of the bulky objects that were being transported under wraps that summer from British workshop to French battlefield. Instead of being discarded when the truth came out, the title stuck, rapidly assuming the formidable connotation it has carried ever since. An early name for them had been 'land cruisers', or, more briefly, 'landships' – these terms were swiftly forgotten; inevitably the Tommies produced their own comic variations.

The phase of the Somme in which tanks were initiated is known as the Battle of Flers-Courcelette; this was a major offensive on a ten-mile front from Combles to the right of the Somme plateau to the Ancre Valley on the left, the tanks to be engaged in the centre. Some progress was made but at much cost, and the Germans moved rapidly to contain the British advance. Forty-nine tanks moved forward on the night of 14 September, but only thirty-two were at the starting line on the morning of the 15th. Of these only about a third played any significant part in taking strong points or trenches. Many broke down or became ditched or were set on fire. Despite this they certainly created panic among the enemy and Haig was sufficiently impressed by them to despatch, as early as 19 September, a request to the War Office for a thousand more.

Corporal White was a tank machine-gunner. He described his experiences of this and a subsequent action in a series of brief, pithy letters, to his sister (unnamed) and to a brother, Harold:

21 September

My Dear Sister

Just a line to let you know I'm quite well, it has been impossible to write before, we have been up in the firing line a week and that is not a picnic I can tell you.

Guess you have heard what a success our 'Tanks' have been, we were in action 14 hours and jolly glad to get back again. We have seen some awful sights I can tell you, impossible to put into words.

It makes one smile to see Germans running over the trenches surrendering they don't half look scared.

28 September

My Dear Sister

I have been in action twice now, but last time we had a terrible time, they shelled us until they sent our car all in flames. I do not know how we got out, but we found ourselves in a shell hole behind our first trench. I had a bullet through the poke of my cap and it just scratched my ear so you can tell it was a near go, but we all got off with a few scratches although they had a machine-gun fire upon us. It is impossible to put into words what it is like on the firing line where the advance is.

We are not in the firing line at present, about 5 miles behind having a good rest, which we all need. I've got a very thick head and still feel shook up. Of course I have not been used to shells bursting in motor cars, only been used to driving them.

After being in action the first time a Brigadier-General sent us about 80 cigarettes each for our good works and am enclosing one which please keep as a souvenir.

4 October

Dear Harold

Well what do you think of our 'Landcrab Cavalry' or Irish Navy for that is what our Tommies call us out here? It has been a great success and the first time we went into action the Hun fled for their lives for they did not understand quite what was attacking them.

It is very seldom we see an English paper out here, but from what we have seen they seem to think a lot of our tanks.

Curiously, although taken aback by the new invention, the Germans were not fully persuaded as to its effectiveness and so they did not hurry to produce their own version – in contrast to the reaction of the British to the introduction of poison gas. The cumbersome vehicles Germany finally produced in 1918 were no match for those on the Allied side; she would reserve the use of tanks as a major instrument for a later war.

Soldiers on the Somme, September 1916.

Above: An exhausted Tommy resting; near Aveluy Wood in the Ancre Valley.
Left: A Royal Fusilier sporting a German helmet, after the capture of Thiepval on 26 September. (Q 1331)

'Over the Top'

Why did men go into the attack, in many cases time and time again, knowing that they risked death or maiming, aware that they might see their friends die horribly in front of them or that they themselves might die in front of their friends? How did they master that instinctive fear which makes a person shy away even from heavy rain, let alone the 'terrible rain' of death-dealing bullets and shells?

Of course, a belief in 'war fatalism' – as discussed already (see pp. 91–96) – was undoubtedly an important factor. But this was perhaps good enough for routine trench warfare, with its daily possibilities of a chance shell or bullet; it cannot always have been adequate for the 'over the top' attack of a major battle, for what all too often became a case of (to quote Churchill's telling phrase) 'fighting machine-gun bullets with the breasts of gallant men'. Everybody knew that there would soon be many dead and wounded among those who were in full health and vigour during the countdown to action. Moreover, it was a common experience of assault troops marching to the front before a major offensive to pass burial pits already dug for those about to fall. They also knew that First Aid Posts, Advanced Dressing Stations, Casualty Clearing Stations (complete with a moribund tent for those for whom there was no hope), Hospital Trains and Barges, and Stationary Hospitals – not to mention the Hospital Ships that would take many cases to 'Blighty' – would have been primed and made ready for the inevitable flood of casualties. Chaplains would be on hand to comfort the dying, or, in the case of Roman Catholics, to offer the last rites. Company and platoon commanders would be well aware that, if *they* survived, they would soon be writing numerous letters beginning: 'It is with deep regret that I have to inform you ...' and ending with the almost standard reassurance: 'You will be relieved to hear that death was instantaneous and that he suffered no pain.'

Yet when told that they were about to be in an attack men appeared not to react with dismay or fear or even grim resignation: on the contrary. Captain Harry Dillon – much quoted earlier in this book – wrote the following in July 1916 on the Somme:

> We must lose a lot more men, but the men are only too willing to take their chance. It makes me awfully proud to belong to a nation who, when they are warned for a show like this, knowing what it means, cheer and start singing and whistling and in fact carry on like a dog that is going to be taken for a walk.

And when it came to the moment of attack, what then? There were doubtless many answers. Captain John Staniforth's was one. Aware that his family would want to know how he had felt during an action on the Somme, he anticipated their question:

Over the Top by **Eric Kennington.** (Art 671)

What does it feel like to go 'up and over'? I don't know. I concentrated my thoughts on keeping my pipe alight. It seemed to be the most important thing at the moment, somehow.

A remarkable attempt to explain why soldiers behaved as they did and how they coped with the challenges they faced has survived in an eleven-page document preserved without comment in the papers of an officer who himself fought in both the First and the Second World Wars. It is undated but would appear to have been produced in 1916. It is entitled: 'A Word from Pte G. Ward 1st 4th Oxford and Bucks Light Infantry: Tommy & His Actions'. It was apparently written under the stimulus of the impossibility of explaining the realities of life at the front to 'people at home' – to whom the document is addressed virtually in the form of an open letter. Somewhat rambling and discursive, written almost in a 'stream of consciousness' style, it nevertheless makes clear what factors, in the writer's view, enabled soldiers to face the 'terrible task' of going into battle: e.g. a crucial comradeship between a man and his mates, a consciously constructed general cheerfulness, and an unquestioned assumption that there was no possibility of shirking one's duty – they all knew what they were there to do and they knew they had to do it. Here are two 'keynote' sections:

> You don't realise, and never will realise, what a Tommy has been through. You know as soon as you see him, that he looks years older and has that War Worn look on his face, and that cannot be so easily got rid of as one thinks. But nevertheless he will tell you that he is lucky to be alive; and you can take it for granted that he is, for if you have any idea what a battle is like, and you could see for yourself, you would never think any human being could escape the Danger. And yet there are always a few of them to go back behind the lines to talk about the Battle he has just come out of. All the same he never forgets his Dear Old Mates, that he has left lying Dead on that Shattered Piece of Ground he has helped to fight so hard for. Little notice is taken of your mates that fall by the side of you when you are in the Actual Battle, but when you get back a little way behind the Firing line, well then, that is the time you miss your Dear Old Chums, that you've marched the side of trying to overcome the Test you have before you, Singing, Shouting as you go along and you puff your Cigarette and march along with a good heart, until you reach a Certain Area and then the Order comes down, 'Cigarettes Out and no noise' and then you know you have not many minutes to go before the terrible clang starts to assist you in the terrible task you have before you and behold it is *hard*! Every man for himself, and not one must shirk his duty, but no never a man thinks of doing such a thing as that. He knows what he has to do and leave it to him, he will do it with all his heart. And would you think for one minute that there is a smile on his face? 'Yes, there is,' and the words come from his mouth, 'Best of luck to you old mate, let's hope you will make a good job of it.'

> Every man must be fully prepared to do the awful task put before him, and for a full two hours every Tommy is busy getting his supplies which he needs for the attack. Late tea is given you an hour before you start. A Conference by your Platoon Officer giving you full details of what you have to do when you reach your Objective, a map is shown to you, showing you the piece of ground you have to attack and by this time then you are waiting ready for the Zero which is told to you a few minutes before you start. 'Right, it will be at 4 p.m., and at 5 minutes to 4 it is passed down to you 'Get out on Top' and sharp at the tick of 4 o'clock you step off and as you put your left foot forward, then your Barrage starts, in which Every Gun on your front Bangs away, and the whole sky is lighted up by the Flash of the Guns behind you, and then you hear shouts and moans, and someone say he is hit. Call for the Stretcher Bearers, and so you go on. Men fall dead right and left of you and you wonder when your turn is coming. All sorts of strange thoughts go through your mind and by this time you have reached your Objective, which you may have to hold on to for 24 or 48 hours whichever the case may be. And when you have held on for those certain hours you begin to look for the Relief. Tired, Wet and Hungry, bumped from one side of the trench to the other, you begin to wonder 'Are we ever going to get out of it?' But with a surprise you hear the

word passed down to get dressed and then with a rush you look for the next Battalion Relief. Behold you will hear someone shout 'There is the Relief. Please hand over', that doesn't take many minutes. 'Well Goodnight boys, best of luck to you' and that is how you finish up the battle.

That officers too could see the requirement to do whatever was ordered in similar 'Hobson's choice' terms is clear from the attitude of the Artillery officer Major Ronald Schweder. There was simply no other way. You went where the others went. Peer group pressure (though it was not so-named at that time), not to mention the whole apparatus of army discipline, dictated that this was what had to be done. Hence his comment of 16 February 1917, after having experienced the rigours of the Somme:

> The papers today gave me the jim-jams. 'Haig on his next offensive'. My métier ain't blood and iron, and I have had one of his offensives. Of course, there is no good grousing. One will go with the herd of other poor idiots.

Not surprisingly, however, there were those who simply could not cope. Staniforth, noting the case of an officer who managed to get himself sent home on medical grounds by feigning illness – a process generally known as 'working one's ticket' – commented scornfully: 'The only disease he was suffering from to any extent was the not uncommon one known as "pedes frigides"' – i.e. cold feet. But sometimes cold feet – or its companion concept 'wind up' (or 'wind vertical') – became not so much an attitude as a condition, virtually a disease. In such cases officers received more sympathetic treatment than men, for what, arguably, were very defensible and logical reasons. Captain Geoffrey Donaldson of the Warwickshire Regiment, on the eve of the Fromelles action in July 1916 in which he himself was killed, reported that two officers of his company had been sent back from the line with nerves, 'as it was essential that they should not be near the men while the sort of ague, which is the outward and visible sign of the disease, was upon them.' He added: 'Some of the men had it too, but I allowed none of them to go back. An officer is a different thing, because on him depends so largely the nerves of the men.'

In extreme cases soldiers resorted to self-inflicted wounds, or – the ultimate sanction – to suicide, and the evidence suggests that these phenomena, well known from previous wars, started remarkably early in this one. Lieutenant Neville Woodroffe noted examples of the first in September 1914, Sergeant T. H. Cubbon an example of the latter in October (see pp. 35 and 19). Other men, in the extraordinary circumstances of battle or bombardment, lost all control; see for example in Lieutenant A. G. May's account of Messines (p. 173) his reference to the two soldiers who went 'completely goofy' during the attack, one of them cradling a tin hat as though it were a child and smiling and laughing in the midst of falling shells. Similarly, Private Alec Reader recorded the reaction of one of his colleagues during a concentrated shelling of their trenches in April 1916:

> One of the chaps, about 25 years old, who came out in our draft lost his nerve and laid in the mud groaning and crying the whole time. A rotten experience.

Getting the dead for burial, Thiepval Wood, 1916 by Gunner Harry Bateman RFA.

The Army's first reaction to any such behaviour was to assume it was simply cowardice, that it showed a deplorable, indeed a punishable, lack of grit. Later in the war the concept of shell-shock began to be accepted as an affliction for which a man could not be held responsible. Thus Lieutenant May himself, in hospital in Blighty:

> After a few days I started to have uncontrollable jerking and shaking of my legs. I was quite upset because I was unable to stop it. The doctor came and told me I had shell-shock but I did not believe this. A day or two later I was told I was to go to a special hospital for shell-shock victims.

Major Schweder was confronted by a shell-shock case (and described it as such) in April of the same year – not during a battle but a bombardment;

> One look-out fellow suddenly went chumpy and dashed away. I chased after him into a dugout where I found him trembling from head to foot. All he could say was 'I can't stand it.' Poor devil. He had shell-shock some time ago.

Typically, Schweder, always humane and perceptive in his comments, had sympathy for this unfortunate man.

Yet the war was won by those who managed to cope and the majority did. Ultimately, there is always likely to be a gap of understanding between our later perception of the special ordeal of a First World War attack and that of the men who undertook those terrifying journeys

Dead German in the trenches at Flers, September 1916. (Q 1284)

across No Man's Land. It was for those occasions they were there; this was, by definition, clause one of the job description. Other factors which assisted included tradition, unit pride, pride in the flag (significantly the only entry in the diary of amputee B. C. Jones after being wounded in 1915 was a reference to the Armistice and the phrase 'God Save the King'); and there was always the hope that what they were about to do would help to finish the war – these elements helped enable them to get up and over.

But in the end the most important element was the simple unarguable fact of military orders that could not be disobeyed. On Friday 4 May 1917 Private A. P. Burke took part in an attack with many casualties during the Battle of Bullecourt, in the later stages of the Arras battle – a 'second round' attack as the first one had failed. In a letter headed '17032 Still Smiling/Sunday 6.5.17', he wrote:

> We spent Thursday in a trench until evening when we got orders that our brigade would attack and try to take the village which a full division and 8 tanks failed to do.
>
> Whilst we were waiting our time to go over, the wounded were coming down in their dozens, and we were under the severest bombardment I have ever known Fritz to send over. We knew it was certain death for all of us – [but] orders are orders in the army and we had to obey them.

The 'Bomb-proof' Canadian

Private Andrew Munro 50th (Calgary) Battalion, Canadian Expeditionary Force, photographed with his mother before leaving Canada for Britain, autumn 1915.
(Q 111701)

Andrew Munro, a bank clerk aged twenty-two when war began, enlisted in Calgary, Canada, in May 1915, and subsequently served for two years as an infantryman on the Western Front. He was a native of Scotland, but the family had emigrated from Inverness to Alberta as far back as 1892, so there was no question of his becoming anything other than a Canadian soldier. His unit, the 50th (Calgary) Battalion, Canadian Expeditionary Force, sailed for the United Kingdom in the early autumn of 1915 and crossed to France in August 1916 as part of the 4th Canadian Division. A member of the battalion's Signal Section, he took part in several major battles, went 'over the top' many times, and was awarded a Military Medal for bravery under fire. In his letters home he admitted frequently to strain and exhaustion, but he was a survivor. His comrades dubbed him, not without cause, 'bomb-proof'.

He served throughout as a private, refusing all offers of promotion. As more and more of the original battalion were killed or wounded, the pressure on him to become an NCO grew ever stronger. 'The Major and others have time and again wanted me to take stripes,' he wrote in September 1917, 'but yours truly is like the rest of the old timers here, too wise to take them. They go about the trenches sometimes with a bag of them, looking for someone on whom to pin them.' Munro would not concede.

The battalion was blooded on the Somme and he clearly found this a very challenging and harrowing experience. On leave after the battle – staying with an aunt in Kettering, Northamptonshire – he wrote the following account in a letter to his parents, plainly feeling the freer for being away from the front and the eye of the censor:

Seeing I am in England I am going to tell you a few little things. I suppose you had an idea that we were on the Somme in the midst of the very heaviest fighting, where the Canadians have won undying fame for themselves. We spent eleven weeks there, which is weeks longer than we should have, but owing to bad weather we had to wait before advancing on our part of the line. We took our objective and held it, against numerous counter-attacks by the enemy, but our losses are heavy indeed, although not to be compared with those of the enemy. The 50th of old is practically extinct, and there are only about 30 of us who are really 'originals' left. Do you remember me telling you about a fellow named Webster who worked in the Commerce in Red Deer? He was a Corporal in the Signal Section. He with our Signal Officer, Hextall, and 4 others were all killed with one shell. Do not know how I managed to come through it. Was blown up once, buried once, and thrown down by concussion of bursting shells, and bombed by Fritz into the bargain. That was an awful day Dad. I was not a bit nervous during it all, even when I went through the German barrage three times, but after I got back to billets my nerves could stand it no longer, and I collapsed.

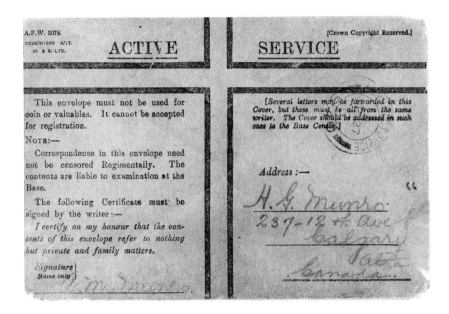

A 'green cross' envelope used by Private Andrew Munro in 1918. From Munro's correspondence it is clear that the understanding that 'nothing but private and family matters' should be referred to in letters sent in such envelopes was subject to generous interpretation. (HU 63261)

The happenings of those few days can never be described, and they are only a sample of what some of our boys have gone through. There are pictures in my mind that I shall never forget as long as I live.

This was not the only time he collapsed; indeed his health seems to have suffered a steady deterioration during his months at the front. But he did not give in easily; a determination to carry on whatever happened to or around him seems to have been an essential part of the philosophy of this thoughtful, sensitive and courageous man. That determination was undoubtedly stiffened by his fierce pride at what the Canadians had achieved on the Somme, a subject to which he returned in a letter of 30 December:

> The boys did good work there, and never once did they forget their duty, and many times we held our captured objective, against overwhelming odds, for our ranks were sadly depleted, yet never once did the boys look back, or grumble.

But side by side with his feelings of pride was something else: the characteristic resentment of Empire soldiers such as the Canadians and the Australians for 'bull', 'spit and polish' and other such phenomena associated with the Army of the mother country to which they were expected to pay respect when not fighting. If there were no grumbles in the firing line, there were many

> when we go back for a rest, and buttons have to be polished, boots shined, clothes cleaned etc. for inspection by some 'big guns', who let out lots of Hot Air, of which the boys have long since gotten tired.

At times he seems to have felt inhibited by the possibility of censorship when writing from France – 'I must close for now,' he once wrote in 1917, 'as there is not much to tell you outside of war news, and the censor does not permit much of that' – but nevertheless his letters are rarely other than frank and outspoken. A substantial number of them were sent in 'green' envelopes (later known as 'green cross' envelopes), which were subject only to spot-check censorship at the base, and therefore allowed a man a greater freedom of expression provided he obeyed the rules and did not give away sensitive military information. But even such of these as were opened – as indicated by the 'passed by censor' label with which such envelopes were re-sealed – bear no deletions or crossings out. He instinctively found the right mix, balancing the good and the bad and analysing his own feelings and attitudes with a clear-sighted honesty to which no one could take exception. This is from a letter written in June 1917:

> My nerves are in a pretty shaky state now, just the same as the rest. They cannot be otherwise under such a strain. Still it is a funny thing. We have time and again been awaiting in a trench ready to go 'over the top' as soon as the barrage starts. Everyone is a bundle of nerves and excited, until the 'show' commences, then all at once everyone seems to get quite calm and over we go, without a qualm, some whistling, some singing etc. It is not the actual 'going over' – it is the suspense of waiting to go over. After that one would think it a picnic.

It was in this letter that he told his parents of his reputation for surviving in the most extreme circumstances:

> Have come through several more tight places, without a scratch. I have been mixed up in quite a few tight corners, and as it were I am becoming 'climatized' – a regular old soldier. Some of the boys call me 'bomb-proof Andy', but of course I know that our lives are in the hands of One, who alone looks after us. We cannot help realizing it in a place such as this is. The more I see of it all, the more I think that, as you say, until the nations appeal to God for mercy and peace, to stop this horrible and wholesale murder, it will not be finished.

His pride in the Canadians' achievements grew steadily as the months went by. Out on rest in July 1917 and seeing much of the French, he reported with relish that 'they almost worship us because of Vimy' – the Canadians had taken Vimy Ridge in April during the Battle of Arras – and in September during the Third Battle of Ypres he could write with the hint of a swagger:

> Am in a recently captured 'Fritz' dugout, so if there are occasional misspelt words or if there are a few scratches you will know that 'he' has lobbed one fairly close. 'He' is quite sore at losing his formidable strongholds, and deeply resents us occupying them, and consequently he 'pounds' away, shoots over his gas and liquid fire, all to no avail, for the Canadians have a nasty habit of hanging on to what they have taken, regardless of Prussian Guards, Bavarians or anybody else.

Such 'hanging on', of course, could not fail to add to the list of fallen comrades – he once wrote that it made him 'lonesome' to think of the many friends he had lost since arriving in France – yet this did not affect his deeply held belief that the war should be prosecuted to its necessary conclusion:

Poor Ernie Smith was badly wounded in the last scrap, and I heard he has since succumbed. He was so cheery too the last time I saw him, and asked to be remembered to you. Yes, Dad, we all heartily wish it was over, but it is just as you say. Not one of us wants peace until we get the right peace, and everyone knows what that is.

Like most other soldiers Munro collected souvenirs. In May 1917 he wrote that he had acquired a Prussian Guardsman's belt with 'GOTT MIT UNS' on it (see p. 91), plus a tassel of a kind only given to prize bayonet men. But he also collected souvenirs of a less obvious kind – reminders of the resilience of nature in a world of ugliness and barbarity. He wrote at the end of a letter of January 1918:

PS. I am enclosing a leaf, don't know what it is, but will tell where I got it some time. It is a very interesting little souvenir.

Some months earlier he had sent home a four-leafed clover and a poppy which he had found on the old battlefield of the Somme. He had been much moved by the area's markedly different appearance, now the tide of war had moved elsewhere:

It is strange to see that place, that only a few months ago was torn and shattered, covered with ruins and shell holes, and now it is covered, or nearly so, with grass, flowers and shrubbery, where one would have thought no green thing would ever live again. I wish you could see that memorable place that I never shall forget.

Occasionally in Munro's letters there is evidence of a quiet, droll sense of humour, for even in situations of extreme danger the soldier's life could have its amusing aspects. This is from his letter of September 1917 written during Third Ypres:

It is a funny thing, but often you will see some poor soldier, worn and tired lying on a pile of bombs, or some other unheard of place in trenches, trying to snatch forty winks. The noise of bursting shells, and whistling bullets, disturb him not in the least, but let some nearby pal start whistling, or chewing the rag, and see what a balling out he gets for kicking up such a 'noise'.

There was a similar light touch in his letter of January 1918, in which, responding to his parent's enquiry, he described how he came to be recommended for his Military Medal:

It was for getting through with a message, through a Hun barrage when we were in rather a tight corner. Got through the barrage, got an answer and back through it again. Was buried a couple of times, and once a piece of shrapnel the size of a hand hit me, flatways, on the bottom. It was coming some too, and laid me flat as a board for a few minutes. It was quite a few days before I was able to sit down again with any comfort, ha ha. If anyone ever asks me to show them where I was hit – I shall show them – but only on the map.

Munro's last surviving letter from the front was written in February

1918. He was at the Canadian Corps training camp recuperating after a collapse that had kept him away from his unit for nearly three months. As ever, however, he was determined not to give in:

> One thing I do know and that is that I am not one tenth as fit now as I was 8 or 12 months ago, but others are carrying on, so I am going to do so too.

But further infantry fighting was now beyond him. At some time in 1918 he transferred to the RAF, and he was still under training when the war came to an end. He returned to Canada soon afterwards and was demobilized in February 1919. He married later that year and was subsequently employed by the Alberta Government Telephones, eventually becoming District Traffic Superintendent at Calgary. He died, of cancer, in 1961.

Winter, and the German Withdrawal

When battles 'closed down', the fronts on which they were fought did not fall silent. There might be a cessation of 'over the top' attacks, but trench warfare would resume, with a notable extra hazard: the reinstatement of the old rituals of mutual harassment in a terrain devastated in the fighting just concluded and littered with detritus and the bodies of the dead. Conditions were notoriously bad on the Somme after the great push ended in November 1916, with a bitter winter, which would win the

A remarkable photograph from a private album showing Trones Wood, scene of bitter fighting in the early stages of the Somme Battle, under a powdering of snow.
(HU 63277D)

reputation of being the worst one in European memory, providing extra hazards in the form of cold, rain and mud. One young officer who had not been long in France and who found the situation more than a little stressful was Lieutenant G. Havard Thomas, a Sherwood Forester temporarily attached to the 11th Battalion The Rifle Brigade; he wrote to his parents on 14 December:

> I have just returned from the line and have had a perfect nightmare of a time. The mud is simply incredible up here. I have been holding a piece of isolated trench with a party of men, no communication trenches up to it or tracks. My tribulations began when the guide they gave me lost his way and was taking me (after wandering for another hour and a half in and out of shell holes and mud) straight for the German lines. Luckily, as we were going over the front line someone shouted where the devil we were going. The guide at this juncture lay down and began crying like a child. I was furious and threatened to shoot him then and there if he did not find his way back to the starting point again. The Hun spotted us and began showering us with shrapnel so I put my men into a disused trench and went forward alone until I came across some machine-gunners who knew the way. I then led them back to Headquarters, the men absolutely exhausted. It then took me two hours to find this wretched trench and relieve the other Battalion. One man of the previous occupiers was left stuck in it and it took us 15 hours to get him out. We kept his spirits up by handing him food and rum on the end of a stick. It sounds stupid but it is absolutely true, the more one tried to move the faster one sticks and of course the weaker one gets. To add to the horror the place is swarming with corpses in different stages of decomposition, some spread out like crucifixes, others doubled up lying there, English and Boche.

Another young officer on the Somme front at this time was Lieutenant B. L. Lawrence, originally of the North Staffordshire Regiment but now with the 1st Battalion Grenadier Guards. In a letter also written in December 1916 (though not dated), he described his battalion's progress to the line:

> In the dark and in the crowd, it took us some time to find the guides who were to take us up to the front line, and when we did they told us we were to go up across the open with five minutes interval between platoons, as the communication trench was too dangerous and too muddy to be used.

Since he had been sent up in advance to reconnoitre access to the line he felt somewhat frustrated. 'All my work of the night before wasted!!!' he commented.

All was quiet when they reached their destination, until midnight, then a heavy bombardment opened up from the German artillery. 'I, in common with everybody else, just crouched in the bottom of the trench and hoped.' At 12.15 exactly the guns ceased as suddenly as they had begun, but simultaneously it started to rain; it would continue to do so until they were relieved:

> The rest of that tour of duty consisted in a fight to save the trench from destruction by the elements. It had not been raining long before the earth fell in at all the places where niches had been cut, and a breach once made rapidly

enlarged itself. We had not a very large supply of sandbags and there was nothing to fill them with except mud, and in addition to this the enemy kept sweeping round the top of the parapet with a machine-gun. The result of so much earth falling in from the sides of the trench was that the trench boards (such few as we had) became buried and the whole of the floor was deep in bog. It was a difficult and exhausting business to make one's way from one end of the company to the other, and one often sunk almost up to one's waist and had to be half pulled half dug out by some of the men.

In a later letter he turned again to the subject of the dismal conditions, this time with regard to their military consequences:

Really it is quite impossible for anyone to attack anything in this winter's Somme mud. The men would be drowned before they could cross 'no man's land'.

The state of the ground was not the only circumstance that made non-sense of any serious attempt to make war that winter. In February 1917 Lawrence's battalion was in trenches at St Pierre Vaast Wood in the vicinity of the Bapaume–Peronne road, on the eastern fringe of the old battlefield; the positions they had been assigned were such that the only sensible reaction was to declare a temporary draw:

From our front posts you could see for miles, and could trace the opposing trench systems right and left of you for a long way. There was a very extensive view over the enemy's back area behind his lines. It was a curious situation as being so close to the Boche and so much above him, we looked down right into his trenches and could see every movement, while we for our part had to cross the sky line (only about 50 or 60 yards from him) to get to our front line. By common consent there was a sort of policy of live and let live and neither side was sniped. If either of us had begun to use our rifles, both front lines would have become untenable.

I spent most of the daytime in one of the front posts with my field glasses, as there was so much that was interesting to watch. There were two German sentries who stood outside a big dugout just opposite us, whom we christened the Bing Boys. They used to greet us most cheerfully when we looked over the top and smiled and waved their hands. One wore a stocking hat, and the other a spiked helmet, but neither of them seemed to have any rifle or equipment that I could see.

In fact, serious fighting was now unlikely in this sector for another reason. There was about to be a major shift in the geography of the Western Front. Ever since September 1916 the Germans had been building formidable new defences to the east of the Somme battlefield, to which they would give the name of 'Siegfried Stellung' (which translated literally means 'Siegfried Position'), but which the Allies, borrowing the name of Germany's veteran Chief of the General Staff, would call the Hindenburg Line. On 4 February 1917 the Kaiser signed the order authorizing the withdrawal of German forces to these defences – a retreat of twenty miles in depth along a front of sixty-five miles in length from Arras almost to Soissons. Code-named 'Alberich' after the dwarf of

Retreat of the Germans to the Hindenburg Line. The ruined village of Athies, with a huge mine crater in the centre — left by the Germans with a view to impeding Allied traffic.
(Q 1941)

Wagner's *Ring* cycle, the operation was also to include the deliberate and comprehensive devastation of the areas relinquished. The process began on 9 March with the removal of *matériel* and the carrying out of demolitions; the evacuation of troops began generally on the 16th, though on one sector, the Ancre, the movement began earlier.

The Grenadiers were out of trenches when the news of this unexpected development began to spread. Lieutenant Lawrence and some other officers were sent up to report:

> We walked up to the old front line at St Pierre Vaast Wood, and found it empty. We could see all round the horizon a glare of the sky from the villages the Boche were burning preparatory to their evacuation. As we walked across what had lately been 'No Man's Land' we noticed that the REs had dug up or wired off a number of land mines which the Boche had laid in the hope that we might set them off when we advanced.

Moving into the line, they installed themselves in what Lawrence described as 'a very good Boche trench', but there was a clear need to exercise the greatest care:

> There were plenty of dugouts in the trench we occupied, but everyone was rather chary of entering them. All sorts of stories of booby-traps, explosive

Evidence of new management: German sign scratched through, British one added. Seven Dials being in a part of London near the 'Tipperary' places Piccadilly and Leicester Square, perhaps there was a subtext of nostalgia as well as wit in the choice of name.
(Q 1929)

dugouts, and so on, were in circulation and some of them were only too true. The battalion we relieved had had several casualties; in one case a man found a full rum jar, which, on being uncorked, exploded. In another case a man picked up a spade which set off a mine. And of course there were several cases of souvenirs, such as helmets which detonated bombs when you touched them.

On occasions, however, it appeared that Fritz was enjoying a joke at Tommy's expense. When the Grenadiers moved forward some days later, they found that a dummy gun had been rigged up behind a trench, with wires from it leading to a 6-inch shell and with the chalked message, 'Please do not touch', while another dummy in the middle of the trench, made of drain pipe with wires attached, bore the legend 'Highly Dangerous'. Strict instructions were issued that these were not to be touched.

> It was pitch dark that night and pouring with rain, and as they shelled us a bit, I decided, when going round the line to stick to the trench. I rather miscalculated the position of the dummy gun, and before I knew what was happening, I fell headlong over it and uprooted most of the wires. It was quite harmless, just what it appeared, a piece of old drainpipe and some rusty wire.

Predictably the German move was mocked by the press back home, but the reaction in the field was more cautious. There were those indeed who were much impressed by the manner in which the Germans had redrawn the trench lines. Major Ronald Schweder, for example, writing on 28 March:

> It is all very well for the papers to sneer at the German retreat, but it was wonderfully well done; they left not a thing behind, and no prisoners.

Eventually the Allies would have to storm the Hindenburg Line, but that time was not yet. In 1917 there would be hard battles fought in sectors away to the north, notably in the vicinity of Ypres. But before that another name would come to dominate the despatches and the headlines: Arras.

Diary of a Battalion Runner

The point of view of the earthy, ordinary Tommy as expressed at the time is singularly rare in books about the First World War. Contemporary newspapers generally portrayed him as endlessly buoyant and uncomplaining, happy to do what he was told (apart from some good-natured grumbling in the manner of 'Old Bill'), and ever ready, if need arose, to lay down his life for King, Country or High Command at the drop of a tin hat. To a considerable extent this interpretation (if perhaps less glibly put) still prevails, with the result that ex-Tommies challenging it in later memoirs have often been seen as responding to post-war revisionist attitudes, as opposed to reflecting the actual attitudes of the war years. One reason, arguably, for the persistence of this simplistic version is that it was widely endorsed by officers who, remote from the Tommy by reason of class and education, found it difficult to understand his real thoughts and motivations. Thus a battalion Commanding Officer of high intelligence and sensitivity could write in a letter to his parents in April 1917:

> The private soldier is really wonderful the way he carries on and is always cheerful, as long as one makes him think that everything is going well. Under these circumstances they will follow one anywhere.

Admittedly this officer was writing in relation to a New Army battalion which had not been long at the front and to which he had been appointed in order to sharpen its performance, and he would certainly have been correct in respect of many or even most of the men serving under him. Yet such sentiments would surely have brought a fierce rebuttal from such as Private Robert Cude, who served as a battalion runner of the 7th Battalion, The Buffs (East Kent) Regiment. (A runner was a message-bearer, a vital and often highly dangerous role in a war in which communication was still extraordinarily rudimentary.) Cude, who joined up aged twenty-one, kept an almost daily diary from his arrival in France in July 1915 until well into 1919 and his 100,000-word account constitutes a marvellously readable view of the underbelly of war. Most importantly, it sifts everything it describes. Although it inevitably contains much that is mundane and routine, it is also packed with sharp, unblinkered observation. For a man who was virtually self-educated – he had little or no formal schooling – he could write with remarkable precision and skill. He could be outspoken, even, by his own admission, 'venomous', with no pulling of punches and a rich line in scathing wit.

A notable example of his 'venom' is his outburst against the press during the Passchendaele campaign in 1917 – an attack on that very attitude which tended to present men like him as devil-may-care automata:

> Tens of thousands of England's finest manhood have been sacrificed, and tens

of thousands more have to be before the war is over, if that is a possibility. Yet to read the various articles from the papers one is taught to believe that War is a glorious thing, and that every man Jack of us is anxious to kill, etc., and, incidentally, is delighted to be serving. I am disgusted with England.

Yet his venom was far from instant. His first encounter with a general in the field, for example, led to a typically earthy entry, but one in the context of an instinctive respect.

2 August [1915] Parade for review by Army Corps General Munroe. Rained like the devil just as we were lined up, and after getting drowned we are marched back, as he is afraid to wet his boots. Incidentally, we are proud to be soldiers, and we are certainly proud of our Generals.

Two years later, however, he could let fly at a brigadier-general who had been dismissed for incompetence. He wrote of the general who took over:

At first sight he suits, for he looks a thorough soldier. The other old woman has gone back to England to act as house-keeper to a Suffragette, at least, that is all he is fit for, and I think everyone in the Brigade is unanimous in that opinion.

Yet in 1916, when a Brigadier-General Jackson was sent home for refusing to commit his battalions to an action which he saw as ill-conceived, Cude was vehement in his support:

He has been relieved of his command, for what? Being a human man. He will carry with him the good wishes of the whole Brigade and we can never forget the man who would wreck his career rather than be a party – however unwilling – to the annihilation of troops under his command.

Cude appears only to have seen the Commander-in-Chief once, in May 1916, but the occasion drew from him a sympathetic rather than a scurrilous comment:

Haig rode through on horseback, with all his staff, a very impressive caval-cade. He is rather nice-looking, but seems to be showing signs of wear. His perhaps is a very harassing life.

The Staff, however, is rarely spared. Thus this entry in early 1917:

Nothing doing today 16th Feb, except Divisional HQ move up. Wonders will never cease. They will get hurt one of these days and it seems such a pity to see such brightly decked men so near the line.

Or this, also in 1917, when the 18th Division's Artillery HQ was shelled:

We laughed until the tears ran down our faces watching the flower of Eng-land's greatness – the STAFF – running for dear life.

His attitude stemmed from two causes. One was the belief that officers given staff posts were those who were not up to the demands of serving in the line. Hence this comment, again in 1917:

An officer who is an idiot can get a staff job as easy as shelling peas.

The other was the belief – widely held – that the Staff, who gave the orders which others carried out, looked down on the ordinary fighting soldier while being spared the dangers to which that long-suffering individual was constantly prone. Searching for a definition of the 'infantryman's lot in wartime' Cude described it as being 'treated as less than nothing by big wigs in scarlet who direct operations without taking a man's share of the burden'.

But it was not only the Staff who aroused his antipathy. He shared the basic hostility of those engaged in the fighting with those who lived a safe life away from it. When members of the latter group were given medals while deserving members of the first group were ignored, his 'venom' could be particularly strong. Hence this outburst in early 1918:

> The officer i/c 18th Div Baths has been given the DSO for his valuable services, whereas Officers (Junior) in the Battn go through the bitterest of the War, unhonoured, except perhaps for a wooden cross! The inequality of it is simply astounding, and one marvels at the courage of the men who wear the medals that were won in Tea shops or over Mess tables, whereas they were instituted for service in the field.

His attitude to the enemy was double-edged. After seeing a killing of Germans at La Boisselle on the Somme (not during the famous battle), he commented:

> It was a wonderfully cheering spectacle, although now and again I am forced to think: 'Every Boche has a mother or wife, or at least someone he holds dear, and they all mourn for him.' Still, such thoughts do not do on 'Active Service'. Rather I set my thoughts on need of extermination of the whole race.

Yet he could also write of the Germans, 'They are brave chaps, as also are his airmen', and he could note with approval the successful escape of a German flyer whose dexterity in a dog-fight with superior Allied forces had won his admiration.

Cude did not ask for or want a comfortable life. Bored when out of the line he could express the wish to be back in it. And he could write thus of an harassing day on the Somme in which his activities as a runner – on this occasion a mounted one on a bicycle – had put him in conflict with one of the constant hazards of the Western Front, the product of its remarkable proneness to rain:

> I have had to push my cycle, in company with other 'Runners', over roads three inch deep in mud! Arrive midnight and drop into sleep straight away, awaking 7.30 a.m. feeling completely washed out, for am still soaked to the skin. It is all in a day's march however, and we are on 'Active Service', so must grumble but carry on.

'Must grumble but carry on': the phrase might almost be a motto for him.

He could also show a keen patriotism. He was much moved by Kitchener's death in June 1916, just before the opening of the Somme battle:

> His Army is missing his leadership, for we always said that 'K of K' would lead

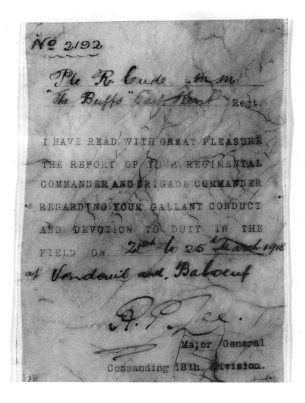
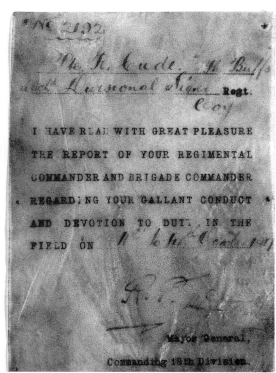

us over the top. I feel the lads will exact full reparation for the death of such a great man.

Cude was plainly no slouch at his job; he was awarded the Military Medal and Bar for bravery under fire and, although he had once vowed he would always remain a Private ('Will not be acting NCO again. Too much hard work and no pay for it'), he finally accepted promotion and ended the war as a Sergeant. However, he retained throughout his no-nonsense attitude and his basic scepticism, whether with regard to his military superiors or to those who guided the political destiny of the nation. Thus he could write in November 1916 at the end of the Somme battle:

> Hurry up 'Peace'. This is undoubtedly the heartfelt wish of all the troops operating on 'Somme'. Let the politician fight the war now, I have had enough. We hear such a lot of talk of 'fighting to a finish', but if they were in the scrap themselves, they would wish for a 'Peace'.

Fortunately for Cude, he was one of those who came safe home, but not until several months after the war. His diary's final pages include numerous caustic comments on the slow pace of demobilization. Long before that he had settled into a steady disenchantment with the whole business:

> Personally, I do not think that anyone out here troubles as to which side will ultimately win, all we ask is to go back quietly and live a life according to our own tastes.

Two commendations sent to Private Robert Cude following acts of gallantry, the first during the Third Battle of Ypres, the second during the German attack of March 1918, as a result of which he was awarded the Military Medal and Bar.
(HU 63262)

Entertainments, for the troops, various

Major Ronald Schweder wrote to his wife in May 1917:

> A leave camp has started for Officers and men somewhere near Boulogne. I should imagine it will be awful – all YMCAs, tinkling pianos and parsons. Enough to drive one crazy wasting a fortnight in such a hole.

One man's poison made another man's meat. Private Robert Cude spent some days in the camp while on rest away from the Third Battle of Ypres and thoroughly enjoyed himself. A concert put on by an entertainment group from 'Blighty' made a particularly strong impression. There were funny sketches, songs such as 'Alice Where Art Thou?', 'Come Into The Garden, Maud', and a skit on 'Excelsior'. Altogether it made a 'grand evening', Cude noted in his diary, adding: 'and if only I had the pluck to speak to the artists, and thank them personally, I should be satisfied. Their hearts are in the right place, for it is easier said than done to cross the channel, and sing throughout the weekend for the troops, and I thank Heaven that there are people that appreciate us for what we are doing and in return, help us to live again, if only for a few hours.'

Lieutenant Kenneth Mackenzie was another who enjoyed himself at the camp, and was equally appreciative of the efforts of the entertainers from afar. 'Yesterday I had a grand swim in the sea,' he told his family in a breezy letter dated 13 June 1917, 'and in the evening Miss Lena Ashwell's party gave a tophole concert.' He went on to list and evaluate the members of the group in some detail; of particular fascination was:

> Miss Norah Blaney. A most versatile American girl entertaining at the piano, and making all sorts of people on the front row uncomfortable by making remarks during pauses in her song. Such as 'Dear Brighteyes' to some stolid Hindenburg-Liner of last week. Every soul, and there are many hundreds here, was in the line a week ago and we are not naturally bashful.
>
> Miss Norah pulled my leg too to make me uncomfortable, and one fellow said he would prefer to be shelled with 5.9s any day than go through the ordeal.

Such entertainments were fully professional affairs, organized as part of an officially sponsored attempt to keep up the morale of the troops. Concerts of a less sophisticated kind had been improvised from very early on, in estaminets, barns, or any place in which performers and an audience could be got together in more or less peaceful proximity. Lieutenant L. S. Lloyd of the 18th Hussars noted one especially memorable occasion in February 1915:

> One evening we had a concert in the nunnery in which the men were billeted. It was held in the chapel – all the old nuns came, for having got their consent we invited them to attend. They seemed to enjoy the show thoroughly and roared with laughter. The performers were mostly dressed as nigger minstrels, having

ENTERTAINMENTS

The Follies

Songs Stories and Dances

by a talented group

of

PIERROTS and PIERRETTES

at the

ÉCOLE PROFESSIONNELLE

(17th Field Ambulance)

ARMENTIÈRES

Turce daily at 4 p. m. and 6.30 p. m.

CINEMATOGRAPH

at the Theatre of Varieties

PONT-DE-NIEPPE

CROSS ROADS

At 4 p. m. and 6.30 p. m.

CONSTANT CHANGE OF PROGRAMME

Films direct foom LONDON

Prices of Admission :

| OFFICERS | 1 FRANC |
| OTHER RANKS | 50 CENTIMES |

A typical 'Entertainments' poster, underlining the popularity of concerts and also of cinema shows which took place in all kinds of venues from variety theatres to muddy fields, Chaplin films being always in great demand. (HU 63263)

found some actors' garb somewhere in the nunnery. It was a queer scene – the grotesque performers in the old chapel, the nuns and the men – yet it was such a mixture that nothing jarred in this rather mediaeval picture.

Handsome young Tommies who could, with the aid of costume, wig and make-up, be transformed into presentable representations of the largely absent sex were especially in demand. Lieutenant G. Havard Thomas, on a course at the 3rd Army Infantry School in January 1918, went to a number of concerts by Divisional troupes. 'One, an especially good one,' he informed his parents, 'acted a pantomime *Dick Whittington*. It was far and away the best I have seen out here. The boy who took the part of the girl acted so well that it was very difficult to believe it was actually a man.'

Such mock pantomimes were especially popular, and if their titles

The 'Follies', as in the poster, seen in performance. (HU 63264)

could twist the military tail – as in one unit's effort, neatly entitled 'Puss in Boots, Gum, Thigh' – so much the better. But one appeal of behind-the-line entertainments was, inevitably, the nostalgic; they made the boys – in Ivor Novello's phrase – 'dream of home'. Hence the almost lyrical entry in the diary of Sapper Harold Brooks, Royal Engineers, on 9 March 1917, he and his comrades having managed a day away at a nearby town:

> After looking at the shops and at the thousands of absolutely indispensable things provided for a man on active service, there was the ritual of the day to be observed – tea – and we finished up with a topping concert. For a modest half franc we had a front seat – at least as much front as an 'other rank' can get. And we had as much as we could assimilate in the space of half an hour from a first class regimental band. I just shut my eyes and slipped back to Eastbourne, with nothing to do and nothing to think of, by the seaside. They played a selection of popular revues. Then the music stopped and the bandsmen hung up their heavy brass instruments (they made an imposing array too!) and, while one settled himself at the piano, the others re-arranged themselves as an orchestra in the little trench in front of the stage. Then came the usual 'ping, ping' from the violin strings and a few bald heads kept bobbing up and down until all was well and away they went again. I shut my eyes again to get the full effect until the curtain went up and the show began. I have seen a good few concerts given by 'Firing Line Parties', 'Divisional Follies', and 'Fancies', but this of the 'Merry Mauves' seemed to be the best I've yet seen. The staging was 'almost human' and the war came in only in the inevitable 'gags' on official life. Ah-lack-a-day, everything comes to an end and we had to trot back six miles on glassy roads to duty, and nights at that.

One form of entertainment encouraged at the highest level was the sports day. Brooks was an enthusiast for these occasions too:

> 18 June 1917. First annual sports of E-Corps Signal Coy. A HUGE success.

The arrangements made were exhaustive and as complete as circumstances permitted. The programme was enlivened by the sweet music of the Ulster Divisional Band. A canteen was open all day for solid and liquid refreshment. All work was suspended for the day, except of course for the Signals Office. No one seems to have suggested stopping the war for a bit!

Entertainments with a more specifically martial purpose were provided by 'Military Tournaments'. The programme for a tournament held by the 110th Infantry Brigade at Moyenneville on 7 August 1917 announced the following events: Wrestling on Horseback; Bomb Throwing Competition ('Dummies'); Officers' Digging Competition ('Dress:– Any order, but Box Respirators must be worn'); Rapid-Wiring Competition ('Points will be given for time, drill and form; form to include silence'); Stretcher-Bearer Competition; Bayonet-Fighting Competition; Physical training competition; Tug of War ('Any weight, 8 men, 3 foot pull'). Also on the card was a bareback race on mules, while there would be competitions for best platoon, best pair of mules in harness, single cob with pack saddlery, and – as the final category in the Transport section – 'Best turnout, Unloaded Limber Wagon, with Mobilization Equipment, complete'. Meanwhile the Divisional Band would play all afternoon from 1.30 to 5.30, at which time there would be a performance by the Divisional Troupe on the Tournament Ground. A Championship Prize, awarded by the Brigadier-General, was to be given to the Unit winning the largest number of events.

The most widespread and popular form of entertainment on the Western Front, and not only among the British, was football – or 'footer', as it was generally called. Football games took place in all circumstances and in the most unlikely circumstances, even with the enemy (as at Christmas 1914), and even under fire. A Company Com-

Men dressed as women were a special attraction at Western Front entertainments. Here a member of a Canadian Concert Party 'The Maple Leaves' is undergoing a sex change prior to performance in September 1917, while two members of 'The Queerios', a Concert Party based at the GHQ town Montreuil, disport themselves for an al fresco photo-call in May 1918. (CO 2013, Q 8961)

mander of 22nd Manchesters, Captain Charles May, described one such match on the Somme just a month before the launch of the attack on 1 July:

> 31.5.16 We played the Borders tonight at footer and beat 'em 2-nil. It was a good game and was rendered a trifle more exciting than some other matches I have been to by the fact that Fritz commenced shelling in the wood whilst the game was in progress, the shells passing over our heads and exploding on the slopes above.

One 'entertainment' rarely if ever described in contemporary writings, and for which one can only turn to a memoir by someone prepared to write frankly and without embarrassment of his experiences, was that provided by prostitutes. Brothels, their existence sufficiently acknowledged by the authorities for there to be a distinction between those for officers and those for men, flourished in a number of cities and towns in the base areas. The following description was written by a former artillery officer in the early 1970s:

> It was always very pleasant to visit Dunquerque, with its crowds of civilians going about their unperturbed business in their unspoiled streets and squares. I recall no ruins in Dunquerque, though there must have been some here and there. Every trade flourished there, even the brothels. There was one reserved for officers, in the Rue de something-or-other in the suburb of Rosendael. This we occasionally patronised; the girls were nothing to write home about, with the exception of a red-head, whose favours were competed for. My young woman was a black-haired, black-eyed wench, whose enthusiasm was quite adequate and whose skill likewise – I stuck to her on the rare occasions when a visit seemed desirable. I remember the house had a paved courtyard at the back, with a rectangular lily-pool in the centre. Here you might stroll, or sit and drink a bottle of wine with your very sketchily clad companion – they all sported extremely gauzy shifts decorated with ribbon and lace, and not a stitch underneath. My young wench confided to me that she was saving up to retire, and already had a handsome sum safely banked. She proposed to get married and buy a practical little shop, perhaps a milliners. An exceedingly practical young lady, she was. I quite forget her name. She couldn't speak a word of English.

Arras: A Senior Staff Officer's View

Brigadier-General Douglas, Lord Loch, had been a virtual spectator during the Somme campaign. In the case of the Battle of Arras, which lasted from 9 April to 17 May 1917, he was heavily involved, and his almost daily letters to his wife Margaret provide an informed and incisive commentary on the course of the action.

His post was that of BGGS – Brigadier-General General Staff – of VI Corps, one of four corps in the Third Army under General Sir Edmund Allenby. As such he was chief of staff to his Corps Commander, Lieutenant-General Sir J. A. L. Haldane, co-ordinating and advising on all matters concerning operations and administration. Aged forty-three, he was an officer of wide experience, having entered the Grenadier Guards in 1893, fought in the Sudan under Kitchener in 1898, and taken part in numerous operations in South Africa during the Boer War, in the course of which he had been severely wounded. After Arras he would serve as a Brigade Commander during the Third Battle of Ypres, though ill health would then force his withdrawal from the Western Front to a less demanding role in Ireland. Promotion to Major-General would follow in 1919.

Just as the Fourth Army had borne the main burden on the Somme, so the Third Army was assigned the major role for the Arras offensive, fielding twenty divisions. Also playing a vital, though subsidiary, role at the northern end of the battle front was General Sir H. S. Horne's First Army, with nine divisions. Of these nine, four were Canadian; these proceeded to write a famous page in Canadian – and Western Front – history by their brilliant seizure of Vimy Ridge in the battle's first two days. (Vimy, a steep whale-back eminence dominating the northern French plains, was a great feature to hold, a hard one to oppose; its value to the Allies would be shown when its possession helped to slow the German advance of March 1918.) Additionally, seven divisions of General Sir Hubert Gough's Fifth Army, four of them Australian, took part on the southern flank, notably in the diversionary attacks on Bulle-court. For the Australians Arras would not have the resonance that it would have for the Canadians; in their attack on Bullecourt on 11 April they were reduced to clawing back the enemy's barbed wire unaided by tanks or artillery.

Overall Arras was a battle with a promising beginning – with a three-and-a-half-mile advance into German ground in addition to the seizure of Vimy – which then mutated into a prolonged attritional slogging-match, accompanied by heavy casualties. Launched largely for political reasons, as a major diversion on the eve of what was intended to be a definitive, irresistible French offensive under the flamboyant but flawed General Nivelle, it was continued for political reasons, as Nivelle's initiative collapsed and the French found themselves coping

Brigadier-General Douglas, Lord Loch, undated photograph but taken while serving as Brigadier-General General Staff on VI Corps (this can be deduced from the fact that he is wearing a VI Corps arm-band). (DOC 425)

with a string of mutinies and, effectively, withdrawing from the scene for
the rest of the year.

There were some notable improvements at Arras, however, as compared with the Somme. On that front the approach to the start line had
been over open ground subject to enemy artillery; at Arras things were
different, as Loch explained once the battle was under way:

> My pet work for the past three months has been to organise the underground
> systems. The old French built their towns by quarrying down till they came to
> the hard chalk and then dug it out. This has made huge caves. We joined them
> up and made entrances etc. Lit them by electric light. Made cook houses –
> Divisional and Brigade headquarters etc., etc. On the day of the attack you
> could walk underground from the centre of Arras to the German front line.
> The last 150 feet we blew out at zero hour. We consequently had communica-
> tion trenches across 'No man's land' in under half an hour. This would have
> been of enormous assistance in case we had had only a temporary success. As
> it was the men lived in quite comparative comfort and comparative safety
> before the assault with no long approach march. The caves are quite a
> wonderful sight and will I suppose be one of the show things after the war.

There were other differences: a shorter front overall (eleven and a half
miles as opposed to eighteen); detailed maps based on aerial photography (though acquired at a high cost in airmen's lives, giving rise to the
soubriquet 'Bloody April' for April 1917); creeping barrages; new,
instantaneous fuses; more guns set closer together and firing a far lower
quota of defective shells. The preliminary bombardment was only
slightly shorter, five days rather than seven; Allenby would have liked a
briefer bombardment still – a mere forty-eight hours; four days was
agreed after a sharp exchange of views between Third Army and GHQ,
but in the event became five when zero hour was delayed by twenty-four
hours. There was no question, however, as to the improved quality of the
gunners' contribution.

> Tell Frank [a relative of Lady Loch's] from me that the artillery did their work
> splendidly in the battle. The way the defences and the hostile gun positions
> were knocked about was wonderful. We had very few shells that did not
> explode, going over the trenches one hardly saw one. *Very* few guns got out of
> order or broke. The prisoners all say that the artillery fire was awful and they
> had nothing to eat from the time the bombardment began until they were
> taken except reserve food they had in their dugouts.

Nevertheless VI Corps made less progress on the opening day than had
been anticipated. Loch wrote on 10 April:

> We did not have the success yesterday that we hoped for – why I can't say.
> Several little things went to stop us. One is that at one place some of our men
> got too far behind the field gun barrage and consequently the Germans had
> time to man the parapets. In another place one brigade lost direction and did
> not arrive at the place ordered. Bitterly cold weather with a gale blowing – we
> have just had a snow storm and all the country is white. This has been going
> on continuously – the ground is very wet and we can't get the guns up, or at
> least they are very much delayed. Though we are disappointed we did not do

Artillery moving to the front through Arras, 12 April 1917. (Q 6191)

so badly. Our Corps captured two systems of trenches and part of another, 1600 prisoners and 59 guns. The other Corps did well, apparently 10,000 prisoners altogether.

On the 11th, however, there was a prize gained: the target village of Monchy-le-Preux, south-west of Arras. But weather conditions were deteriorating, there had been strong resistance, and the attempt of the Cavalry to play their traditional exploitation role had ended in failure. (He did not expand on this latter subject at this time, but his wife knew his views from the Somme period, when he had described talk of 'pushing cavalry through the gap' as 'all nonsense' unless there were an advance substantial enough to offer a genuine prospect of being able to 'break the line'.) There was a reasonable tally of captured guns and men, and there were plaudits from above – the Commander-in-Chief had been 'very complimentary' over the performance of the Corps – but Loch was more concerned about profiting from the mixed experience so far:

> We have learned one lesson which we learnt before but were not allowed to profit by and that is that the same men cannot attack from trenches and advance for more than 5000 yards at the outside. The physical and mental strain will not allow of it. Therefore if we want to succeed we must have fresh

Arras enjoying its freedom from enemy bombardment. A British military band playing on its famous Grande Place, 27 April 1917. (Q 6444)

men in such a position that they can pass through the tired ones and carry on. It is easy to say this but it is very difficult to carry out in fact, nothing could be more difficult but it is not impossible. Simply a question of staff work.

There were also anxieties about the air war – 'The Germans have not been beaten out of the air in spite of all the newspaper claims. Their aeroplanes are very much in evidence' – but there was good news in relation to Arras itself, now restored to some semblance of normal life after months of being at the enemy's mercy:

Arras is a wonderful sight. Last week a city of the dead and hardly anybody to be seen in the streets and though we had thousands of men there they were all underground. Now the town swarms with soldiers and civilians. Shops that have been carrying on their trade underground are now opening above ground. Shop windows where such things exist are stocked. It is a transformation scene.

The Nivelle attack, in the Aisne area to the south, opened on 16 April. On the 17th Loch wrote:

Rain all yesterday and heavy sleet showers today. It's most unfortunate, for the French attack began yesterday. From what I can see it seems to me as if the

Germans had made up their mind to accept battle from the French to make it one of the decisive battles of the war. They think they can hold us in the field and starve us with submarines. If they hit the French very hard it may finish things. However it ought to be just the sort of battle to suit the French. If the Germans counter-attack the 75s should account for most of them. It just depends on whether the French have got their tails up and mean to fight. If they have they will defeat the Germans. Oh what a pity it was we could not do our little bit better. We got forward 3½ miles but could not quite manage to do it in one day. If we had we would have been another 15 miles on now and the French would have had a better chance.

By the next day, however, he had heard that Nivelle's advance had met with a serious rebuff – not to the surprise, it might be added, of the British Commander-in-Chief:

I am afraid the French have not got on as well as they expected. I think their objectives were too big, the weather has been against them and the Germans were ready with big reserves. I heard the French are very jealous of our success and unless they get on and we get stopped there may be friction. It seems rather hard to understand. Doctor describes the situation as follows. The Frenchman is divided into 3 parts, 1 part a man, 1 part a child, 1 part a woman. It is the French woman part that does the mischief.

At Arras a major new effort began on 3 May (to be known to historians as the Third Battle of the Scarpe), but in the wake of a serious conflict of opinion as to when it should be launched: by night, as the Australians wished, or by day, as preferred by Allenby, who felt that his men had insufficient experience of night fighting. The result was an awkward compromise, an attack just before dawn with neither side satisfied. Worse, the planning had been hurried and the briefings inadequate. Loch was firmly of the 'daylight' school. He wrote on 4 May:

I am very sad about yesterday as it was to my mind the best chance of gaining our objective and I felt confident of success in spite of the men being tired and the ranks full of drafts. Now I am afraid we will not be able to do what we want to do. I do wish those in high places would take the advice of those in front as to how an attack is to be carried out. If we had been allowed to do the attack in daylight I think we might have succeeded. We were given no warning that it was to be a night attack until very late – too late for any reconnaissance to be carried out. But now I am grumbling so I must stop.

As the battle continued into May, slowly moving away from the old defence systems, he became anxious about the capacity of troops conditioned by months of deadlock war to cope with the new situation. He wrote on 14 May:

One division goes in tonight. This semi-open warfare is much more difficult for the untrained men than the trench warfare. At the commencement we had no men who knew anything about trench warfare and now we have no men who know anything about open warfare. However I think we are tiring the Germans very considerably. The 4th Ersatz Division seems to be the most pleasing adversaries. Three nights ago four or five hundred surrendered as soon as they were attacked.

Lord Loch by no means fits the stereotype of the desiccated, uncaring staff officer. His focus was always forward, with the men who were doing the fighting. He wrote of one intelligence officer's tendency to distribute material irrelevant to the needs of those in the field, 'It is the sort of idiotic policy of a man who has never been with soldiers.' He was never a courtier of GHQ and went there as rarely as he could; he stated in August 1916:

> They usually annoy me there by talking rot. Opinions based on considered knowledge is the best thing in the world but opinions based on ignorance or unconsidered knowledge is the most poisonous.

Yet although he was continuously engaged with the matter in hand and discussed aspects of the campaign almost every time he put pen to paper, his letters were far from being simply arid analyses of military situations and problems. They were also the love letters of an ardent husband very much missing his wife, Margaret – herself a person of distinction, being the only daughter of the Marquis of Northampton and a woman of high intellect and independent mind. This is from a letter of 11 May, during the Arras battle.

> Seeing all the spring green and listening to the birds makes me long for you. I believe it is called being Homesick. To think that I have been away from my darling for nearly three years.
>
> I am afraid from your letters that you think I am unhappy and dissatisfied with my job. I am not in the least dissatisfied, in fact I do not know of a job I would like better. I sometimes grump about it, but that is when I am grumpy. The only reason why I am unhappy is because I am away from you.

His letter of 28 May, by which time awards were being distributed relating to the recent battle, now judged overall to be a reasonable success, might be quoted as a fitting postscript to this section:

> They have gone and given me a Legion of Honour. I don't know what class. I am to go and be given it on Friday by Pétain. I am pleased at getting it – I can't help it though, I feel it is wrong any staff officer being given these things. The Regimental officers are the men who have the bad time and they are the ones that should get the rewards.

Liaison Officer with the Portuguese

Portugal entered the war on the Allied side in March 1916 and the first Portuguese troops landed in France in January the following year. Since it was intended that they should be integrated into the Western Front alongside the British, the BEF undertook to provide liaison officers who would assist in this process. Their function was to play the role of advisers, instructors and, in effect, public relations consultants. A vital qualification was, of course, a knowledge of the language. Lieutenant (later Captain) R. C. G. Dartford, 1/19th London Regiment, whose family was in the fortified wine trade in Oporto, was well suited to undertake such an assignment; he spoke the language well and he had seen service in the trenches. He had also fought in a major battle, at Loos, and had been severely wounded, with a bullet to the head. Now recovered, and with no permanent disfigurement from his injury, he had returned to the front able and eager to contribute further to the war. He became one of some sixty officers who formed what was officially known as the British Military Mission to the Portuguese Expeditionary Force, he himself being one of nine officers attached to the 1st Infantry Brigade, 2nd Division.

Unfortunately, the Portuguese were not to win any great reputation on the Western Front nor to distinguish themselves by their military zeal. For them this was a quarrel far from home; arguably, they were almost a token rather than a serious fighting force. The usual British name for the Portuguese was the 'Pork and Beans'. Dartford never uses that term, however, in the vivid and detailed diaries which he kept through the many months he served with them; he calls them 'the geese'. It was a convenient shorthand; it also suggests that he did not necessarily hold them in the highest regard as soldiers.

He wrote eight diaries in all of which five have survived. Diary no 3 begins in March 1917 with him about to go on leave to Britain; his experiences with the Portuguese begin on his return. By this time the new arrivals had been through various training establishments and were having their first taste of the trenches. They were assigned to the Neuve Chapelle area, doubtless because this was now considered to be a quiet sector. Its time would, however, come again in 1918.

By early May Dartford had begun serious trench training. He noted on 3 May: 'I made the geese do some firing during the important 10 mins or so when it's light enough to see the parapet but not to distinguish heads', adding: 'I took great delight in taking the geese officers over the open to the front line.'

Teaching his new pupils the necessary routines was plainly no easy task. After attempting to 'show the geese the job of an officer on rounds, examining sentries, etc.' he was driven to comment 'I get sick of explaining things again and again to Captain Pissarro.' This on 10 May.

A frame from the 'comic' scene arranged by Captain Dartford during the visit of the Official Cinematographer to the Portuguese lines in May 1917. (FLM 2367)

On the 13th he noted, not without a touch of hyperbole:

> The first Port batt to go alone in the line is the 34th and it went in on the 11th. The first night they let off 700 Very lights and 500,000 SAA! [Small Arms Ammunition, i.e. bullets]

By the 15th he was beginning to feel moderately encouraged:

> The geese seem to be getting into the way of things fairly well, cleaning rifles and staying to their ports.

One important skill to be imparted to the 'geese' was that of installing and repairing barbed wire entanglements. Although, as Dartford put it, this was 'hardly a thing to learn in No Man's Land', it had to be done.

> 19 May (Sat) At 10 p.m. the wiring party started work – 10 men with 2 English corporals covering patrol. The wire isn't bad really but we found a suitable place to put up an 'apron'. The men worked fairly well and it was the funniest bit of interpreting I've done. Whispering and stumbling about. All went quietly till 12.30 when the Germans started dropping RGs [rifle grenades] all along the wire, evidently having heard or seen something. The Boche soon seemed to know where we were and several fell near. Got the party in just in time before a regular bombardment of RGs and TMs [trench mortars].

The arrival of the new ally required recording by the official media of the time. Over the next weeks Dartford's brigade was visited in turn by both a film cameraman and a stills photographer. Dartford collaborated fully and enthusiastically on each occasion, helping to arrange suitable scenes.

> 21 May Mon During afternoon a cinema operator turned up and caused great

The photograph of Captain Dartford and the Portuguese Captain Burn taken by the Official Stills Photographer during his visit in June 1917. (Q 5568)

excitement. He took various things in the front line. I stage-managed for him and arranged men to walk into fire-bay and then distributing dinners from the portable containers. A 'comic' was got by 2 geese eating out of the ladle at the same time and smiling. Unknown to me somebody threw 2 bombs over the parapet and I'm afraid I shall figure in the photo as having considerable wind-up.

He need not have worried; in the film – which has survived – he is not in the frame when two soldiers react to the throwing of the bombs; he does appear, however, at the edges of certain shots while 'stage-managing' one or two of the set-ups. The high point of the sequence is the 'comic' scene with two soldiers eating out of the same ladle.

24 June Sun Came back to lunch and to find the official photographer of the Western Front awaiting me. Wanted to take snaps of good infantry for the papers. Took him round and he did a dozen snaps, my grouping the geese for him. One of Captain Burn and myself which he says he'll try to get hold of and send me.

The photographs have also survived, including the one referred to above.

These were enjoyable interludes but were soon forgotten as Dartford turned again to his often frustrating task. On 24 June, just two days after the photographer's visit, when reconnoitring his brigade's left sector, he found himself making his way along 'very exposed' trenches and being subjected to the personal attentions of the German artillery. 'Nobody works on deepening the trench', he exploded in anger that night 'and then I find the 2nd i/c is spending all his energies building himself an extra dugout at HQ, it's really criminal.' He went on to record an episode told him by a British artillery officer about a raid on one Portuguese battalion three weeks earlier, after which the CO 'wept copiously and bewailed that he had lost the front line and was disgraced – but did nothing', while when a British trench mortar officer went up to the front to see the commander of the company against which the raid had been mounted he was confronted with an even more bizarre response:

> The company commander was under the table with his gas respirator on (no sign of gas). The British officer kicked him out and asked him if he had sent an SOS. No. So he hauled him along to the rocket stand and sent one up (about ½ hour late). After they had re-occupied the front line – during night – gas-shells came over and they were ill-disciplined enough to get 40 casualties.

Overall the learning curve of the new arrivals would continue as an erratic one, with Dartford swinging constantly between exasperation and optimism. On the one hand there are references such as that on 11 September to a raid which had proved 'a complete failure', while on the other hand he could write on 1 October: 'Everybody is pleased with the energetic way the brigade is going ahead.'

As Christmas approached, however, it was clear that the high command surmised that the Germans might see the Portuguese as likely collaborators in some kind of seasonal cease-fire along the lines of the great truce of December 1914. This was reflected in the following entry written on Christmas Eve:

> Fear of fraternising this evening so British officers had to go to the front line and report if there's anything unusual in enemy's attitude. As a precaution there was a lot of harassing fire carried out during the night which annoyed everybody very much.

Arguably, it was reasonable of the British commanders to be concerned. If they sensed that the Portuguese Expeditionary Force was not seen by the Germans as the doughtiest of opponents on the Western Front, this assumption would be amply justified some months later when the sector held by the Portuguese was chosen as a prime target for a major enemy offensive.

Messines, June 1917

The most spectacular and effective use of mines on the Western Front took place on Thursday 7 June 1917 at Messines, in Belgium.

Messines lies at the southernmost point of the Ypres battlefield. The whole Ypres area can be roughly likened to a huge question mark, the Salient forming the semi-circular curve above, the Messines ridge the vertical stroke below, St Eloi providing the pivotal point. Looked at from Ploegsteert ('Plugstreet') Wood to the south, Messines, with its jumble of red roofs about its ugly, rebuilt church, appears tall and dominant above the featureless horizontals of the Flanders plain. It was this rare geographical situation that made Messines an appropriate location in which to carry out a major experiment in underground warfare.

Mining seemed to offer the only means of dislodging the enemy from a vantage point which he had used to great effect since seizing it in late 1914. When in August 1916 a rumour that Messines had been taken was found to be false, Battery Sergeant-Major Douglas Pegler, RFA, commented in his diary: 'Messines is one of the strongest points in the German line. I should think the only way to capture it would be to surround it and starve it.' By the following year a better way had been found.

At 3.10 a.m. on the 7 June, nineteen huge mines, in mine shafts prepared over months and containing almost a million pounds of explosives, were detonated under the German positions. (There should have been twenty-one, but two failed to explode.) The two northernmost mines were under that much fought-over vantage point, Hill 60, on the Salient's southern boundary. Their detonation was in the hands of the 1st Australian Tunnelling Company, AIF; the officer responsible for activating the mines, Captain Oliver Woodward, wrote this graphic account of the final minutes before zero hour:

At 2 a.m. all troops were withdrawn from the dugout and mine systems, and posted in their position for attack. At 2.25 a.m., I made the last resistance test, and then made the final connection for firing the mines. This was rather a nerve-racking task as one began to feel the strain, and wonder whether the leads were properly connected up. Just before 3 a.m. General Lambert took up his position in the firing dugout. It was his responsibility to give the order 'FIRE'. Watch in hand he stood there and in a silence that could almost be felt he said, 'Five minutes to go'. I again finally checked the leads, and Lieutenants Royle and Bowry stood with an exploder at their feet ready to fire should the dynamo fail. Then the General, in what seemed interminable periods, called out 'Three minutes to go, Two to go – One to go – 45 seconds to go – 20 seconds to go' – and then '9, 8, 7, 6, 5, 4, 3, 2, 1, – FIRE!!' Over went the firing switch and with a dull roar, accompanied by a heaving of the ground, the mines exploded. We had not failed in our duty.

Just prior to the actual firing of the mines, probably a second or two, we

began to feel the earth tremors resulting from the firing of the other seventeen mines on the Army front. In those fractions of a second, arising from the variation in the synchronisation of watches, I realised how quickly the mind functions, as I distinctly remember the feeling of envy of those officers similarly situated as I, who had brought their task to a successful conclusion, while mine had yet to be performed. I grabbed the handle firmly, and in throwing the switch over my hand came in contact with the terminals, so that I received a strong shock which threw me backward. For a fraction of a second I failed to realise what had happened, but there was soon joy in knowing that the Hill 60 Mines had done their work.

The blowing of the mines was part one of a sophisticated battle-plan, devised by the commanding general at Messines, General Sir Herbert Plumer, a favourite among the troops for the thorough and meticulous way in which he planned his battles. It was to be followed first by an intensive bombardment from over 2,000 artillery pieces and then by a mass infantry attack, with tanks in support, by a mixed force of British, Australians and New Zealanders. Ahead of the explosions there was quiet along the front, with no hint of anything unusual. As Brigadier E. Craig-Brown, commanding the 56th Infantry Brigade, 19th Division, put it in a letter to his wife, 'The night was normal. The Boche was evidently not anxious, otherwise he would have shelled our front line system and inflicted heavy casualties on the lines of men who had got into the assembly areas after dark and were ready to go forward. They were pretty thick on the ground.'

Private Albert Johnson, 11th Royal West Kents, was one of the 80,000 'thick on the ground' infantrymen poised to go into action that spring morning. Writing to his father about the event on the following Sunday, he was already aware that the noise of the great explosion had reached southern England and had numbered in its cross-Channel audience the Prime Minister himself:

The press mentions that Mr Lloyd George distinctly heard the detonation of the numerous mines which were sent up with such clockwork precision and at the same time acting as a signal for the guns to belch forth their unceasing rain of iron at the German trenches and beyond. At this point I was crouching in a trench with the rest of my companions waiting for the word to go up and over. We had been waiting there some time and in fact I began to get a trifle dozy but this speedily vanished when the mines went up. Our trench rocked like a ship in a strong sea and it seemed as if the very earth had been rent asunder. What the Germans thought of this is better described without words.

Craig-Brown was at his Brigade-Headquarters, which had been established in a deep, specially constructed dugout. Having been warned that the explosion might cause the dugout to collapse, he and his staff had come to the top at 3 a.m. and had marshalled themselves into suitable vantage points:

All our watches had been synchronized. Punctually at 3.10 a.m. the mines went up, magnificent sights in the dark, and, we hope, sending the mangled fragments of many Boches sky high. The ground shook as in an earthquake

Opposite: *Sappers at Work: The Canadian Tunnelling Company, St Eloi.* Charcoal drawing by David Bomberg. (Art 2708)

After Messines: a former German front-line trench, one mile north-west of Wytschaete, captured during the battle. The trench-board, centre, bears the name 'Oblige Trench', its new British name, but the words have been obliterated by the censor to prevent identification. Below the board a German notice indicates a telephone exchange, entry to which was permitted only to men on duty. (Q 3088)

exactly. Immediately all our guns and howitzers opened on carefully prepared lines on his front system, his support and reserve trenches, his communication trenches and his back areas. The row was terrific and the sight wonderful. It was not light enough to discern the advancing infantry from where I was, and, once started, there was nothing to do but to go below and wait for the first messages to come in.

Sergeant F. E. Collins, 1/22nd Battalion London Regiment (known as 'The Queens'), was one of the advancing infantry. The battle produced the following terse, almost routine, entry in his diary:

3.10 a.m. We go 'over the top'. Zero is marked by many mines going up. Our bombardment was terrible and the German front line was one line of flame and when the barrage lifted we went forward. We go across and take all our objectives without much opposition and dig ourselves in by joining up the shell holes. We hold the new position for two days; Fritz shells a great deal and we lose some men. I get a Military Medal.

Even this pre-eminently successful action, however, was not a complete walk-over. The blowing of the mines could be a two-edged weapon, destabilizing British attackers as well as German defenders. A machine-gun officer, Lieutenant A. G. May, who went over the top opposite Wytschaete and who would end the day with a wound sufficiently serious to lead ultimately to his discharge, has left a vivid account of what happened on his sector:

When I heard the first deep rumble I turned to the men and shouted 'Come on, let's go'. A fraction of a second later a terrific roar and the whole earth seemed to rock and sway. The concussion was terrible, several of the men and myself being blown down violently. It seemed to be several minutes before the earth stood still again though it may not really have been more than a few seconds. Flames rose to a great height – silhouetted against the flame I saw huge blocks of earth that seemed to be as big as houses falling back to the ground. Small chunks and dirt fell all around. I saw a man flung out from behind a huge block of debris silhouetted against the sheet of flame. Presumably some poor devil of a Boche. It was awful, a sort of inferno.

There was confusion on all sides, many men were lost to sight. While looking for my men to get them together again I came across Sgt Riddle and Private Davidson but where were the rest of them? Continuing to look around and futilely shouting I eventually found enough of my men to get together a gun team and sent them off. After waiting a few more minutes hoping some of the others would show up – none did – I decided that Riddle, Davidson and I would try to make up for a gun team. Riddle carried the gun and one box of ammo, Davidson a small chap carried three boxes of ammo and I carried five. We had no tripod but anyway ammo was more important.

At the same time the mines went off the artillery let loose, the heaviest group artillery firing ever known. The noise was impossible and it is impossible for anyone who was not there to imagine what it was like. Shells were bursting overhead and for no known reason I thought they were some of our shorts and then I realized the Boche was putting up a barrage on our front line and no man's land. I had forgotten it was not necessarily going to be all our own show. Not far in advance of our front parapet I saw a couple of our lads who had gone completely goofy, perhaps from the concussion. It was pitiful, one of them welcomed me like a long lost friend and asked me to give him his baby. I picked up a tin hat from the ground and gave it to him. He cradled the hat as if it were a child, smiling and laughing without a care in the world despite the fact that shells were exploding all around. I have no idea what happened to the poor chap but if he stayed there very long he must have been killed.

Crossing no man's land I had a narrow squeak. I was carrying two boxes of ammo in one hand and three in the other when a bit of shell went through one box and stopped in the next. Can't understand why the ammo did not go off but it did not. Would have lost my leg but for the boxes. Telling the others to wait I went back and got two more boxes and then rejoined the others. Surprisingly enough there in the middle of no man's land there was some green grass and I also saw one or two yellow iris though how these plants and grasses escaped destruction I cannot imagine.

From here on the ground was completely torn up, not a square inch left unturned by shells. The Boche wire was completely destroyed, only a few strands lying about. Their front line was utterly napoo, blown to bits and more or less filled with dirt from the mines. A bit further on and we had to rest for we were carrying heavy loads and dripping with sweat. It was just breaking dawn and the dust was still falling. Where we rested there were two dead Germans and believe it or not Davidson used one for a seat to rest on. They had been killed by m.g. fire, ours I hoped. All this time I realized that I had not been a bit windy though maybe I should have been. Probably too anxious to do a good job and too interested in all I saw.

Some gas shells had been coming over and both Riddle and I were feeling the effects of them badly. We tried a cigarette to see if it would help. It did not. Further on some more gas and we had to put on respirators but due to heavy sweating it was impossible to keep the nose clip on. Private Davidson for some reason hardly seemed to be affected by the gas, but Sgt Riddle and I were having a bad time now.

I was leaning over vomiting when an officer came up and asked 'Are you hit?' I straightened up and said, 'No, just gas'. Then I was bowled over like a rabbit. I felt as if a whole shell had hit me in the back. Maybe I was out for a few minutes but certainly not very long. It was painful to breathe and one of my legs was jerking and kicking and I had no control over it. I wondered if I could carry on but with the leg unmanageable and the trouble I had breathing decided I had done all I could. It was a terrible disappointment to realize I would never get to my objective but I thought Riddle would probably do so. Then I thought about how upset mother and father would be when they heard I was a casualty – nothing I could do about that at the moment. Stretcher-bearers came and dressed the wounds, actually very little blood and as far as I could see no apparent damage to the leg. The bearers rolled me on a stretcher, a painful process but my breathing was easier. I told Riddle and Davidson to carry on and said Goodbye to them. The bearers started off with me on the stretcher – an awful task on the chewed-up ground.

It was now getting lighter and as the stretcher party reached the British front line May observed the tanks coming up:

I had never seen these in action before, like some prehistoric monsters as they lurched and rolled over this chewed up terrain. We waited in a shell hole till the tanks had passed for the Boches were shelling them.

Second Lieutenant T. C. Eckenstein, an infantry officer with the 3rd Battalion South Lancashire Regiment, was another witness of their slow but purposeful progress. 'They looked very curious,' he wrote to his mother, 'coming along over the fields and ditches. They look rather like a tortoise. You know how a tortoise stops and has a look round with its head and then moves on a bit and stops again. Well that is what a tank does. When it comes to a big ditch it stops and pushes on over the obstacle.'

The tanks merely added the *coup de grâce*, as it happened, for the Germans had already virtually conceded. Eckenstein was delighted at the competence with which the whole complex operation had been executed:

The attack was very well carried out and the furthest objectives reached according to programme and there were very few casualties.

May's experience suggests that this was a relative statement, though overall losses were light on 7 June – indeed, in comparison with other notable 'first days' they were almost negligible. Private Johnson was also a casualty, though his wound was not serious. Recuperating at his Dressing Station he was able to tell his father, with much satisfaction at a battle which had been well planned and well executed at all levels:

After Messines: photograph taken on 11 June 1917 of soldiers of the 36th (Ulster) Division, out on rest near Dranoutre and displaying their victory souvenirs. (Q 5496)

Taking everything into consideration from my point of view we gained what we set out to get and one great point which was related to the success was the confidence which was placed in the NCOs and men. I do not think I should be giving you any restricted information if I tell you that we had the task thoroughly learned at heart so that each man went over the top knowing his objective and the various orders he had to perform in going and when he got there.

The explosions and the subsequent bombardment had caused exceptional devastation. 'We passed many terrible sights', wrote Corporal William Ebsworth, 1st Battalion Royal Fusiliers, whose unit advanced over the captured ground later the same day: 'huge craters caused by the mines that had been exploded in the morning, men paralysed by the shock, slabs of concrete from shell-proof shelters hurled fifty or sixty yards, and other evidence of the power of scientific warfare. The enemy trenches had been absolutely levelled by the shell fire of our artillery, and the few positions that were left intact were strewn with German dead.'

Despite the shattering impact of the opening attack, however, the enemy continued the fight, determined that the British would have to pay some reasonable price for their success. Nevertheless Messines was a notable plus for the Allies, and when the last counter-attacks ceased Ebsworth was able to write with considerable pride:

We had exactly five days in the greatest and most successful attack of the war.

The Treatment of Prisoners

During the advance at Messines, as Lieutenant A. G. May moved forward with his machine-gun team, the first German prisoners began to pass, being conducted under guard to the POW cages. They were, he noted 'green with fright, as well they might be'. Shortly afterwards he approached some German concrete strong points which had been blown up, either by mine explosion or artillery fire:

> From the remains of one of these I saw a miserable little Boche run out. Here was my chance to shoot a Boche personally but he raised his hands when he saw me so of course I could not. I judged him to be about fifteen years old, weak and about half my size. He looked at me like a dog that knows he has done something wrong and croaked 'Kamerad'.

May ordered the German to help with the carrying of ammunition boxes, which he did with astounding agility considering his physical condition.

Soon afterwards another batch of prisoners came by, with two Tommies in charge. If the reports which May subsequently heard were true, these men were to be treated with considerably less regard for the correct behaviour towards prisoners of war than was the case with his 'miserable little Boche'. His account continues:

> The Tommies reported back without any prisoners. After being much questioned it was learned that the two men had killed the prisoners. 'All right,' said the Staff Captain, 'you'll be court-martialled for this.' 'We don't care, we expected it.' 'Well why did you kill them?' 'They killed my mother in an air raid,' said one. 'When they bombarded Scarborough they killed my sweetheart,' said the other one. This of course was nothing but revenge, though it is possible though unlikely they thought they had justification for this. Anyway killing 30 men in cold blood is straight butchery.

May states that this version of events was 'later vouched for by Divisional Headquarters'.

Such a story, heard at second hand, should perhaps be viewed with a certain caution despite the alleged verification from above: the Tommies' reasons are arguably too neat, too tidy – a mother killed in an air raid, a girlfriend in a famous bombardment – to be entirely convincing.

If it did take place, such a killing would have been one carried out 'in cold blood'. More plausible perhaps are accounts of killings carried out under the influence of what might be termed 'battle-rage', following an action in which no quarter had been expected or given.

As already indicated, the Second Battle of Ypres in 1915 was to gain the reputation of being especially murderous, and later episodes in the Ypres Salient continued in the same brutal vein. On 16 June 1915, just after Second Ypres, the 1st Battalion Honourable Artillery Company took part in a 'charge' at Bellewaarde near Ypres, in the vicinity of the

German prisoners coming into Fricourt, Battle of the Somme, July 1916.
(Q 3970)

Hooge Château. Charles Tames, a private in the HAC, serving in the Transport Section of 2 Company, took advantage of a 'green envelope' (see p. 117) to write an account of subsequent events which almost certainly would have been vigorously deleted had the envelope been opened by the Base Censor – indeed, it is most unlikely that the letter would have got through at all.

> Now this is my private letter, I therefore intend to tell you everything concerning this Great War and myself. We have just been through a very rough fight at Ypres, we were in the charge with the Royal Scots, Irish Rifles, Worcesters and South Lancs. I am sorry to tell you that two officers have been killed (Hoare and Tatham), ten officers wounded, including the Colonel, the Doctor, Capt. Lancaster, Capt. Osmond, and Capt. Royle, 250 men killed, wounded and missing. Thanks to you for your good prayers, I am unhurt, the chap next to me had the back of his head blown off, and the fellow next but one on my left was shot through the right lung, seven of our transport horses were killed, three were blown to atoms.
>
> We were under shell fire for eight hours, it is more like a dream to me, we must have been absolutely mad at the time, some of the chaps looked quite insane after the charge was over, as we entered the German trenches hundreds of Germans were found cut up by our artillery fire, a great number came out and asked for mercy, needless to say they were shot right off which was the best mercy we could give to them. The Royal Scots took about 300 prisoners,

their officers told them to share their rations with the prisoners and to consider the officers were not with them [sic], the Scots immediately shot the whole lot, and shouted 'Death and Hell to everyone of ye s----' and in five minutes the ground was ankle deep with German blood, and this is the life we have had for two days, men and horses all mixed up in death.

Here again, however, caveats must be entered. As a member of the Transport Section Tames would not normally participate in a charge (though the death and wounding of men next to him might suggest that he might have done in this instance), so that it is unclear whether he witnessed or merely heard about the alleged killings. That some Germans emerging from their trenches were shot down while crying '*Kamerad*' is not improbable – it is not easy to switch instantly from bayoneting warrior to benign gaoler – but more solid evidence might be required before his claim that several hundreds were eliminated by the Royal Scots could be accepted as reliable evidence. Scottish regiments, like the Canadians and the Australians (though not the New Zealanders), won the reputation of being especially fierce fighters, but this is not to say that they were capable of massacre. There is also more than a hint of exaggeration in such phrases as 'ankle deep in blood'.

A more convincing story occurs in a letter of Lieutenant John Staniforth, written to his family after his battalion, the 7th Leinsters, had mounted their first major trench-raid near Vermelles in June 1916:

> They went straight for the throats of the Prussians. One little chap was found on the top of three dead Prussians, with his hand gripped round the throat of the tallest. Another wee drummer came back over no man's land under a torrent of shells and machine-gun fire with a hapless Sapper on his back. Oh they were great. Of course they were all quite mad. Three lads were sent back to our trench with six prisoners. On the way they stumbled across the body of one of our officers. Those prisoners will never reach any internment camp now, I'm afraid. As I said, we were all quite mad.

What is persuasive about this story is that it offers the more likely scenario of a small-scale affair with a handful of Germans shot on impulse and in anger.

In Tames's defence, it might be argued that, just as Staniforth claimed 'we were all quite mad', so he also used as key terms in his description the words 'mad' and 'insane'. The terror and elation of an attack, combined with an awareness of the horrific nature of what was happening to one's comrades and might so easily happen to oneself, could act as a powerful destabilizer, whether the situation were that of a major attack or a minor, but still very intense one, such as Staniforth's raid.

That stories of the killing of prisoners were accepted as true at higher level is clear from the diary of Captain A. M. McGrigor, staff officer to Lieutenant-General Sir William Birdwood, who though British served as the commander of I Anzac Corps at Arras and Third Ypres. On 6 October 1917, following a major action in the latter battle, McGrigor noted in his diary:

> The 2nd Anzac Corps got over 2000 prisoners in the battle and are very elated at getting over double the quantity that we did. It appears though that our

Bringing in Prisoners: **drawing by war artist Eric Kennington.** (Art 672)

fellows took a great number at the beginning and then suddenly got news that the Boche was massing to counter, so the unfortunate prisoners had to be disposed of.

What gave credibility to such stories, whether true or false, was a widespread belief – doubtless with some evidence behind it but also greatly fuelled by rumour and a xenophobic press back home – that the Germans were capable of every kind of evil, thus giving rise to the feeling that it was acceptable to disregard the rules of war in the matter of prisoners. The following is from a letter written by Lieutenant Gordon Bartlett in October 1915 towards the end of the Battle of Loos:

> The German Barbarities go from bad to worse. I have heard officially that having repulsed one of our attacks they piled the dead and dying in a trench and bombed them till all were dead; doesn't induce *us* to take too many prisoners, does it?

In similar mood Lieutenant Kenneth Mackenzie wrote this in June 1917, after hearing some tale of German wickedness in a letter from his family:

> Atkin's yarn makes me hate the Boche even more than I do, and the idea of giving them mercy is out of the question. They don't get much I can tell you unless you have no time to deal with them, and must press on to the next objective! Then they are made prisoners, otherwise ———.

Such attitudes could produce a climate in which it was possible for the killing of prisoners to become – no doubt unofficially and presumably on a strictly limited scale – a matter of stated policy. A conscript infantry-man who fought in the last hundred days of the war, T. G. Mohan, described in his diary a pre-battle briefing in September 1918:

> The whole thing was pointed out to us on a map, and detailed instructions were given; *one of which was that we were to take no prisoners* (Mohan's italics). I might add that this order was given by a man who was a coward himself, and certainly not an Englishman.

In the end, it must surely be acknowledged that so many instances cannot be dismissed entirely as smoke without fire. Either all the soldiers quoted were guilty of self-deception or gullibility, or there were situations here and there in which 'atrocities' against prisoners occurred.

Yet these were doubtless exceptional events. Moreover, it would be wrong to assume that animosity against Germans was universal. 'I did not hate the enemy,' wrote Second Lieutenant Cyril Rawlins in October 1915 after visiting a battlefield strewn with enemy corpses. 'I was as full of pity for those scattered bundles which had been men, in their grey-green uniform, as I was for our own dead; they were men, somewhere a home waited for them, a mother or sister prayed for their safety, to the same God!!' Normally, when taken prisoner, disarmed and no longer a threat, Germans mutated with impressive speed from dangerous enemies to vulnerable human beings. G. Macleod Ross, a junior officer in 227 Field Company Royal Engineers (39th Division), was present at the successful action against Beaumont-Hamel in November 1916 in the final phase of the Battle of the Somme, after which, he recorded in his diary, 'prisoners [were] coming in galore – on quite an unprecedented scale'. He noted particularly the way they were treated:

> One Boche comes down with a shattered arm – looks ashen grey or green. One of our chaps gives him a drink from a water bottle and the Signals who have billets there produce a cup of hot tea.
>
> I never saw the slightest hint of bad feeling against the Boche and there was quite a different atmosphere. Almost a sort of one-sided comradeship, i.e. on our side only, as the Boche were too done up to do much more than walk aimlessly along.

There were many, indeed, who did not subscribe to the vilification of the enemy and saw no evidence of a general hatred. One such was Private A. R. Williams, 17th Battalion Royal Fusiliers, in whose view the soldiers of *both* sides were victims – prisoners, as it were – of a grim situation not of their making. He wrote this thoughtful passage in a letter to his parents in October 1916:

So much is written about the war nowadays, and in proportion so little of it strikes a right and wholesome note – and yet it is so clear. It is nothing but an intimately personal tragedy to every British (and German) soldier concerned in the *fighting* part of it. Also it is quite the exception to note any ill feeling towards the individual German. I saw today a sentry pointing out our Lewis gun with animation to a prisoner working by the road side, expatiating on its qualities, to all appearance as to an interested listener. In many cases it is impossible not to feel pity. The belief at home that the individual enemy is an incurable barbarian is simply wrong, however black his record has been in the war organisation. I confess to some distrust (and here you may differ from me) of the attitude which consents to, and even demands, a permanent European estrangement. Germany has got to be beaten, and, in that way, since it is the only way, shown the error of her ways. *Then*, we must not only tolerate the return of the whipped child into the family circle again but, if we sincerely want peace, not only for our own advantage but for the sake of peace itself, we must even be prepared to lend a helping hand.

'Hot tea and biscuits being given to Boche prisoners.' A Canadian photograph dating from the Third Battle of Ypres (CO 2216)

The First Day of Third Ypres

In the category of 'first days of famous battles', 31 July 1917 has never been in the same league as 1 July 1916. This is in spite of the fact that the campaigns which followed those dates have become equal contenders for the palm of the most horrific or, alternatively, the most heroic battle involving British forces in the First World War. The results achieved on the later date, though modest, were greater, and the casualty lists, though considerable, were much smaller, so that its story does not carry the same sense of drama or raise the same sense of shock. Nevertheless it was a major landmark, and it was a portent of the struggle to come.

Knowing how the action was to develop over the following months gives a special resonance to accounts written at the time. The following letter was written to his sister by the Artillery officer Colonel Bill Murray on 1 August. It shows the mood of confidence in which the battle began; it also highlights, significantly, the untimely intervention of the rain. The time would come when the Germans, in the words of Crown Prince Rupprecht of Bavaria, would call the rain 'our most effective ally'. It was the rain, also, which would give this battle (generally known as 'Passchendaele' from its final phase) its controversial sub-title, coined by Lloyd George, of 'The Campaign in the Mud'.

My dear Claudine

Just before dawn yesterday we began our final attack. Never has there been such a barrage and bombardment. From the sea to Lens thousands of guns were firing as hard as they could for five hours. The barking of the field guns in front formed a sort of treble to the deep booming of the heavies behind us. And the air was one long screech of shells passing overhead. The sky was lit up like a continuous streak of lightning and the effect on the Huns on the other side must have been paralysing for when our men advanced they just ran away like rabbits and the waves of our infantry drove them in front like a flock of sheep. We went through about 3 miles and then stopped which was all we wanted to do today. So the Pilckem Ridge is in our hands and all the ground lost in those early days of May 1915 when we had to retire is again ours – our casualties are small and our morale splendid. As always happens the rain came down to save the Boche and it has poured ever since making it almost impossible to move. They tried to counter-attack us twice but are entirely broken up by our gunfire. They will try again today but they have got the Guards to reckon with and they are unbeatable.

Murray added an exuberant postscript:

My first battle as a Colonel was a success! Not like those when I was just a Major.

Sapper David Doe, Royal Engineers, also marvelled at the opening barrage. What he saw from a vantage point behind the lines inspired a vivid and, literally, colourful description in his pocket diary:

At 3.45 a.m. the great bombardment commenced in full power along the whole front from Warneton to Bixschoote. I went out at 3.55 a.m. to watch it from the hill near here and human eyes never saw a more terrible yet grand sight. The guns were flashing in thousands and one could see the big bursts of shrapnel. Flashes of every kind of explosive were seen and were of different colours. High in the air I could see the Germans' frantic signals – for artillery assistance – clusters of red rockets. They were going up in an absolutely frantic manner one after another. The noise was frightful. My word – *what* a bombardment. It was the very greatest massed artillery shoot in this war.

31 July 1917: scene at an Advanced Dressing Station near Boesinghe, on the left of the British Fifth Army. (Q 5730)

Lieutenant C. L. Overton went over the top on 31 July as a platoon commander in the 1/7th Battalion King's Own (Royal Lancaster) Regiment. He was to win an MC for his gallantry on that first day. His letter to the young woman whom he would eventually marry, written on 4 August and covering the whole of the first phase of the action (known as the Battle of Pilckem Ridge, 31 July–2 August), paints a somewhat less optimistic picture than Murray's – of a moderately successful advance at high cost:

I have been having quite an exciting time lately. We have been in this recent stunt, in about the same part of the line as we have been all along. We reached our objective all right, but the people on our right didn't which put our right flank in the air, the Boches got right round us, and then our lives became pretty cheap. We had three officers killed, two missing and several wounded. I was left in command of the three right companies, the Germans twice counter-attacked against us but we drove him off. The sniping was awful and the weather too, we were in two feet of water. However we hung on to our line for two days until we were relieved which was satisfactory. In my Company I had three sergeants killed and the other two wounded. I brought out 74 men out of 240. I had extraordinary luck myself, I had a bullet through my steel helmet and one through my water bottle but wasn't touched actually myself. We could hardly stand when we did come out, not having eaten since the attack began, or slept.

For Private Walter Hoskyn, 5th Battalion King's Liverpool Regiment, 31 July was his first experience of fighting, let alone of battle. The following account is from the diary he wrote up some short while after the event:

31 July 17 Tuesday: At 3.50 a.m. exactly we got over our front line and made our way towards the enemy. It became dark and a terrific din on all the time, I managed to get entangled in some barbed wire and on freeing myself I could not find the Lewis Gun team of which I was no. 2 and carried the spare parts bag. On two separate occasions I was blown off my feet by our own bursting shells but got up untouched, though I found I had lost all direction and was in the middle of the N. Lancs who were on our left so I took a half right turn and eventually stumbled on the team in a Communication Trench of the enemy.

Ralf Tyson had just been hit in the right hand. We did what we could for him and passed on, and established ourselves in what we thought was our correct position, but were informed later that we should be a little further forward. I accordingly left the gun and went scouting out in front for the party digging our strong point in front of Plum Farm. Finding the party I went back and brought up the gun and team. We got into a shell hole, cleaned the gun etc. and dug deeper and connected up with the strong point. It was about 6 a.m. now and the 9th Battalion had passed through us. We noticed Plum Farm (which was a strong point of the enemy and well concreted) shake. The enemy had it mined and had tried to blow it up, but this failed. He shelled it heavily during the day, but I think it was too strong for him.

The tanks were an absolute failure, the ground being too soft and their progress being exceedingly slow. Fritz put several out of action. We changed our position several times during the day, and one of the team (George) having gone down the line with sprained ankle we were only four strong. Towards the evening the enemy put heavy fire all over the captured ground and landed a shell on our trench killing two men next to me and wounding Pickering in the left arm, myself being stunned only. The next I remember was being told by Sergt Lewis to go for stretcher-bearers, so I got out and rushed back to our supports and gave the necessary message. I remember nothing further till early next morning when I woke up sitting next my pal Jack Sharp up to the knees in water and raining hard. I believe I fell exhausted and rather shaken after delivering the message. I was the only man left of the team. My rifle, ground sheet and valise were blown up with the Lewis Gun. So I consider I had a marvellous escape.

Lieutenant Harry Yoxall, normally of the 18th Battalion, King's Royal Rifle Corps, but now temporarily attached to the headquarters of the 123rd Infantry Brigade, saw this opening phase as a time of mixed fortunes. There was some ground gained, but because the first advance had fallen behind the creeping barrage owing to the condition of the ground, the enemy had been 'able to get his head up after it had passed and put up considerable resistance'. More, in the evening he 'started coming back'. This is from Yoxall's diary account written up on 2 August:

> At about 6 p.m. the Germans counter-attacked against our left. Our artillery and machine-gun barrages got on to them as they formed up and caused heavy losses, but they were two battalions strong and came on. Meanwhile it had begun to rain very hard. Soon the whole terrain was in a dreadful state and this combined with the pitchy darkness prevented the 2 battalions of 124 Bde (26th RF and 10th Queens) who were moved up in the night to re-attack the Green line at dawn from getting into position and the attack was never launched. The rain continued all day and the ground got worse and worse. It became impossible to use either rifles or machine-guns.
>
> Wednesday 1 August Fortunately these same conditions prevented the Germans from counter-attacking though they did once form up in the evening but were dispersed. During the day and night 124 Bde took over the whole front except the extreme right, where the reserve 2 companies of the 23rd Middlesex were. Owing to the ground in the centre having become an absolute bog of liquid mud the 11th Queens withdrew their line to the posts which had been consolidated in front of the Red Line which were in a fair condition still. South of the Canal 122 Bde had rather a tough journey too (especially my battalion – poor Gibb was killed, as also was Neil Shoobert with the 23rd Middlesex: all the best seem to go), but finally all got their objectives. Further up the Northern offensive went well, though both the 24th Division and 30th Division of the IInd Corps did not get to the furthest objective: but we hold Celen and St Julien, and the *Armée Française* have Bixschoote.

Captain Harry Yoxall, MC and Bar, 18th King's Royal Rifle Corps; present on 31 July 1917 as a Staff Officer with 123rd Infantry Brigade with the rank of Lieutenant. (HU 63266)

Yoxall's diary also records an early example of what would become all too commonplace in this battle, instances of men dying in the mud – on this occasion with a tank rolling over them and delivering the *coup de grâce*:

> Two poor devils of 123 Bde have been found drowned, or rather suffocated: they must have been stuck in the mud, become exhausted, and fallen face forward.

It was clear that the new offensive was going to be a hard-fought fight, with the same mixture of heroism and horror as before. Murray's 'final battle' was still to come.

'Only Murder': A Stretcher-Bearer during Third Ypres

'It is only murder attempting to advance against these pill-boxes over such ground.' Thus Sergeant Robert McKay, 109th Field Ambulance, 36th (Ulster) Division, writing in his diary on 16 August 1917 – a typically forthright comment by a thoughtful, well-educated soldier who would become a university professor in later life, and who did not mince his words when it came to describing conditions of life and death on the Western Front. The account of his experiences at this time, though it covers only a three-week period in the first month of a four-month campaign, focuses sharply on some of the distinctive characteristics which would give Third Ypres so grim a reputation.

McKay had been with the 36th Ulsters on the Somme, where the division had fought with great bravery and distinction (notably on 1 July at Thiepval) and had suffered very heavy losses. The Somme was much on the minds of the Ulstermen as they prepared for what they hoped would not be a repetition of the hard pounding of the previous year.

Two days before the battle opened, on 29 July McKay with a small party of officers and men went up the line from the ambulance's billets east of Poperinghe to see the advanced aid post which they expected to occupy when the division went into action. Their journey took them through Ypres itself, the sight of which filled him with a sense of foreboding and unease:

> There is something curious about Ypres. Right well has this been called 'The City of Fear'. As soon as one approaches the town, a strange feeling comes over everybody, and indeed all those who have once been in the place hate the thought of going there again. The whole place seems to be cursed with a malevolent curse. After visiting the post we returned as quickly as possible to the unit. Here I was asked what it was like up the line. I told them, but some of them laughed and said it could not be worse than the Somme. I said if the infantry get away as they did at Messines it will be all right; if they are held up, God help us.

Unfortunately, the infantry did not 'get away' as at Messines, and Third Ypres would, by general reputation, prove to be worse than the Somme.

The 36th Division was not involved in the first phase, the Battle of Pilckem Ridge. They moved into the line three days later and went into action during the second phase, which began in mid-August and would bear the name of the Battle of Langemarck. The 109th Field Ambulance set up its advanced aid post in a mine shaft near the village of Wieltje, which lay in the Salient virtually midway between Langemarck and Ypres. (This was not a place of pleasant memory; it was near here that poison gas had first appeared two years before in 1915.) Despite a stream of water four to six inches deep, requiring the constant use of pumps to prevent the mine from flooding, the post was considered safe from shell fire. However, McKay was not happy with the medical situation overall:

> Arrangements for the wounded are bad. Battalion Aid Posts are all in pill-boxes which have been taken from the enemy during the past few days. The stretcher-bearers have got to bring the wounded from the First Aid Posts to the Mine Shaft where they are redressed and then carried down to St Jean Corner, a distance of about a mile. At St Jean the wounded are placed in motor ambulances and conveyed down to Red Farm from which they are finally shifted to the Casualty Clearing Station.

McKay was ordered to St Jean to take charge of the party loading the wounded; he would later comment that it was the worst job he ever had. Things were not helped by the presence of a heavy gun only 200 yards away, which virtually guaranteed regular reprisals from the German artillery. Even the graves behind the house which he and his men occupied were blown open in all directions, with bits of bodies lying everywhere. Walking wounded leaving St Jean Corner had to make their way on as best they could, trusting to be picked up by motor lorries further down the road.

The prospects, in fact, were not good, and given the iron determination of both sides, it was clear there would be difficult times ahead:

6 August Today awful: was obliged to carry some of the wounded into the graveyard and look on helpless till they died. Sometimes we could not even obtain a drink of water for them. Working parties are repairing the road so that the ambulances will be able to go right up to the Mine Shaft. Yesterday and today have been the most fearful couple of days I ever put in. We are waiting every minute until a shell lights amongst us. We would not mind so much if there were no wounded. Went up to Wiltje at night: ambulances now going right up, one at a time. As a rule, I am not very nervous, but I don't wish to spend another night at St Jean Corner.

7 August Bringing the wounded down from the front line today. Conditions terrible. The ground between Wieltje and where the infantry are is simply a quagmire, and shell holes filled with water.

A German concrete pill-box near Honnebeke captured during the Third Battle of Ypres; an Australian photograph dated 20 September 1917 and captioned 'A Boche residence that is practically shellproof'. The photograph shows the fatal flaw of such structures when converted by the British into Aid Posts: a substantial entrance on the German side wide open to enemy guns. (E(AUS)760)

Every place is in full view of the enemy who are on the ridge. There is neither the appearance of a road or path and it requires six men to every stretcher, two of these being constantly employed helping the others out of the holes; the mud in some cases is up to our waists. A couple of journeys to and from the Mine Shaft to the line and the strongest men are ready to collapse. All the Regimental Aid Posts are in pill-boxes which have been wrested from the enemy and they are of great strength. Some of them have had as many as five direct hits from 5.9s and are nothing the worse. Unfortunately, all of them have a serious fault, their door being towards the German line. It is a job getting into them as they are all under enemy observation, and once in it is worse getting out as he puts a barrage round them when he sees anyone about.

14 August Bombardment by British heavy, enemy retaliating; many casualties. We can only get up to the First Aid Posts early in the morning (3–4 o'clock a.m.) and at twilight (8–10 p.m.). One party of stretcher-bearers was bringing down a wounded man when an airman swooped down and dropped a bomb deliberately on them. The enemy shells the stretcher-bearers all the time.

16 August The 36th (Ulster) Division attacked this morning at 5 o'clock a.m. Owing to the state of the ground tanks were unable to move. The 108th and 109th Brigades only took part in the attack, as the 107th had held the forward positions on up to the morning of this attack and it was too weak to take any part in it. The casualties the 107th suffered holding the line has been something terrible. The infantry took a few pill-boxes and a line or two of trenches from the enemy in this attack but at a fearful cost. It is only murder attempting to advance against these pill-boxes over such ground. Any number of men fall down wounded and are either smothered in the mud or drowned in the holes of water before succour can reach them. We have been working continuously now since the 13th inst. and resulting from the renewal of the attack today, more wounded are coming down than any day since I came up. Wounds are nearly all bad. The stretcher-bearers are done up completely.

The 109th Field Ambulance has suffered many casualties here. Today the enemy put a shell in through the door of a pill-box called Bank Farm,

killing practically all inside. Cpl Greenwood, Private Barrett and Private McCormick were all killed. The enemy have nothing but pill-boxes on this front; as soon as the infantry capture one, they find themselves faced by another.

17 August Smell of the Mine Shaft worse than ever. There is a heap of dead lying up at the entrance where they have been thrown out. I was told by Captain Johnston that the Division was being relieved tonight and to warn men of the 109th Field Ambulance that they could make their way down to headquarters. One man, B. Edgar, asked me when I was going down, and I said in the morning between two and three o'clock. Edgar then said he was going to have a sleep and not to go down without calling him. I looked at him and said, 'Where in Heaven's name are you going to sleep here?' and for answer was told that there were two dead men at the entrance with a blanket thrown over them, and I would find him in under the blanket, and here he would not be disturbed, as all three were lying in the open above ground.

19 August Came down from Mine Shaft at 3 o'clock a.m. I have had no sleep since I went up on the 13th, and when I took my boots off my feet looked as if they were par-boiled. Never do I want to be in such a place again. The enemy still keeps throwing shells into Ypres day and night and the thoughts of going through this town of desolation is a continual nightmare to nearly everyone. The oftener one passes to and from the battle line through the town the worse the dread becomes. Why it is so, I cannot say. All the 36th Division have been relieved now. The 109th Field Ambulance alone had over thirty casualties, killed, wounded and gassed – and this out of one hundred men who were doing the line.

The War in the Air

The air war provided the most public fighting of all on the Western Front. It could offer gripping entertainment for the men in the trenches, who if they could not look out could at least look up.

Private Raymond Grimshaw and his comrades of the 1/7th Battalion West Yorkshire Regiment watched a duel between a British and German pilot from front-line trenches in the Ypres Salient on a summer Sunday in 1915:

> 25 July: Today we have been treated to one of the most thrilling yet awful sights imaginable – a fight in mid-air. Shortly after noon one of our airmen was scouting over our trenches when a 'Taube' put in an appearance and flew straight towards him. The British aviator immediately turned tail and was apparently making off – much to the disappointment of the German in hot pursuit. Ascending to about 3,000 ft, the Briton became hid by a cloud. Here he outwitted the German by remaining almost stationary until the 'Taube' passed along underneath him. He then flew down as though he would crash on top of his opponent, but when quite close above him, he dropped a bomb. The effect was awful. The 'Taube' burst into flames, and dived downwards. We expected to see it crash to the ground but with wonderful skill the German got control of his machine – although it was blazing furiously – and tried to volplane back to his own lines. He got to within 1,000 ft of the ground, when he was suddenly seen to fall or jump out of the machine. He dropped like a stone, and the aeroplane – now out of control – dived straight down – turning over and over in a mass of flames. Though he was German we admired the gallant attempt he made to get back.

BSM Douglas Pegler saw a dogfight in August 1916 in which the German was also the loser:

> A thrilling air fight took place over Maricourt today. A 'Boche' was up and our Anti's fired at it for about twenty minutes without success, and Fritz eventually escaped into a cloud. Presently one of our planes entered the same cloud and we heard machine-gun fire. Suddenly a flaming mass hurtled through the air to the ground. Fritz had made his last flight. He fell from 3000 feet.

In May 1917 Major Harry Dillon watched a British aeroplane being shot down:

> The Hun must have got him through the petrol tank as he burst into flame. The pilot by nose-diving and not planing seemed for a moment to have put the fire out but the machine suddenly broke up when still about 5,000 ft. and one could see the pilot and observer falling side by side which was rather sickening as it must have taken minutes before they reached the ground. They were of course both killed outright.

Parachutes were supplied to the crews of observation balloons in the First World War but they were not supplied to crews of aeroplanes. There were few possibilities for the flyer whose aircraft came off worse in a dogfight; either he burned, or he fell. Doubtless it was the sheer starkness of these options that helped to produce the spirit of bravado, even bluster, with which the airman has come to be associated. Indeed, the tradition of the brave, devil-may-care knight-errant of the sky eager for his next brush with the 'brother Boche' is not only strong, but justified, in that undoubtedly there were many who fitted that image perfectly.* Others, however, did not, and being only too aware of the risks they ran and the odds against their survival they lived lives of great tension and strain. One such was an officer of 66 Squadron, Royal Flying Corps (first name Oliver, surname unknown), who, after his first two months at the front, wrote frankly about his work as a pilot in a letter to a friend dated 9 August 1917:

> I haven't the slightest hesitation in deciding that this war isn't nice to know. Even at the end of these two months, I'm sick to death of France, and machines and above all the lines, and the look of

*See for example the section 'Sportsman of the Air' in the present writer's *Imperial War Museum Book of the First World War*.

The officers and aeroplanes – SE5A Scouts – of Mannock's 85 Squadron RAF, at St Omer Aerodrome, 21 June 1918, with Major Mannock himself pictured in the photograph alongside. The officer in the extreme right of the photograph, in which the CO is not present, is Lieutenant Donald Inglis, a New Zealander, who flew with Mannock on his last patrol. (Q 12050, Q 60800)

the area we work over. This flying job is rotten for one's nerve, and although one is supposed to last 6 months with a fortnight's leave half way, quite a lot of people's nerve completely conks out after 4 or 4½. I don't know whether you know what it's like to feel your nerve going. I've felt it several times but one gets it back by pulling oneself together or a stretch of dull weather like we are having now. No one can imagine the strain of 2½ hours over the line. Firstly one has to keep one's place in the formation – this necessitates wangling the throttle and petrol supply continuously, then one has to watch the leader, who does all the scientific dodging of Archie [i.e. anti-aircraft fire], there's nothing more nerve-racking than getting really badly archied for a long time. Then there's every single machine in the sky to be suspicious about, until you've proved it isn't a Hun. As a matter of fact with all this wretched aerial activity we get a dogfight nearly every time we go out now, too often for my liking. The evening dogfight is the only one which is at all amusing when we send out a 'circus'

of our machines, 30 perhaps, as a counter-strafe to old Baron Richthofen's circus of red brutes. It's always a terrific dog fight, and everyone seems to be going down in spins all round one, but somehow it's more cheerful with a lot of our machines out. You see hardly anyone realises what the RFC scout squadrons do out here except themselves and the staff. It's all so high up that it's clean out of sight of the ground. 15,000 ft is the minimum we ever go over the line. No, this flying job out here is by no means a soft one, but it's certainly a gentleman's job, as there is no dirty work, absolutely none.

We've just had a very cushy show, never saw a

Hun until we went down on some 2-seaters just before going home. Extraordinary how warlike one feels before you get to the line, and how suddenly it comes out when you want it. As a matter of fact I and most people live in a perpetual state of wind up during a patrol – a most unhealthy frame of mind.

For the British the greatest air ace of the war was Major Edward (Mick) Mannock, VC, DSO and two Bars, MC and Bar, who died in action in 1918 after being credited with a record number of enemy 'kills' – seventy-three. Yet his brilliance and commitment did not exclude him from an acute awareness of the dangers facing men of his unique profession. So much is clear from the following letter (believed to be hitherto unpublished) which has been preserved with other letters written to a Miss Mary Lewis, who was the correspondent of several officers in the latter half of the war. The main purpose of the letter, however, was to state its writer's belief in the high virtue of war and its value to humanity, with the conquest of fear as part of the equation. The letter was written from France, where Mannock was commanding 85 Squadron, and dated 7 June 1918:

> Dear Mary
>
> Greetings!
>
> Your cryptic note of the 1st inst is still puzzling me very much. I cannot for the life of me understand how or guess where I have 'putten' my 'foot in it' during the course of my last unfortunate (alleged) letter to you. If possible, please send it back so that I may analyse it thoroughly and prepare my defence.
>
> On one or two of your points (letter enclosed) I do not agree. I do not believe that *War* or the '*Great Push*' are things 'rowdy and superficial'. Don't you see that strife and bloodshed and physical 'exertion' and mental anguish are all good, glorious, wonderfully beneficial things for the human race, just exactly the same as you and I experience when we are called upon by our sense of righteousness to resist some animal temptation. These boys out here fighting are tempted every moment of their day to *run away* from the ghastly (externally) Hell created by their maker, but they resist that temptation (Heaven only knows how strong it is) and die for it, or become fitter and better for it, or because of it.
>
> I love music. None better. Therefore it is not difficult for me to listen to it. In other words, I am pandering to my sensuousness when I listen to good music. And I question whether listening to good music – that is, music which pleases the senses (soul, if you like) – I question whether it improves the soul, character, outlook, sense of justice, or in blunt language, I doubt if it makes a man a better man – as man should be – or woman a better woman.
>
> Here endeth the first and last letter dealing with this impossible subject.
>
> Yours E. Mannock

Mannock was reputedly greatly afraid of being burnt to death in an air fight, and carried a revolver to despatch himself if he found himself in such a situation. It is not known whether he used it when he was finally shot down in flames by ground fire some six weeks after this letter was written, on 26 July 1918.

The Battle of the Menin Road

The Battle of Third Ypres has acquired so negative an image that it is important to emphasize that not all its actions were desperate assaults in impossible conditions or were fought knee-deep in mud.

Harry Yoxall, who had been with 123rd Brigade at the start of Third Ypres (see p. 185), was back with his battalion, the 18th King's Royal Rifle Corps, with the rank of Temporary Captain and serving as Adjutant, when it was involved in an attack on a German strong point known as Tower Hamlets on 20 September 1917. This was part of a major offensive by the Second and Fifth Armies which would become known officially as The Battle of the Menin Road Ridge, though the troops called it by the simpler, but more resonant, title of the Battle of the Menin Road. Devised with great care and ingenuity by the victor of Messines, General Sir Herbert Plumer, this was a largely successful operation. One particularly notable innovation was that the practice of sending long lines of men over the top was abandoned in favour of an advance based on small fighting groups, with 'mopping up' groups following on. The attack was also favoured by reasonable weather; indeed, far from taking place in pouring rain, this battle, like Plumer's later action at Polygon Wood in early October, has been described as having been 'won in dust clouds'.*

For his role in the attack Yoxall was awarded a bar to his MC. As soon as he was out of the line, he wrote the following graphic account of his experiences to his mother:

Fate or chance or whatever Gods there be have again shown me great kindness in bringing me safely through this latest offensive. From the 18th to the 23rd of September I spent the six most intense days of my life. It was a time of grandeur and terror, very awful in the experience and very inspiring in retrospect. Now, in its happy event, not to be regretted, rather a time to be thankful for. At least I know that I have never been more useful in my life and that I was doing something to help all the while: so what would it have mattered if death, ever near all the time, had come. But – it didn't.

The Battalion went into the line on the night of 17th/18th. It attacked at dawn on the 20th, advanced a thousand yards with its right flank exposed all the way, captured and consolidated both its objectives, beat off three counter-attacks on the 21st, and was fully relieved in the early morning of the 23rd. Now as I write it is back under canvas 12 miles behind the line, conscious of duty done, and basking in the sunshine of this late September afternoon. And it is good – now.

We fought over ground made sacred to the Rifles by the exploits of the 2nd battalion there in the early days of the war. And we were worthy of them: never have men or officers fought more magnificently against a definite

---

*Cyril Falls, *The First World War*, Longmans 1960, p. 284.

resistance. We lost very heavily but the cost was paid for by the splendour of its manner and the magnitude of its result.

Now it is all mostly a mass of confused memories. There were two nights before the show, on the first of which I pegged out the tapes for our forming up and on the second of which the assembly took place. We had to form up in pitchy darkness, during a fall of rain, across a marsh. After seeing the ground by daylight I wonder how we ever did it. Twice I went into the water over my waist. But somehow the battalion got there into its correct formation without being heard or seen: just with an hour to spare I was able to return to my colonel and report the assembly finished. In my mind that formation was perhaps the most difficult part of the whole operation: certainly it was the most anxious period of all those days. If we had been detected or if we had not been ready at dawn . . . but we were not and we were.

Next was the awful moment after the attack started when the troops on our right were held up and wavered. But our own men went on with their flank in the air: were held by strong points to their front, took these and went on, only to be checked again by enfilade machine-gun fire from the right; then rallied and went on again to capture their first objective. After a pause our supporting companies advanced again, with enemy all round their right flank, pushed across the stream and the morass on its eastern bank, fought their way up on to the plateau which was their objective, and there dug themselves in.

Waiting to go into action: Men of the 13th Durham Light Infantry before their attack on 20 September 1917, the first day of the Battle of the Menin Road, 1917.
(Q 5969)

Then about noon I remember lying in a shallow and wrecked German communication trench, with my colonel, the colonel of another battalion, his adjutant and signalling officer, and a few runners of all regiments, engaged in a sniping duel with a German machine-gun some six hundred yards away, firing till our borrowed rifles were hot and clogged. The East Surrey colonel and the officer on my left were hit. Then a German plane came over flying low and spotted us. Half an hour later they began on us with 5.9s and shrapnel, and we were shelled out and had to go: so we went forward.

Then I remember the three counter-attacks of the next afternoon and evening. They were preceded by the most intense bombardment I have ever experienced from the Hun in my now fairly long knowledge of this war. First they came on down the Menin road crowded in close mass, and we scattered them by machine-gun fire. Then they tried again in more open order, supported by *flammenwerfer*, which fortunately never came into action. Finally in the twilight they made the most determined effort of all, after a terrific bombardment: this time in the outpost line which another regiment, passing through us, had formed in front of us, but our men held fast, used their rifles, and the attack collapsed.

Yoxall also wrote a diary account of the episode and the two put together make interesting reading. He would himself concede later that his diaries rather than his letters were a more faithful record of his thoughts and activities during his time at the front, since he was constantly at pains to reassure his family that he was not taking unnecessary risks. In the present case the diary gives a greater sense of the difficulties and confusions of the battle, while in no way reversing his reaction to it overall and his pride in having performed well. A notable absentee from the letter, however, is the following event, which took place shortly after zero hour, and after the first of the walking wounded had started coming in 'bringing contradictory stories [from which] it soon became obvious that we were not having it all our own way':

Then a terrible thing happened. An enormous crowd of 124th Bde suddenly appeared, retiring in disorder. We formed a battle stop with headquarters officers and men, and assisted by the gunner liaison officer and a stout MGC captain, and drove lots of them back. What things we did and what language we used during that awful half hour I do not remember. We stopped as many as we could, but many got around us. It subsequently appeared that 124th Bde had come right up against it badly at the beginning, had wavered, and that then some 500 had retired in disorder. The results were nearly disastrous.

'The six most intense days of my life' was Yoxall's verdict on this episode; 'the greatest day of my life' was the description of 20 September by Major J. R. Webster DSO MC, Acting Commanding Officer of another battalion involved, the 16th Sherwood Foresters. He stated this in a postscript to the copy of his report on the operation sent to Brigade which he wrote out in his own hand in his personal diary. His account makes no reference to any loss of morale on the part of the troops in his sector; on the contrary. His postscript continues:

The dash of the men was simply amazing, and nothing could stop them. They came out with their 'tails right up' and every man had stories to tell of the Boche they had killed.

On one soldier's performance he commented:

> Corporal Egerton's attack on the dugout known as Wellbeck Grange was the most reckless piece of gallantry I ever saw and I have recommended him for the VC.

His recommendation would be accepted and Egerton's 'gallantry and initiative' is recorded in the Official History. 'Owing to the mist, some German dugouts were not cleared by the leading groups, and fire from them was causing heavy losses. When volunteers were called for, Corporal Egerton at once dashed to the dugouts under heavy fire at short range, and shot 3 of the Germans, after which 29 surrendered. His bravery relieved in less than thirty seconds an extremely difficult situation.'[*]

In his 'Observations on the Battle' with which his official report concludes, Webster noted that there had been much success in dealing with the concrete strong points which had been the cause of so much havoc at the Battle of Langemarck. Thanks to their 'keenness to get on', his troops were usually within a few yards of the creeping barrage, and though this led to some casualties, he considered these were worth the cost as the men 'were on most of the concrete dugouts before the Enemy had a chance to get out of them. In one instance,' he added, 'an officer's servant advanced in our barrage and entered a dugout at Chatsworth Castle, where there was a German officer and 8 men. The German officer congratulated the man on his bravery.'

A third perspective on this action survives in a letter written to his sister on 23 September by the battalion's chaplain, Reverend J. F. (Jack) Bloxham. During the advance to the start line Bloxham was in company with Major Webster, who had been newly appointed as CO from a fellow battalion, the 17th Sherwood Foresters. 'So far I like him greatly', wrote Bloxham in his letter. 'He is very tall, far taller than I am and quite a gentleman.' Sadly Webster was to lose his life some months later during the German offensive of March 1918.

Bloxham was more concerned with the sights and sounds of the battle rather than its military aspects. Of the ridge, already taken during previous fighting, where they were to spend the day before the attack, he wrote:

> I think I have never seen (or imagined there could be) such appalling desolation as this great ridge where so much fighting has taken place. Not a single sign of vegetation, not a blade of grass. Nothing but shell holes and dry clay and pools of water and broken wreckage of all kinds, and wire and everything hideous that can be imagined.

As the battle began, he was immensely impressed by the power and precision of the British barrage:

---

[*] *Military Operations France and Belgium, 1917*, Vol II, p. 262.

It was of course simply tremendous falling just in front of us. As it went forward, we all crept forward too, through the fog amongst the trees, which were quite bare by the time we reached them. The light was perfect, just light enough to see our way (of course by compass) and to recognise one another, while the thick mist hid us from view. I cannot tell you much by way of an account of the attack; I simply followed the CO and the adjutant, sitting down in a shell hole when told to do so and pressing on when they went. It was all weird and exciting in a way. Suddenly we met the first 3 of the German prisoners coming back, sent down by our companies just in front.

A chaplain's place of duty in such circumstances was with the battalion's medical staff:

The CO selected an excellent little dugout for the advanced first aid post and there the doctor and I established ourselves. It was a good dugout very nearly high enough for me to stand up in, with a table right across one end about 5ft wide, and a lower shelf of the same size beneath it about 10 inches from the ground, really beds for German soldiers, but we used the top for a table on which to lay out dressings etc. and kept the lower half for a bed for three. There were benches, very narrow, round the rest of it against the concrete walls, leaving an open floor space of 4ft by 5ft or less. So there was not much space for the doctor and his orderlies, numerous patients and various visitors! Most of the stretcher cases had to be treated outside. Of course it was only a case of first aid, and then send them back by stretcher-bearer as quickly as possible. As the Germans were on the side of the ridge opposite and the dugouts were in full view they gave us a fairly lively time for the next 40 hours or so that we remained there, and shells came bumping round us all the time. During the next day I had a fine view of the Germans massing in their trenches and running up the hill bent double just on the side of the opposite ridge, through a big telescope. You could see them as clearly as if they were only a hundred yards away and see them chatting to one another and pointing out things and creeping out of their trenches and running up the hill bent double to avoid danger. Very few people, even those who have been out for years, have had such a view, so I was extraordinarily lucky.

Despite the relatively dry conditions, however, mud was so much part of the Salient that it was inevitable that it should have its victims – although in the case described the outcome was benign:

While up there we had many adventures, some tragic, some humorous, though there was an element of tragedy in all that was humorous. The really funny thing was when I slipped into a shell hole and got stuck in the mud. It was only up to my knees but it took 3 men to pull me out, partly because we were laughing so much, even a poor boy with a broken thigh beside us could not help laughing and I really think it cheered him up for a bit.

Above: The Ypres Road, September 1917: 'Limbers going up' — loaded with ammunition for the front. (E(AUS) 829)

Left: 'Coming out on Blighty Leave' — Australian soldiers leaving the battlefield. (E(AUS) 846)

'Great Days These':
The View from Passchendaele

Major C. E. L. ('John') Lyne, RFA, was a cheerful, up-beat and forthright soldier. When a letter he wrote describing conditions during the Arras battle in May 1917 prompted a sympathetic reaction from home, he replied:

> Don't dare to think that I'm having a dreadful time. It's not, it's grand and splendid, but there are times when one feels that the war is a bit oppressive, intrudes itself too much, as one might say. One such occasion to me was when they took away the remains of our Sgt-Major, one of the best. Another was when they carried off H——— all smothered in blood.

Yet Third Ypres crushed even his remarkable optimism. He wrote four letters during its final 'Passchendaele' stage which suggest that, whatever the military-cum-political arguments for the continuation of that battle to the top of the ridge and into November, the morale of those who had the task of continuing it was never so low. It is also clear from them that Passchendaele's reputation as the worst place on the whole Western Front was not a hindsight invention by post-war critics but was the view of the fighting men at the time: Lyne calls it 'absolutely *the* most unholy spot from the North Sea to the Mediterranean'. The extracts, from two of the letters are printed verbatim as typed after the war; they were not datelined at the time but a later hand, presumably the writer's, has added 'Passchendaele' to the first two, plus the information that he was then in '119 Army Field Brigade' (i.e. 119th Brigade Royal Field Artillery).

> 2 November 1917 The events of the last week have succeeded each other with such rapidity that I am absolutely dazed. I can't remember how long it is since I wrote you on what I was doing at that time. I think I did tell you we had been sent hurriedly upwards, and how we battered mightily with mud and other discomforts and various treks to and fro. Well anyway, here we are, in absolutely *the* most unholy spot from the North Sea to the Mediter-

ranean, when I say it's about the most lively spot on the map, you'll know where to look for me.

> I'll forgo description till I'm feeling a bit more optimistic, they say first thoughts are best, but I know darn well they couldn't be worse, anyway I'm dead tired, so—

> 4 November 1917 I'm feeling a bit tired and muzzy in the nut, so not much in the way of a letter. Shall be glad of that new shirt, have lived in the present one for the last three weeks, have had *one* hot bath since last leave and at present moment am saturated in mud and dirt. Had your letter containing budget on psychical research today, a subject which cuts no ice with us at the present moment as materialistic matters count just nineteen to the dozen. We are properly up against it here, we've struck the liveliest spot on the Front. I've never yet struck a proposition which filled me with less enthusiasm than the present stunt. The conditions are awful, beyond description, nothing we've had yet has come up to it, the whole trouble is the weather which daily gets worse. One's admiration goes out to the infantry who attack and gain ground under these conditions. Had I a descriptive pen I could picture to you the squalor and wretchedness of it all and through it the wonder of the men who carry on. Figure to yourself a desolate wilderness of water filled with shell craters, and crater after crater whose lips form narrow peninsulas along which one can at best pick but a slow and precarious way. Here a shattered tree trunk, there a wrecked 'pill-box', sole remaining evidence that this was once a human and inhabited land. Dante would never have condemned lost souls to wander in so terrible a purgatory. Here a shattered wagon, there a gun mired to the muzzle in mud which grips like glue, even the birds and rats have forsaken so unnatural a spot. Mile after mile of the same unending dreariness, landmarks are gone, of whole villages hardly a pile of bricks amongst the mud marks the site. You see it at its best under a leaden sky with a chill drizzle falling, each hour an eternity, each dragging step a nightmare. How weirdly it recalls some half formed

Passchendaele after the battle; a photograph from the album of Captain E.G.F. Boon MC, Royal Garrison Artillery, who captioned it: 'Passchendaele ridge general View – in foreground our trenches and Infantry – everything smashed to bits.' (HU 63277E)

horror of childish nightmare, one would flee, but whither? – one would cry aloud but there comes no blessed awakening. Surely the God of Battles has deserted a spot where only devils can reign. Think what it means, weeks of it, weeks which are eternities, when the days are terrible but the nights beyond belief. Through it all the horror of continual shell fire, rain and mud. Gas is one of the most potent components of this particular inferno. Nights are absolutely without rest, and gas at night is the crowning limit of horrors. The Battery that occupied the position before we came was practically wiped out by it, and had to be relieved at short notice, and the battery that relieved them lost 37 men on the way in. You can imagine how bucked I was when they handed me out these spicy bits of gossip on the way up. I daren't risk more than three men per gun up here at the same time and only 2 officers besides myself, at the moment they are rather sorry for themselves after last night's gas stunt, and doing unhelpful things to their eyes with various drops and washes. I've got a throat like raw beef and a voice like a crow.

They shot us up in style last night, hardly got 30 minutes sleep and I was dead tired. We've got a dugout for our mess with 4 inches of concrete on top, last night there were our 3 selves, our servants, a stray officer and his servant and one of my wounded men. I kept on telling them the roof would not stop a splinter, but no one seemed inclined to go elsewhere.

6 November 1917 Very troublous days, particular hell all day, shells of many calibres have descended upon us, aussi rain. I lost a corporal, killed, also a bombardier and best gunner wounded. I thought the war was over when a shell burst 5 yards away and projected a 12 feet beam on to me. Two guns out of action. Altogether what you'd call a rosy-hued outlook. We're up against it here, more than any place I've struck yet. Up firing most of last night, a very disjointed and hand to mouth existence on the whole. What price Xmas dinner in peace! Had to send C off down to wagon line, he was quite bad from the gas, and would have gone to pieces with another night like the last few, and he's a real tough nut as a rule. Great days these.

Cambrai: Hopes Raised, Hopes Deferred

On 20 November 1917 Captain George Samuel, an officer in the Royal Field Artillery, wrote in buoyant mood to his future wife:

> Now you will know why I was so much in a difficulty as to how I could write to you! The results of the push that we started about 6 hours ago I cannot say (you will know before me), but I do know that it *has* been an absolute triumph for SECRECY. No one has dared say a word (in fact very few have known a word) about it. Since the 8th when we left our last home I have been on the move every day and have not had my boots off for several nights at a time. We have done all our marching by night and hidden ourselves by day. No fires have been allowed – in fact it has almost been a crime to show an *electric torch* at night! *But* – it's been worth it. The six hours pure joy we have had today have repaid every bit – and I am confident that we shall get further when we want to!

At 6.20 that morning the artillery had opened fire along a sector of the front many miles south of Ypres in the vicinity of the German-held Picardy town of Cambrai. Nineteen divisions of the Third Army under General Hon. Sir Julian Byng were poised to advance, and they did so almost immediately, without the extended artillery bombardment which had taken place before most previous battles and which had both signalled an impending attack to the enemy and broken up the terrain over which the attack was to be made. There was a special need for this change of plan: good dry ground was as vital to the concept of the offensive about to be launched as was the secrecy with which it had been prepared, for it was to be spearheaded by a massive force of tanks. Fighting under the personal command of the GOC of the Tank Corps, Brigadier-General Hugh Elles (he himself went into battle in one of his own machines), some 300 tanks crushed down the barbed wire of the Hindenburg Line and by the end of the short winter's day an advance of three to four miles had been achieved

on a six-mile front. Captain Samuel was writing as the advance was still in progress and no doubt his prediction was correct when he stated:

> Tonight I may sleep and dream of you where a Boche Officer last night never dreamt of the trouble awaiting him at dawn. Think of the hundreds of 'tanks' – think of the hundreds of guns – all got up quietly and secretly and let loose at the Hun without a thing to warn him of coming trouble. I can't get over the wonder of it.

It was so sudden and overwhelming a victory that it was hailed in Britain by a ringing of church bells; but it was not enough. Once again the virus endemic in this kind of siege warfare asserted itself – the loss of momentum following the initial attack. The advance was not reinforced, the hoped-for gap for the cavalry was not made. The enemy bent but did not break.

Ten days later, at 8.30 a.m. on 30 November, the Germans mounted a twenty-division counterattack. Over the following days in fierce fighting they gave as good as they had got. The British were able to hold most of the ground they had gained on the first day but they conceded an area almost as large to the south of it. The battle closed down on 3 December. Hopes had been raised; hopes were now, yet again, deferred. It was a kind of draw, but a draw where a victory had seemed to be there for the grasping.

Captain Samuel wrote to his fiancée on 8 December about the outcome of the battle. He offered no apologetic climb-down, however, rather a robust defence of what had been achieved:

> I suppose people at home are more 'down' than ever over all recent 'evacuations' etc. – but there is not too much need of it. I have always admired the Hun as a soldier and he saw a very good chance of taking all our recent gains from us with about 50,000 prisoners. The fact that he failed should be enough to keep the folks' 'pecker up'.

Above: Mark IV Tanks, carrying 'fascines' to be dropped into enemy trenches, waiting to move forward by rail to take part in the Battle of Cambrai. (Q 46940)

Left: A restful moment in the Cambrai Battle; 235th Brigade (47th Divisional Artillery) watering their horses in Flesquières, 24 November 1917. By seizing and holding Flesquières the British created a Salient which would come under immediate and heavy pressure in the great German attack of March 1918. (Q 6316)

PART THREE

BREAK-OUT

March – November 1918

We are encamped in a field of daisies . . . It seems so curious to have the war in this peaceful countryside, without any of the curious accessories of approaches to the trenches, shelled areas behind the lines and so on. I wonder if they felt like that in 1914.

> Captain John Staniforth
> *7th Battalion Leinster Regiment*
> *2 May 1918*

We are progressing fast in ripping country.

> Major Ronald Schweder MC
> *Royal Field Artillery*
> *20 October 1918*

A 13-pounder Battery of the Royal Horse Artillery at full gallop near Inexent, 20 June 1918.
(Q 6728)

INTRODUCTION TO PART THREE

20 March 1918 – the day before the opening of the great German offensive known to the Germans as *Die Kaiserschlacht*, the 'Kaiser's Battle' – has been called 'the last day of trench warfare'. In some ways this is incorrect. Countless battalions would find themselves in entrenched positions in the weeks to come. In essence, however, the kind of warfare institutionalized from late 1914 ceased to be the significant norm with the German attack of 21 March and things would never be quite the same again.

The March offensive was brilliantly planned and made use of carefully thought-out means of overcoming the deadlock. These included: surprise achieved by marshalling men and *matériel* to the front by night; deep infiltration before zero hour by storm-troop groups who bypassed front-line defenders leaving them to be dealt with by subsequent waves; and a concentrated, devastating bombardment on all the key power points of the British resistance, including headquarters establishments, dumps, magazines, even individual guns. The weather handed the Germans a further weapon by providing a cloak of fog at the vital time.

The offensive was launched against the British Third Army, reasonably strong and in good positions, and the Fifth Army, which was under strength, in less satisfactory positions and – having just been obliged to take over a substantial slice of front from the French – with too large an area to defend. A further problem for the British was that the BEF had just been through a major reorganization, with infantry brigades being reduced to three battalions and numerous battalions being disbanded or reduced to cadre; these moves, though necessary, had been widely resented and had done nothing for morale. The setting was the vast open area to the north and south of St Quentin, at the rear of which lay the old battlefield of the Somme. Thus when the British began their retreat they found themselves abandoning places which they had won by bitter

fighting almost two years earlier. But there was a positive side to this: by definition the Germans were seizing territory ravaged not only by battle but by their own scorched-earth tactics of early 1917 – an area impressive on the map but largely useless on the ground. Their advance also inspired a long-overdue development on the Allied side: unity of command, with the French general Ferdinand Foch being appointed as supremo. Significantly, this was achieved a mere five days after the attack began, on 26 March. There would be difficulties and conflicts of interest in the weeks ahead, but basically the change brought a new dynamism and purpose to the Allied cause which boded well for the inevitable counter-attacks to come.

These began in earnest in August and, a hundred days later, ended the war. Now it was time for the Allies to produce their own master plan. The British achievement in all this is well summarized by a recent historian:

> Infantry, artillery, machine-guns, tanks, aircraft and wireless telegraphy all functioned as parts of a single unit. As a result of meticulous planning, each component of the offensive was integrated with, and provided maximum support for, every other component. Here, more than anywhere else, was the great technical achievement of these climactic battles. It was not that the British had developed a war-winning weapon. What they had produced was a 'weapons system': the melding of the various elements in the military arm into a mutually supporting whole.*

Part Three tells the story of this amazing year through the experience of numerous participants many of whom are, so far as this book is concerned, new players on the stage. There is a section on the American involvement, increasingly significant as the year went on, and on WAACs – uniformed women soldiers – now increasingly visible and playing a much valued supporting role.

*Trevor Wilson, *The Myriad Faces of War*, Blackwell 1986, p. 586.

The 'Kaiser's Battle': First Impact

21 March 1918: this first day of the German attack would join other occasions such as 22 April 1915 (the first use of gas) and 1 July 1916 (the first day on the Somme) as one of the great landmark dates of the war. 'A famous anniversary for ever', *The Times* would call it, commenting on the event a year later.

Second Lieutenant Gilbert Laithwaite was serving as a Signals Officer with the 10th Battalion Lancashire Fusiliers, 52nd Brigade, 17th Division, on the Third Army front. 17th Division was in the Havrincourt Salient, in the vicinity of the Canal du Nord. Unfinished and waterless, this man-made ravine had been turned into a strong point in the British defence system; it would now become a prime target for the German artillery. As the following description, from the account which Laithwaite wrote up from rough notes as soon as he was out of the line, makes clear, the attack was massive, comprehensive and meticulously planned. It was also aided, as already stated, by fog:

> In a thick mist, at 5 a.m., on the morning of 21 March, the storm broke. Front and support systems were deluged with thousands of gas shells, mixed with high explosives: communication trenches and junctions barraged, all avenues of approach for reinforcing troops blocked by a chain of fire. Simultaneously, all rear Headquarters, transport lines, and heavy guns of which the positions were known, were subjected to a heavy bombardment from long-range high-velocity guns. Corps was shelled into its dugouts at Villers au Flos; Division into its cellars at Bertincourt; in the bank of the Canal du Nord the deep dugouts of 52nd Brigade were blown in, and their locality so thoroughly dealt with that no message by a Brigade Runner reached us in front all day. Dumps were fired by mapshooting as far back as Haplincourt and Villers. Brigade Transport Lines and the Quartermaster's Stores in Velu Wood were shelled with high velocities and amidst great confusion started to apply the defence scheme and move backwards across the open to prearranged stations.

The precision and sheer force of the enemy's artillery onslaught can be gauged from the fate of one gun in Laithwaite's area, a 12-inch railway gun positioned in Velu Wood which became the target of a host of shells as soon as the barrage opened:

> Its crew drew it out from the wood and towards the Canal, and, ignoring initial casualties, it started to fire at its greatest rate – the enemy shells bursting all around. First the Major was killed, and then one by one, his men, the gun firing gallantly all the while: finally a lucky shot lighted right on the muzzle, knocked the gun out, and killed the remainder of the crew – there it lay disabled, muzzle forward on the rail, the dead men around it, till late that night the ROD [i.e. men of the Railway Operating Department] stealthily brought round an engine, hitched it to the carriage, and dragged the gun back behind the lines.

Despite the intensity of the opening bombardment, it was still not clear whether this was the feared mass attack, a large-scale raid, or an attempt to pinch out the so-called Flesquières Salient. Laithwaite, at battalion headquarters, went 'up on top', to help assess the situation:

> The mist still hung, and the air was clogged with gas. I have never seen such a concentration: overhead was a most extraordinary hissing sound – our shells whistling over without any semblance of a break; his guns replying vigorously; loud crashes from a 5.9 barrage falling on the Havrincourt–Moeuvres Road immediately to our rear. The noise was so great, and the whole thing so immense, that one's nerves steadied automatically.
>
> At 7.55 a.m. a message from A Coy reported heavy shelling of the front line, and ten minutes later a runner from the West Yorks – timed 7.15 – from their company on our side of the canal reporting heavy trench mortars on the front line and several enemy aircraft over it. We felt that things could not much longer be delayed, and made arrangements for the destruction of all papers and the mustering of Headquarters as soon as word should come from the front.

The 'word' would come not from the Battalion's own front-line companies but from the Divisional Scouts who were out in No Man's Land manning a forward Observation Point.

> I was writing a message for the CO and had just signed it when a last message came through from the OP – 'Enemy coming over on our right'. It was 10.25 a.m. We all jumped up, shook hands and wished good luck.

Front-line vigilance, early 1918, before the March attack. A Gas-Sentry in 'Railway Alley' communication trench at Cambrin, Loos sector; he was provided with two sign-boards, 'Gas Alert OFF', displayed here, and 'Gas Alert ON', in case of emergency. (Q 8480)

It was becoming evident that this was no minor trench skirmish, but a major onslaught with profound implications, and with the prospect of surviving far from guaranteed. 'We saw little hope,' wrote Laithwaite, 'of finishing the morning.'

Another participant who thought he would not live through that frightening first day was Captain C. J. Lodge-Patch, medical officer of the 8th Queens (officially the Queen's Royal West Surrey Regiment), a battalion in 24th Division, Fifth Army. The battalion headquarters was at the village of Verguier, while the Aid Post which was Lodge-Patch's chief concern was some way forward at a point called Piumel Quarry, where the battalion's C Company was also entrenched. As the bombardment intensified, a runner was despatched to C Company ordering it to withdraw to the line of the village. The move spurred Lodge-Patch, who had been at headquarters at zero-hour, into urgent action:

> This would have left my Staff altogether exposed and in advance of the remainder of the battalion, so I decided to run the gauntlet of gas and shells, and warn them to retire at the same time, with C Company covering their withdrawal. But on my way, I was deflected from my course by a Trench Mortar Officer, who recognised me, and asked me to come and see his wounded servant, some hundred yards away. When I left the dugout in which he lay, I was as completely lost as a ship in mid-ocean with neither compass nor steering gear; and found myself wandering round and round in circles in the fog. The shelling had become fiercer, and the fog seemed more dense in the smoke of each fresh explosion, which threw up the earth on all sides of me. A 5.9 seemed to land at my very feet, and buried me waist deep. I was not wounded, but felt temporarily stunned, so sat down to get my breath and rest for a few minutes. Hardly knowing what I was doing, I lifted off my Gas Helmet to see things better; and took in a mouthful of Phosgene. I had been fairly calm and collected before, but this made me almost panicky and I felt it was now, indeed, all up with me. However, I pulled myself together, and tried to locate the points of the compass from the direction in which the Hun shells were travelling. This gave me the Orient, and I struck a line that would, I estimated, lead me in the direction of Piumel Quarry. This line I checked every hundred yards or so, when I had to rest for a few moments, as my breathing was becoming difficult.

Still some way short of his destination, Lodge-Patch stumbled into a broken dugout manned by some of his medical staff where he collapsed on the floor. As he lay there one of C Company officers came into the dugout with bomb wounds of the arm and sides, having left Piumel Post only a few minutes before. The officer confirmed that no orders had been received for its evacuation. Lodge-Patch sent a stretcher-bearer to deliver the message to retire:

> He came back to say that the Post was full of Boche, that none of our own men were to be seen, and that we had no time to waste, if we were to get safely out of that death-trap.
>
> Meanwhile our Field Guns had been brought up to a point called Apple Tree Walk, a few hundred yards away on the summit of the hill in front of us, and they were setting up a very brisk barrage along the path by which we had

to return. We were between the Devil and the Deep Sea, but to stay was certain capture, and to go gave us a fairly good chance of getting back alive, so we went. I sent the rest of my Staff on ahead with as much as they could carry in the way of medical impedimenta, and followed with Corporal C———, as I did not feel able to walk without assistance. Again and again I fell, and was half dragged, half carried by my companion. We had traversed about half the distance, when I again collapsed and felt I could go no farther. I urged him to go on alone, telling him I would make my way back, in my own time, when I felt able to do so. He was a very gallant stretcher-bearer, and had already won the DCM and the MM, but he too was slightly gassed, and I could see that he was badly shaken. He refused to leave me alone, and I realised that there was nothing for it but to struggle on to the village, which I did mainly on my hands and knees.

British prisoners captured during the March attack, St Quentin area. Some 21,000 British were taken prisoner on 21 March, out of an overall casualty figure of about 38,000. (Q 55578)

Even a day as grim as this had its moments of wry humour. On Third Army front Laithwaite's battalion was suffering mixed fortunes, with A Company overrun and D Company still holding out stoutly when a Lance-Corporal Davies arrived back from a mission to Brigade Head-quarters.

He gave an astonishing account of the effects on Brigade HQ of the barrage. Brigade were, he said, literally imprisoned in their dugouts in the canal bank, and so thoroughly that a wretched Staff Officer who in the early morning had gone there in his pyjamas was still stuck there. We were pleased to hear of the aesthete in pyjamas, and more pleased to hear that Brigade was getting its share of the war, but this was nothing to our satisfaction when on opening the letters which Davies had brought the first turned out to be a chit from the Staff Captain asking us whether we wished to use the vacancies allotted to us for a course at Auxi-le-Chateau!

'When we could hold old Fritz up no longer,' wrote a Tommy in a Midlands Battalion on 31 March, 'he came over in thousands to take us or kill us.' The second phase of 21 March 1918 was the mass injection of infantry into the British defence system, both by storm-trooper groups bypassing the front lines and other forces following on to complete the killing or capture. Second Lieutenant P. D. Stewart was in the Forward Zone with the 1st West Yorkshires on the Third Army front that morning; he wrote a detailed description of the events of 21 March in a German school exercise book purchased for 20 pfennigs from his guards when in a prisoner of war camp in Germany:

> It was about five minutes past ten when I was talking to the Captain and discussing the situation, and he was just suggesting sending two Runners to Battalion HQ, when we heard the sentry shout that the Germans were here and we all made a grab for our arms and manned the trench, but there was very little that we could do as we were surrounded by hundreds of them. A party of Germans came behind us and called on us to surrender. Well, we hadn't anything to say in the matter as there was hundreds to one. We were on the look out for Dirty Work but they shouted 'Bon Tommy' which meant that they wanted to take us prisoner. Seeing that the case was hopeless we were taken, very much against our will.

Also taken prisoner, after having been wounded, was Stewart's CO; his battalion was to be one of seven in Third Army who lost over a hundred men killed that day.

Not only many men died on 21 March; whole units ceased to exist, some never to be reconstituted, while brigades, even divisions, were effectively destroyed. Laithwaite would recall overhearing an Adjutant of a neighbouring battalion telling a colleague: 'I suppose you know our friends the 51st Division are gone to glory', while Captain John Staniforth, away from the line at the time, wrote in anger and grief about the fate of the 16th Irish Division of Fifth Army:

> The Division has ceased to exist. Wiped off the map. You know where they were; they took the Boche attack full smack, the first day they were in the trenches. They died fighting, while I was hanging round a base depot. I'll tell you about it later. I don't want to just now.

There were even cases of the fighting strength of a whole battalion being described as 'missing'.

One result of the confusion stemming from all this was that over the ensuing days many men, no longer in touch with their units, joined up in random fashion with other men or groups equally disorientated by the turn of events. This was the experience of Sergeant Albert Slack of the 117th Machine-Gun Company in 39th Division; when a full month later

A pathetic consequence of the German offensive: refugee women and children leaving their homes in a farm-cart, Brétencourt, 23 March 1918. (Q 8636)

he was at last able to fill in the details of his recent adventures for his mother, he sent her the following dramatic if understated account:

From Mar. 21 to Mar. 25 it was 'touch and run' all the time. We got into action first on Mar. 22 early morning. The enemy attacked at dawn and we held him back for several hours till our ammunition was exhausted. Fritz suffered terribly. We were firing at point-blank range and couldn't miss, and when our ammo was finished and our flanks were surrounded we skilfully withdrew.

In the meantime another line had been prepared in rear and we fell back through this line which was held by a Battn. of my old Regt. After a roll call and getting a fresh supply of ammo. the Section Officer, myself and three teams were sent to reinforce a certain place and that was the last I saw of the Coy. The next day (23rd), we held off another attack till our flanks were penetrated and then we fell back slowly, keeping our line intact.

We managed to get a fresh supply of ammunition and took up another defensive position with the 2 remaining guns. Here my Section Officer was killed and after holding Fritz back till all ammo was finished I gave the order to retire and got out with 5 men, 1 gun and self.

We attached ourselves to a scratch mob of all sorts and with a fresh supply of ammo. again 'took the field' the same night. The next morning (24th) I haven't a clear idea of what really happened – I was too exhausted. I know we fought and retired, counter-attacked (and I can distinctly remember shooting a big 6-ft Fritz with my revolver and doing all sorts of mad things) then retired again. I slipped and something went wrong with the works in my ankle so I got away as soon as I could – God knows how.

I wandered about trying to find some trace of the Coy, as I had only 2 men left in my Section. Eventually I landed in 42 Hospital, Amiens, and you know the rest.

Yet although the Germans had sent shock waves through their opponents and made massive inroads into British-held territory they had not made the immediate, decisive breakthrough for which they had hoped. Captain Lodge-Patch, having survived the experiences of that grim first morning, could write not long after in almost triumphalist terms, in spite of hard, sacrificial fighting which was to win his battalion, the 8th Queens, one of the day's ten VCs:

At present we are passing through the most critical time we have yet experienced. This Hun is a wonderful fighter and he has a wonderful organisation behind him. But I think we have got him seized up now and more or less held; and we are waiting only for Foch's counter-strike.

As a Battalion, we bore the initial attack on the 21st. It is no secret; for the papers have all extolled the achievements of the 24th Division and praised particularly the Queen's, who, according to the accounts of the war correspondents, fought to the last man. According to the Hun programme, the village was to have fallen in two hours and we held it for thirty. Post after post was occupied by the enemy and reoccupied by us after a determined counter-attack. Trench after trench was taken and retaken. The enemy artillery was magnificent. They brought their field guns to within a few hundred yards and blazed away at us with open sights. We replied with machine-guns and slaughtered the gun teams and the parties which carried the ammunition, for we had and held the high ground.

In essence, Lodge-Patch had judged the situation well overall and would be ultimately proved correct. But for many his elation would have seemed premature as, particularly on the Fifth Army front, the British had no option but to turn their minds to their second great retreat of the war.

The March Retreat

For many units not in the immediate line of fire, the reality of what was taking place on 21 March took some time to become clear. In the case of Private J. L. Bramley, 2/7th Battalion Worcestershire Regiment, in Fifth Army's 61st Division, he and his comrades greeted the first news of the German attack without dismay. 'Everyone was optimistic', he noted in the diary which he kept regularly throughout the following weeks, 'and thought we were scoring.' However, this upbeat mood soon changed as they began to hear 'reports of all kinds, which spoke of retreat and disaster'. On the following day he and his comrades realized there must be 'some truth' in these reports when they were told to pack up and prepare to be off at any time:

About 10.30 p.m. came the order and off we went leaving the camp we had improved so much for the Germans. It was a lovely moonlit night for which we were thankful and what a tramp it was. Everywhere the roads were full of troops and transport and guns of all descriptions moving back in one continuous stream. Scores of times we were held up and had to stand there with packs on and blankets too. Out on our left great fires were burning – an aerodrome being destroyed before the Huns could get there. His aeroplanes were over us bombing and if they could only have hit the road would have done some damage.

After a good breakfast on the morning of the 23rd we had to fall in for off at 9.30 a.m. It was a lovely day, but very hot for marching and everywhere the roads were packed. The last bit before dinner was up a steep hill and scores of our chaps dropped out up there. I felt like it but stuck to the finish at the top of the hill. We stayed about an hour for dinner, then on again and reached our destination, Maricourt, about 3 p.m. We sat down in a field and had tea served, after that we were taken along to some old trenches and told we should have to stay the night there. There was plenty of grass so we made a nice bed among it and having our blankets slept nice and warm, but we had not been down long when Jerry was over bombing and dropped six very close. Of course there was a rush and scramble for the trenches, though for my part I think the safest plan is to stay where you are. We got settled down again but in an hour or two he was over again and I awoke to find all my chums rushing for the trenches again and to see the flash of the bombs exploding close by, luckily we all escaped damage and got down again to sleep.

We were awakened at 4 a.m. and told to be ready at 4.30, our blankets were rolled and taken to the wagons and that is the last we saw of them as I think the next day they were lost. We were marched off nearer the village and close to a large field hospital and here had to stand to in a sunken road until daylight. They were just preparing to clear out of the hospital and I slipped across with a chum and got some tea. Oh how delicious it was, later our kitchens came up and we had some breakfast.

The roads were still full of traffic, tanks, guns and all kinds of stores

British defence. The Battle of the Somme Crossings; Gordon Highlanders in support lining a bank, 24 March 1918. (Q 10787)

moving back. It turned out a lovely day and later when they turned out of the hospital we were able to have a wash. They left behind any amount of stores, food, clothing, fittings and equipment, pots and pans and all manner of things, a splendid library of books too, we were able to help ourselves. They left dinner cooking too so we had a good feed, some of the fellows carried whole cheeses away, boxes of dates, biscuits, meat and tinned stuff of all kinds, there was plenty for all. I got a new suit and clean pants.

Such episodes were not unique during the retreat, as is clear from the diary of Bombardier Dudley Gyngell, then serving as a clerk in the 2nd Divisional Artillery. 'On our way', he noted under 27 March, 'we passed a YMCA canteen, which had been abandoned, and we stopped and raided it. I carried away as much as I could including half a dozen tins of sardines and several tins of fruit.' There was also a piano which Gyngell would have liked to have acquired, but he decided that their battery's wagons were too overloaded to carry so large an item of booty.

If Bramley's diary indicates the trials and hazards of the infantry during the retreat, Gyngell's illustrates those of the artillery, especially in a situation of constant movement and confusion. On 24 March in the vicinity of Albert his battery found itself heading down a road with a steep bank on one side and a hedge on the other, when the column was abruptly halted:

We then saw two infantrymen who had come along in the ditch by the side of the road. They told the OC that we were in 'no man's land' and that the Boche was about a kilometre away and coming over fast, and that we were heading straight into him. The order was given to turn the column at once and this we could not do as the road was too narrow to turn the GS wagons in. We had to go forward a good distance to an opening in the bank and turn the wagons off the road. There one wagon became ditched and we worked feverishly and silently to get it out and only did so after hooking in about twelve horses and manhandling it. Anyhow we got away in time and went back. This time the OC made no mistake and took the road for Albert.

German advance. A column of German troops marching towards the battle front during the March offensive. (Q 29902)

The near presence of the enemy was sometimes a rumour, sometimes a reality, resulting in ill-prepared attempts at counter-attack which found little favour with the men ordered to carry them out. Bramley's battalion was thrown into such an action near Maricourt on the morning of the 25th:

> Fritz had evidently got his guns up for he kept up a terrible barrage, one division who were counter-attacking on our left were flying in all directions before it, then came the order for us to up over the top and the 'damned fools' took us with full packs on too [sic], it was terrible, shells bursting and bullets whipping all around, however most of us got through and gained another trench which we occupied for a bit until too warm and then kept on the move

all day from one trench to another; hundreds of men got separated from their Batt, and were mixed up hopelessly, a good many of us were surrounded and missing, a few officers too.

Some counter-attacks, however, were extremely successful, inflicting many casualties and severely jolting the advancing Germans. One such action was mounted by Captain Cosmo Clark, a Company Commander of the 13th Middlesex, in the XIX Corps of Fifth Army. On the evening of the 25th he was able to ambush a company of the enemy, in circumstances in which overconfidence put them virtually at his mercy. The incident happened as his company was about to leave its briefly held positions at a village called Punchy and continue the apparently endless retreat. Clark an exuberant account of the event in his diary wrote:

> Just before falling back I saw about a Company of Boche cautiously advancing in the positions in advance of and around where 'C' Company had been holding. They had small parties of scouts out creeping in front who reconnoitred the ground and then ran back and larger parties crept up.
>
> I got my Company into an old trench running through Punchy by the time it was dark. After about half an hour we could hear large numbers of Boche on the roads in front. Their transport was rattling down the roads, and the clatter of the horses hoofs on the road was as distinct as could be. Also we could hear large parties of Infantry marching along – the tramp, tramp, tramp made one imagine the whole German Army was advancing against my Company.
>
> Suddenly the tramping of infantry became louder and louder and we could hear them shouting to each other. We heard names called and Companies called out – 'Carl' – 'Kompanie!' The moon was not strong enough to see anybody. It was an anxious moment for me and in fact for us all. Not a man fired a shot though they were anxiously looking at me as much as to say I was leaving it too late.
>
> After a bit I could hear them coming marching along in column straight down a road leading to our position, shouting out orders and other things I couldn't understand. When they were about fifty yards away I gave the order to 'rapid fire' and we let 'em have it.
>
> Every machine-gun opened at once and every man fired rapid fire, for three minutes. The silence of the moment before became an ear-splitting roar, and we heard them screaming and scrambling about the woods and bushes. When I gave the order to 'cease fire' we could hear moans and groans in front and people softly calling. The proud brazen tactics of marching in column of route shouting as they came had suddenly changed, and I think that little part of Boche learned to have a wholesome respect of 'rapid fire' from a bunch of very tired Middlesex men.

A thwarted attempt by the Germans to play the ambush card is described in the account by Private W. A. Hoyle, 24th Royal Fusiliers, written from the sanctuary of a hospital bed in England to which he had been despatched after receiving a 'Blighty' wound to the hand:

> Six men rose out of a trench just in front of us. They were all bareheaded and wore English equipment and overcoats. They shouted out to us, 'Come on you bastards.' Our officer yelled 'Don't fire they are our own men', but a Corporal

who was in a trench just in front of us shouted, 'Fire, they are Fritzes', so we cheered and let rip with our Lewis guns and rifles. Those six never got up again.

This was at Beaumont-Hamel on the old Somme battlefield, now the setting for numerous small-scale rearguard actions, many of them undertaken with great bravery in circumstances where survival was the least likely outcome. Such a one was witnessed by Lieutenant Kenneth Mackenzie, 9th Battalion, Duke of Wellington's West Riding Regiment; as he watched in admiration five British tanks headed gallantly towards the superior enemy force:

It was a hopeless task, and we saw each tank in its turn hit and put out of action by the field guns at point-blank range. It was a thrilling sight to see the tanks advance spitting M.-G. and 12-pounder fire. In one case I saw the officer in command standing on the top of his tank as she was going into action. The sight cheered the troops who realised the difficult position we were in.

What of Second Lieutenant Gilbert Laithwaite and his 10th Lancashire Fusiliers in Third Army? It had extricated itself from its vulnerable position of the grim first morning and had been moving back ever since. Laithwaite had noted many remarkable sights as they crossed the old battlefield: a string of wagons, filing westwards from Martinpuich across a wide valley for two whole hours, the carts and their horses silhouetted against the sky; also silhouetted, a train on fire at the dump at Carnoy on the Montauban–Carnoy road. He had not himself visited Albert, but a fellow officer had brought a vivid report of its 'extraordinary confusion' – food shops full, people loading their carts and getting out, troops passing through – a 'bad mess' in the Cathedral square, where transport had been bombed, dead mules across the road near the dip down to the town on the Albert–Bapaume road.

The night of 25–26 March found the battalion HQ, to which he was attached, in the Mametz–Fricourt region of the Somme – virtually on the old front line of 1 July 1916. By this time despite the uncertainty and general chaos there was a growing assumption that the retreating was at last over and that the time had now come to turn and face down the advancing Germans. This, however, was not to be:

We were all dead asleep, tired out after the night's patrolling, and anxious to get a rest before the uncertain morrow, when at 4 a.m. we were awakened by CSM Smith of D Company with the startling news that the left had given way, that orders for general retreat had been issued, that he had come with this message from Brigade, had warned three companies, which had moved off, and seen that the Manchesters had the order to warn the fourth.

The message was received with incredulity; the CO first cross-examined Smith, but found that he held to his story, then wanted to go forward himself to make sure that the companies had all got safely away, but after argument was dissuaded, Smith urging that all had gone. Once this had been decided, there was no time to be lost, and none was lost. In the haste and confusion, the CO's horse, borrowed the night before from the West Yorks, was left behind.

It was twilight, still chilly, dew on the grass – the train still burning on the skyline at Carnoy behind us. We were of course still without maps and had only a general idea of the road for which to make. We were, I fear, a disorderly mob – quite heartbroken at this new turn – officers dragging along in silence like the men. I got them at last, once we reached the main road, to march in fours, and after that to keep step and keep their dressing: once this had been done they found marching much easier and began to recover their self-respect.

Crossing the track of various parties moving N.W. from Bray to Albert, we marched into Méaulte. Méaulte was a curious scene – many civilians still about – some lackadaisically standing before their houses – men and women: some women crying as they loaded up their carts with beds and mattresses, others almost at the end of their packing, others driving off.

Some looked bitterly at us, and did not hesitate to say what they thought. Howarth (who knew no French) interpreted their glances, and was afterwards declared by the CO to have heard a woman call us 'bloody shits' in the vernacular.

We took the road towards Dernancourt. At this stage I talked to RSM Newman. He was very depressed. I said, trying to cheer him up 'We don't know the reason for all this – but there must be something behind it. Besides, we've got away from the desolated country, and when we fight, we'll fight in comfort.' It was no good. He said, 'I'm an old soldier, sir, it's over twenty years since my first campaign, and I'll say that it's not a soldier's part to fall back like this, not knowing why or wherefore, and without striking a blow. Yesterday I thought we had stopped, and could turn and get our own back, and just as we had got settled, off we start again. I've lost all heart.'

The long march continued. They were in open territory now – Dernancourt was 'very quiet, clean and empty – like any country village on a bright morning in early spring – the sun shining on its whitewashed houses'. Half way between Dernancourt and the next village, Buire, they caught up with a straggler from one of the companies, who confirmed that, as they had been told, the bulk of the battalion was up ahead; despite delivering this reassuring news he was severely 'strafed' by the CO for 'venturing to fall out on the ground of sore feet'. Moving further west they saw, as Private Bramley had done, a field hospital in process of being abandoned, with, this time, a hospital train in similar straits; 'no doubt it was inevitable, but the sight was disgusting and depressing.' About 9.30 they reached Henencourt, catching up with what they took to be the remainder of the battalion. There was a great sense of relief – 'cookers all lined up, etc.', and in a corner, for Laithwaite and his fellow officers, 'a white tablecloth spread on boards on the ground, cups, plates, forks, jugs, and civilization.' There was also the news they wanted above all; that they were now back at the main line, and that there would be no further retreat.

There followed a muster parade, and then the calamity. Checking my signallers, I was suddenly aware that there were none present from D Company (Wood's). Enquiry showed that there *was* no D Company. The CO was horror struck. CSM Smith was called in, and piecing things together, it transpired that the Manchesters had been charged with warning D Company, and had

A train load of British reinforcements en route for the front, Mont St Eloi, 1 April 1918. (Q 327)

apparently failed to do it – very depressing to men and officers alike, for good friends had gone with D Company (and for me particularly Wood/Cassington/ Handley, and many of the HQ signallers – Walton, Avery). The Colonel went off to report to the Brigadier.

It was borne with – there was nothing to be done – and we had all become inured to losses even of old and close friends.

About noon Avery, Wood's signaller, and other stragglers and wounded, in from D Company. Wood dead, the Company had fought hard against overwhelming odds, but was cut off – alas.

For the 10th Lancashire Fusiliers, there was to be no further fighting – although there were several alarms; they were relieved on the night of 2/3 April and went out on rest. Cosmo Clark's 13th Middlesex was involved until the last day of the retreat, 5 April, all ranks becoming increasingly exhausted. At times Clark 'literally slept while marching'. 1 April produced an amusing diversion, however, when, in the afternoon of a day of pouring rain, Clark noticed three or four cars motoring down the main road from Amiens to Berteaucourt near where his company was dug in:

They stopped just near my extreme left post and a number of civilians and French and British officers got out and walked towards my post.

I walked over towards them with Offord and found Horsford talking to them. One man in a trilby hat I recognised as Winston Churchill. He came towards me and asked me if I was in charge of the support line. I told him I was and he continued as follows: 'Ah yes my boy, and what is your name? Here is Monsieur Clemenceau. Come along and I will introduce you to him.' I then noticed old Clemenceau who was wearing a large black cape. I saluted, clicked my heels, and the old boy shook hands with me. He spoke very good English, and asked me what sort of time we had had; whether I was tired, etc., etc. Then he told us that thousands of French troops were behind us, and thousands of British troops were coming out from England daily. I shall never forget his brilliant shining eyes. They seemed to pierce right through one. After generally cheering us up and repeatedly saying 'They will never get Amiens', he left after a general hand-shake all round.

Before going, I tackled one of the British officers about a smoke. He emptied his cigarette case for me, and Winston gave us some fine cigars.

When they had gone we retired to a little old shooting box in the marshes, and shared out the smokes.

The French President was right; the Germans never did get Amiens. The great advance subsided almost at its gates. One contributing factor was that the German soldiers themselves gave a notable sign of their own exhaustion and battle-fatigue when they reached Albert. They raided the shops, particularly the wine stores, and exchanged campaigning for carousing. It was a yielding to temptation on the part of a normally highly disciplined force on a massive scale; it was also virtually an acknowledgement that the great advance had failed.

As the German effort faded, at last news came through from men of those divisions in the extreme south of the area held by Fifth Army which had found themselves separated from the rest as a result of the German breakthrough. It was not until 4 April that Gunner Harold Coulter RFA, serving with the X/36th (Medium) Trench Mortar Battery in the 36th (Ulster) Division, was able to write to his parents. The letter he sent was not only one of reassurance, it was one of confidence and pride, showing an eagerness that was doubtless widely shared for the British as soon as possible to exercise their right of reply:

Now don't worry at all about us. We are not beaten, if we are well bent. Old Fritz is beaten. I think it has been his dying kick, which you know is always more powerful than any other. What would one expect when he threw twenty divisions against ours and the one on each side of us? He was simply rotten with men. They were like flies. He did not attack in mass formation, but in slightly extended order, wave after wave. As fast as one wave was mown down, another rolled up behind it. Our machine-gunners say they were absolutely sick of killing them. In addition, he put up a hurricane barrage on all our batteries, a rolling barrage on the trenches, a cross-barrage on the roads, and shelled all the villages behind with high velocity armour piercing shells. So what hopes had anybody? Anyhow, it has not done what he expected doing – he said he would be in Paris by 1 April. Good April fool for him when he found himself mile upon miles away on Monday morning!

Well cheer up! All will turn out well before long. Wait till the British have their say!

'Backs to the Wall'

The end of the March Retreat at the gates of Amiens was only the end of the beginning: the Germans were not going to renounce their ambitions after one attempt only. On 9 April they struck again further north, against the part of the line held by, among others, the 2nd Division of the Portuguese Expeditionary Force, to which Captain Dartford was still attached as a member of the British Military Mission. His base was in quarters assigned to the Mission in the little town of Laventie just behind the Allied lines.

9 April Tues: Woke at 4.10 a.m. very heavy shelling. Guessed from the start it meant an attack. Phoned to brigade – every communcation cut already. Dressed hurriedly and set out for brigade. The Rue de la Gare was dangerous for shells were falling in it. Smelt gas and put on my respirator, dodging into doors as shells fell. Reached bde dugout. Next 3 hours we could do nothing, but nearly got asphyxiated by lack of oxygen owing to having to keep gas blankets down. Runner from battalions came nearly dead with fatigue, but their message was nothing more than SOS. Heavy fog on and everybody seemed isolated from others.

About 9 a.m. a shell hit the corner of the dugout and wounded Branco the signals officer in the face. I had my gumboots off at the time and later found my left foot had several small cuts probably pieces of brick. We then all made for the Aid Post cellar. Gas was not hanging about then but the road was a pretty sight – houses down and fog and dust. I persuaded the others to go to the mission cellar. There three civilians were saying prayers in a corner and odd wounded were being treated in another and the rest of us wondering what to do. Impossible to send messages forward. We kept sending mounted orderlies or cyclists back to division but it appears few ever got there.

I think the Boche must have taken our front line about 8.30 and the B line 8.45 and was up to batt H.Q. by 9.15 or so. One message from X. de Costa (CO 29th Batt.) said he no longer had any command and that it was now a question of individuals fighting out. He was killed we learnt after. So was Captain Montenegro, OC 20th Batt. (right) and nothing is known of Montalvao (left) and Woodrow and Sgt Ransdale.

Stragglers passed thro' Laventie but most of them chose the open fields and wisely. We got hold of one and he said 'Everyone was running from the B line so I did too', though he hadn't seen the Boche. We put 2 sgts to try and collect stragglers but they soon came back saying it was impossible to stop them and that officers were getting away too. Was very surprised to see Captain Valle CO 3rd Batt. come in, all of a tremble and nearly fainting. He said his batt. was all out of hand. M.-Gs were reported playing on roads leading S. out of Laventie so we decided that we should move to avoid capture and to try and get in touch with division. Meanwhile I had put on my high boots and Sam Browne and got my stationery box down into the cellar. Tore up most secret things and took my diaries and cheque book out of my writing case. The rest was left.

Dartford would later note opposite this entry for 9 April that he was in the middle of John Buchan's novel *Prester John* when the Germans struck and lost the book that day with his kit. 'Must read it again some time,' he reminded himself.

It was unfortunate that the Portuguese were about to be relieved on the day of the attack, so that they were as much concerned with leaving the line as defending it. Apart from one battalion which fought hard to hold its ground, they fell back in complete disarray, pulling the adjacent British Division on their left back with them. The Division on their right, however, the 55th Territorial, stayed firm and kept the Germans at bay over the critical days that followed. Captain C. L. Overton MC ('Neville' to his family and friends) was a Company Commander in 1/4th Battalion King's Own Royal Lancaster Regiment in 55th Division. The letters he wrote to his future fiancée at this time during what became known as the battle of the Lys, give a vivid impression of the rigours and satisfactions of a battalion fighting for its very existence, and surviving, at a time of hard pounding and high tension.

4.45 a.m. 10.4.18

My dearest Muriel

I am writing this in what might be called the middle of a battle. The Boches attacked us yesterday morning, he got within 200 yds of my Coy HQ before I knew there was an attack on (as you know I am in support). There was a very heavy mist and apparently he got right on top of our front line people before they knew he was there.

We had a terrific battle round my line, he took my Coy HQ for a time, then we bombed him out again. Incidentally before the attack he put gas over and shelled us with heavies and heavy trench mortars for four hours. It was the worst I have ever been in, I got goodness knows how many casualties during that time. However we drove him right out again and hold the original line. 6 of us captured 85, they simply gave themselves up, I think our battalion captured over 400.

Poor old Collins, one of my officers, was killed and Lyon very badly wounded in the head. There are I'm afraid several casualties both officers and men.

We are expecting the Boches to attack again this morning, we have been well reinforced however and feel pretty confident.

We were fighting hard yesterday from 8 a.m. to 4 p.m. We didn't get any food until about 5.30 p.m. We were pretty tired after it, in fact I still am a little.

12 noon

He didn't attack us again this morning after all.
Believe our Brigade got 2,000 prisoners yesterday.
Lots of love Neville

This second letter was written one week later.

12.20 p.m. 17.4.18

My dearest Muriel
I have been up about ½ hour now. Our division came out of the line last night,

or rather early this morning, and we are now in a village about 10 miles from the line.

I have had a good sleep in a proper bed with sheets on it, have had a bath, clean change etc. and feel now as fit as a fiddle.

We have jolly good billets. Our mess is a big room with a fireplace, large table, umpteen chairs, including an easy one, sideboard, cupboard etc. My bedroom is a nice little room, with a good bed, 2 tables and a chest of drawers. The men all have dry, clean billets, so altogether we are very satisfied at the moment.

Powell, our Quarter Master, has just turned up with champagne, fruits, red wine, flour, lime juice, soda water, sardines, milk and all sorts of gifts for the mess, so we ought to be all right.

I only need you to make it paradise.

Lots and lots of love from Neville

At the level of the British High Command, the period covered by Overton in the above letters had been one of supreme crisis. As the battle front extended to take in the area from the La Bassée Canal to the environs of Ypres, the threat to break through to the Channel coast became a very real one. Field Marshal Haig appealed to the Allied Generalissimo Marshal Foch for assistance, but Foch initially refused to transfer any reserves, stating that the British Army must 'hold on where it stood'. On 11 April Haig issued his eloquent and legendary Order of the Day, with its keynote message:

There is no other course open to us but to fight it out! Every position must be held to the last man. With our backs to the wall and believing in the justice of our cause each one of us must fight on to the end. The safety of our Homes and the Freedom of mankind alike depend upon the conduct of each one of us at this critical moment.

The line held. As with the first attack in March, this second German effort expired without achieving any significant gains, though at a huge cost in casualties on both sides as the fighting dragged on until virtually the end of the month, with a late flurry on the 29th.

The steady rise in hope and confidence is reflected in the letters of Colonel Bill Murray, who had been in France throughout the war and was now commanding 15th Brigade, Royal Horse Artillery, attached to the 29th Division. 'It is all fearfully thrilling,' he wrote on 17 April, 'and everyone is in the best spirits. It doesn't matter losing ground if we make it as expensive as we have been doing.' By 30 April he was in a triumphal mood:

Yesterday was a great day. The Germans began at 5 a.m., and throughout the whole of the northern battlefield they continued to hurl great masses of men against our line till evening. Not in a single spot did they succeed and are smashed right down the line. At times the fighting was furious and the roar and din throughout the day is beyond description. My brigade fired thousands of rounds and were very steady though badly shelled at times. Stripped to the waist they worked like demons and it was more like one of those fantastic pictures in *The Sphere* than anything else. In many ways I think yesterday was

one of the best days of the war. It was a critical day because if the line had not held it would have meant a very dangerous withdrawal. And it is a wonderful thing that those masses of Germans didn't get through anywhere. They came over in 4 or 5 waves with fixed bayonets. Very few got back.

The Germans, however, had still not given up. Held on the Franco–Belgian border, they would try their luck elsewhere. From the British point of view, there was a special irony in that when a month later on 27 May they threw an attack against the Chemin des Dames area in Champagne, it fell on a Corps containing three divisions which had been sent there to recuperate after being severely mauled in March. This had been thought a safe area, unlikely to be subject to the enemy's attentions, as is clear from the diary of Captain P. H. B. Lyon, 6th Battalion, Durham Light Infantry, written in the German prisoner of war camp in which he would very soon find himself. His division, the 50th, had, as he put it, 'been through two offensives and was certainly very weak'. Prospects seemed favourable, however, to within hours of the attack.

He spent the evening of the 26th in the front line, improving one or two posts, and arranging work for the night. 'The only activity apparent was in the air, several German planes crossing and reconnoitring our lines under spasmodic fire from our "Archies".' There seemed nothing unusual about this, however. He returned to his company HQ; only then was there the first ominous sign:

> Halfway through dinner came the cloud like a man's hand, in the form of a signalling corporal with a message from Battalion HQ. 'Brigade wires: "Take precautionary defensive measures." All ranks will stand to, and special vigilance will be observed.' Raids had been rather frequent lately, so we deduced that somebody had got wind of one in our neighbourhood. There was not much to do, and the necessary orders were soon issued, and dinner resumed. At about 10.30 p.m. came the message which eventually dispelled all doubts as to the nature of the coming blow. I made a rough précis of it and sent it out to all platoon commanders.

Lyon subsequently attached a carbon copy of the message he had sent out that evening to his diary, having found it crumpled in his jacket pocket some weeks later; it had escaped his own notice, as well as the attentions of several German searchers. Its text ran:

> Prisoner states that attack is coming at 4 a.m. Bombardment probably with gas at 1 a.m. Tanks may be used. Troops must fire at infantry and not at tanks. No fighting men to carry wounded. Issue extra 50 rounds per man and inspect pouches to see No is complete. All Lewis Gunners over 4 per team to come to Coy HQ at once. Destroy all maps and important documents.

Events began to unfold almost precisely as predicted:

> *27 May* At 1 a.m. exactly came the beginning of the German bombardment. I had a lance-corporal on sentry at the head of my dugout, who reported a great concentration of trench mortars and aerial torpedoes on the front line, accompanied by the fire of what we were afterwards told to be 400 guns on the front

Opposite: Backs to the wall; a British six-inch Mark VII gun firing, near Caestre, 23 April 1918, during the Battle of the Lys. (Q 6568)

and support trenches. I went out to him occasionally, but there was nothing I could do till the attack came.

At about 4 a.m. G-S [i.e. one of his junior officers], whose platoon had escaped the worst of the shelling, reported that the barrage had spread to his trench, and that he was awaiting orders. I went up but saw no signs of the expected assault. It was about 20 minutes later, just after I had heard the first round of machine gun fire, that G-S himself came in and said the Germans had broken through on the right. I moved his platoon up to make a defensive flank and meet this attack: by now the barrage was heavy over the reserve area which meant that the infantry could not be far behind. I decided it was time to move, and took out my company HQ with the object of moving up to the supports and seeing what was doing. When I came out into the open I found to my dismay and surprise files of Germans immediately to our front and level with our line on the right. The Germans came on leisurely, meeting with little or no resistance. The air was full of their planes, which went before them and swept the trenches with machine-guns. A few tanks had broken through, and were now well behind us.

Lyon decided to attempt a withdrawal. Under constant fire, he made his way to Battalion HQ; by the time he got there he was 'practically alone', his men having dropped off as they were hit. The CO led him and various others away from the lines through a wood which was being heavily plastered with gas shells, with a view to reaching Brigade HQ. On the way down Lyon met a reserve company from the 5th Battalion of the DLI coming up, and attached himself to it. But they too soon ran into horrendous fire and when they in their turn attempted to retire they found that, as he put it, 'the way back was as bad as the way in'. The situation was rapidly becoming hopeless.

Some of the men crept into a dugout in spite of my language and I found very few still with me. We came to a road which I crossed unhurt, but of the others who tried nearly all were wounded or killed. I saw 2 Germans through the trees about 20 yards to my right, and one took aim at me. Beyond this I found some cover, where 3 or 4 men followed me, all but one wounded. By now I saw Germans all round the hill, and looking up I saw half a dozen of them 10 yards away, shouting and raising their rifles. The wounded men were shouting at me to surrender, and indeed I saw nothing else for it – so I just stood up, and in a minute we were prisoners.

The shame of that moment has proved ineffaceable. I suppose that every man taken in battle must feel that smart of indignation and remorse, for every such man has chosen life before freedom. And such a choice, even in the most desperate conditions, is a falling off from the ideal (so often in men's minds) of 'resistance to the last shot and the last man'. For myself, I only know that it seemed inevitable, and that in similar circumstances I should almost certainly do the same again. It may be a taint of cowardice, or merely an unheroic common sense.

The battle was over for Captain Lyon, as for many thousands of others, killed, wounded or taken prisoner. Again, however, the German attack ran out of energy, delayed by stubborn resistance and harassed too from

1 June onwards by a new and potent factor, the appearance in the field of a battalion of the United States 3rd Division. The great aim of the Germans in launching their 1918 attacks had been to beat the Allies already engaged in France before the Americans came in with their virtually limitless manpower. Now they *were* in; for Germany and her co-belligerents this meant that there was no longer any real hope of victory. Indeed, the logic of the concept of attrition suggested that they would suffer a humiliating defeat. There was as yet no acknowledgement of this, however, and there would be much hard fighting ahead. But the tide, at last, was beginning to turn.

Being taken prisoner, Armentières, April 1918, by Private E. Stoneley. An ordinary Tommy's record of his capture, as sketched in a Prisoner-of-War camp in Germany.
(HU 63267)

A World of Rare Women

The mere presence of women could cause a sensation, particularly when men had not seen any representative of the other sex for a long time. In March 1918 during the Great Retreat the 20th Lancashire Fusiliers arrived at Méaulte, near Albert. According to the account of one of the battalion's officers, Second Lieutenant Gilbert Laithwaite:

> As we got inside the village some civilians appeared; Davies, the runner, called out, to the general amusement, 'Hey boys, there's a woman!' – she was the first many had seen since December 1917.

The diary of Sapper David Doe, Royal Engineers, records an earlier sighting. On 30 August 1915 he noted the discovery of 'a girl dressed as a soldier in the 5th Gordon Highlanders. She was in kilts and had been in the trenches even. She had got into the Army as a result of a bet and after court martial was sent back to England.' Assuming this story to be true and not just a trench rumour, there was surely a special bravado in her appearing in one of the kilted regiments allegedly known to the enemy as 'ladies from Hell'.

The best year by far for woman-spotting was 1918. Women had been long visible as nurses in hospitals or as drivers of the ambulances that met the hospital trains, but now they were appearing in military uniform and in growing numbers as members of the Women's Army Auxiliary Corps. Inevitably they were known as 'WAACs', and when the service was retitled QMAACs – Queen Mary's Army Auxiliary Corps – 'WAACs' they remained. How that combination of initials was pronounced is clear from the riddle passed on to Captain C. L. Overton by his girlfriend in a letter of May 1918: 'What is better than a blow in the eye? Answer: A WAAC on the knee!'

WAACs had been recruited since early 1917 when the service was founded with the purpose of sending uniformed women across the Channel to relieve uniformed men of a range of non-military tasks. 28 March that year saw the publication of the Army Council Instruction which brought the Corps into official existence and three days later its first party left London for France to take up employment initially in BEF canteens. As the number of WAACs increased their functions diversified, with the result that eventually they would work as clerks, cooks, bakers, storekeepers, even printers and map artists – helping to produce the mass of print and paper without which the administration of the Army would have completely congealed. They also tended war cemeteries. In military jargon they were assisting along the so-called Lines of Communication. In more general terms, they were helping to oil the wheels of a huge, multi-faceted organization. They were also, though this was not part of the intention, greatly cheering the hearts of the fighting men. The following is from a letter by Major Ronald Schweder dated 15 July 1918:

'Mosquitos and "Some" Bird': A Tommy's acknowledgement of the rarity and attraction of the fair sex in France, as drawn in the autograph album of a nurse, Miss E. G. Tomlinson, who served in a hospital at Wimereux, near Calais. (HU 63268)

Latham, one of my Subalterns, came back today after a fortnight's rest cure by the seaside. He was full of WAACs, VADs, etc. It seems to me to be on a friendly footing, the male and female army in the back areas. One might almost call it 'matey'.

A priceless idea is that buses are run from the rest camp to Wimereux for the 'Tommies'. At Wimereux there is nothing to do or see but WAACs, but 'peeping Tom' tells me the lorries are crowded. Female forms are gazed upon disporting themselves in the briny.

It was, however, one thing for women to dazzle the Tommies when they were relaxing; it was different if they produced the same effect when the Tommies were seriously employed. Private Maurice Gower, at a Base Depot after being wounded, wrote the following to a sister on 6 June 1918:

WAACs tending graves of fallen British soldiers in a cemetery at Abbeville, 9 February 1918. (Q 8467)

We have a good many WAACs about the Base, they work in Cook-houses, etc.

I happened to be on fatigue in our Cook-house only yesterday and noticed that they did their work all right, but delayed the work of the men to a certain extent especially in the case of the casual fatigue man such as myself. One youth of our party I noticed doing nothing but stare at them whenever they came in sight. Perhaps the poor chap hadn't seen an English girl for several months, but that is no reason why I should wash up 3000 plates on my on.

The new service might have a military uniform – albeit a distinctive dull brown rather than khaki – but it eschewed military overtones in the names chosen for its ranks. Officers were called 'Administrators', NCOs were 'Forewomen', while ordinary WAACs were simply known as 'Workers'. Doubtless intentionally, there was no whiff or hint of martial glory in such downbeat nomenclature.

Dorothy Pickford went to France as an Assistant Administrator in January 1918 and stayed until February 1919. She became the manager of WAAC Hostel No 1 at St Omer, later fulfilling similar duties at WAAC Hostel No 2 at Rouen and then, from June 1918 (following the Corps's change of name and the decision to allow servicewomen to live under canvas), at QMAAC No 7 Camp, on the outskirts of Rouen. Basically her work was to look after the accommodation, discipline and welfare of the ladies in her charge. It was especially necessary to keep a

sharp eye on their morals, since there were many critics on the watch for the first sign of licentious behaviour among these new women warriors and the men whom they would doubtless tempt. By and large, it should be said, the cynics were discomfited, the optimists vindicated.

Miss Pickford described her experiences in a series of letters to her elder sister Molly (a person of distinction in her own right who later became a Member of Parliament). The following extracts give some idea of the satisfactions and problems of her new way of life:

30.1.18. I have just made an enemy for life by refusing a pass to a woman to go out with her 'friend' alone. This is strictly against all rules, they may go for walks with their best boys but they must be two together. It seems rather a strict attitude as of course they separate at the gate and only meet again when the pass has to be given up. No one is allowed to go out after 7 without a pass, and the gate is then shut. The exception is when they go to the YWCA Hut, for they are all marched back together by the Forewoman at closing time. I have not been down to the Hut yet, but I gather the lady in charge is a trial, they always are! When an entertainment is on at the Hut, no passes are given for walks or other entertainments, and this is a cause for grievance, most of the girls would far rather go out with their young men. I rather sympathise with them, as there seems to be something on nearly every night, and the concerts are not always particularly good.

WAACs bathing at Paris Plage, 29 May 1918, a sensational sight for men deprived for months on end of feminine company. (Q 11057)

Unit Administrator Dorothy Pickford. The daughter of a distinguished lawyer, who was elevated to the peerage as Lord Sterndale in 1918, she had done some ten years' voluntary work in girls' clubs before joining the WAACs. She died in 1971 at the age of 90.
(HU 63269)

14.2.18. After lunch I went down to the allotment – and dug furiously for an hour and a half, aided by about six Tommies and four girls. They all worked together well with no nonsense, and the corporal in charge, who was too grand a man to dig himself, kept off the crowds of small French *gamins*. The close of the perfect day was a party at the Hut. It was given by the Major of a battalion to his NCOs before they went up to the line again, and he invited so many WAACs to dance with them, and I think it was a great success. Of course he wanted me to dance, but it is one of the points that the UA [Unit Administrator] is adamant upon, we may never dance when the Workers do. I see it on the whole, that it wouldn't do for officers to dance with the Workers, but when it is like a Sergeants' dance at home where officers always dance, I don't quite see it, however, as you know, there is no questioning points on which she feels strongly.

In March there was a visit by the Commissioners, a group of five ladies whose somewhat severe attitude Miss Pickford found unnecessarily censorious:

14.3.18. They addressed the workers on the necessity of correct deportment, but they, conscious in their own rectitude, are only furious that a word should be said against them.

By contrast, there were certain light-hearted occasions for her WAACs to attend. On 28 August she described a visit to the Indian Base Depot sports day, which offered traditional sub-continental events such as Tent Pegging, Rings and Pegs, and Wrestling on Horseback, plus a driving competition and physical drill – the latter for recruits and 'quite wonderfully good'. Her party was made most welcome, nor was it confined merely to a spectator role:

There were musical chairs for WAACs, VADs, Administrators and ladies – as the Subaltern in charge rather unhappily remarked. I was not for it, though they tried to persuade me, for one thing I never could run, and for another I had field boots on.

In October they were visited by a well-known concert party:

3.10.18. We had a riotous evening at the mess on Saturday night after the Lena Ashwell concert. The performers are generally invited to supper and we go too. I had the second place of honour on the CO's left and on his right a Mrs Hodsall, who conducts the party and accompanies the singers. The conversation went with a swing, and it was well after midnight when we left. Service at 8 but 20 minutes' walk was rather an effort next morning.

Miss Pickford finally attained the rank of Unit Administrator. On 1 March 1919 she was given the honour of being mentioned in a despatch by Sir Douglas Haig, 'for gallant and distinguished service in the Field'.

Americans

Americans were different, there was no doubt about that. On 19 January 1918, the commander of the British 33rd Division, Major-General Reginald Pinney, visited Ypres and that evening wrote in his diary:

> 3.30 p.m. Walked to the Square. Met a group of American officers sitting on their baggage. Shook them warmly by the hand and found they were servants – no matter, equally welcome.

Some months earlier, Captain A. M. McGrigor, staff officer to General Birdwood, commander of the 2nd Division AIF, had become aware of the arrival at the front of some more senior representatives of the new ally. He noted under 9 October 1917: 'It appears numerous American Generals are being sent round to all the Corps to look into Staff work and administration.' One of them came to stay with the Australians for a few days, together with his Chief of Staff. 'Got a lot of information out of them as to how far on America is with her preparations; July is about the earliest that she will have an appreciable force in the field and then it should be about 21 Divisions.' McGrigor thought the General (Clements) a 'typical Yank, too old by far I should think to take the field in command of a Division', but the Chief of Staff seemed 'a very capable fellow'. He added: 'The old man very taciturn, but when he did speak he kept us in fits of laughter simply.'

McGrigor went into Ypres the following morning with the American General and General Birdwood. He was a little disappointed at the visitor's lack of reaction to the scenes of devastation. He commented: 'The old man was not quite as struck with the awful appearance of the town as I thought he would be, at least he did not say much.' He was much reassured later that day, however, when their other guest returned from a visit to the Salient:

> Colonel King, the American Staff Officer, came back bubbling over with wonderment from a trip up the line where he got a pretty fair eye opener coupled with a moderate amount of shelling. Everything was just 'bully' wonderful to him, particularly the enormous traffic and how it was controlled. He has quite impressed us and is, I should think, very capable.

Once again, as often happened in these early tentative interminglings of allies both linked and divided by a common language, it proved difficult to keep a straight face. McGrigor's diary continues:

> Some of these American expressions are just killing to our ears. They both said when they thought it was time to go to bed, 'Waal, I guess we might do worse than go and hit the hay for a spell.'

Not all such encounters were so benign. In a letter written, as it happens, that same week, Captain A. J. H. Smith, a British Staff Officer attached to HQ Fifth Army, told his mother of an encounter between a less than

Men of the American 77th Division under training with the British 39th Division, near Moule, 22 May 1918, with a member of the Machine-Gun Corps demonstrating British bulldog tenacity.
(Q 9076)

entirely tactful American and an Australian not so well disposed as McGrigor and his colleagues to welcome the new arrivals:

> There has been one American casualty so far. An American soldier met an Anzac in a bar and remarked that when the Americans arrived the Huns would run away. The Anzac replied that in any case, he (the American) would not be there to see it and brained him (literally) with a wine bottle. The story was told me by an American who took the Anzac's side. Otherwise the Americans seem to be delighted with the British Army and with the reception by Douglas Haig and the Army Commanders. I think that the relations between the two Armies will be excellent.

This was not always the case. Private Cude had a row with one which ended with the American being sent packing with oaths and curses. This seems to have soured his view of them. 'I wish them luck,' he growled into his diary in January 1918, hearing that some 'Yanks' had been attached to 8th Corps, 'and hope it is not long before they get what they deserve, a good hiding.' Private Maurice Gower, by contrast, came away benignly disposed from his first contacts with them when out on rest in May 1918, though his letters show evidence of a certain culture gap. He wrote to a sister:

We see a good many American troops round these parts. One of their bands performed in our village and played mostly ragtime including one fearful Indian war piece, in which the performers make noises and comic gestures; no doubt they could have played something decent, but the programme was evidently for our benefit. They played 'Rule Britannia' through four times, which was very nice of them, and finished up with the 'Star-Spangled Banner', which is the first time I have heard it played on a band.

I have had one or two talks with them and they strike me favourably, there is no 'swank', they seem anxious to learn and profit by our experience.

American and British troops fraternizing at a camp near Pas, France, 18 May 1918, with advice being offered about America's national game. (Q 8847)

In a letter to another sister, having now heard a second band in performance, Gower compared the American style with the British:

The American bands are perhaps more musical, if not so martial, their instruments are peculiar and unfamiliar to my eyes, but the men are evidently skilled musicians, most of foreign and in most cases Jewish appearance. The drums are the funny men of the party and indulge in juggling feats with their instruments. Of course they play mostly ragtime, but when they do indulge in a little civilised music, they play extremely well.

It was perhaps inevitable, so early in the 'special relationship', that a

Britisher should claim adjectives such as 'decent' and 'civilized' for the music of the Old World and listen with some wonderment to that of the New, but the vibrations were clearly favourable overall. So they were too in the experience of Brigadier-General The Hon. A. M. Henley of 127th Infantry Brigade, with which certain American units were in training at this time. Henley wrote to his wife on 28 May:

> My baseballers are active and intelligent people. They have a tendency to practise those arts at which they are already proficient – such as physical training and bayonet fighting, and to neglect tactical exercises of which they know less. Both their officers and men mix in the most friendly terms with mine – and they are constantly competing at bomb-throwing, rifle shooting, and so on – while they delight to give instruction in baseball especially in the conversational part. They are very keen to come up into the line with us, and I hope that they will. That experience is just what they want now – they are ripe for it, and will mature very much more quickly after it.

He returned to the same theme two days later:

> You cannot imagine how well my soldiers get on with my cousins. I was drawn into a concert with the latter this evening. The concert was quite vulgar and light-hearted – and an American Jew made fun of Jews in general, a new type of Semitic humour in my experience. But our men and theirs were all mixed up together, and talking intimately together, and though not more than 500 could have heard, there must have been 1500 on the hill side. I should like to fight next door to these fellows, and they would like to fight next door to me. They have beaten one of my battalions to a frazzle in bomb throwing, and we have beaten them with the musket – 'So – So – Together We Go'.

Lieutenant G. Havard Thomas, an infantry officer temporarily at Divisional HQ, also took a positive view when he found himself in regular contact during the preparations for the Allied advance. He wrote on 9 July:

> I have come across quite a lot of Americans and to all outwards appearances they are excellent troops and keen to learn.

Captain Arthur Gibbs, an officer of the Welsh Guards, spent some days with an American battalion actually in the line that summer. He described his experiences in a letter to his mother on 16 August:

> I quite enjoyed my four days with the Americans, and had an exciting time. They were raided twice; the first time the company I was with was in reserve, so I didn't see anything of the show. But Fritz put down a very heavy barrage and then came over. Two of the Americans were killed, but they killed the Boche officer, and none of the Americans was taken prisoner; a real good performance. The Boche officer had got into the trench and had had a duel with an American corporal: the corporal was wounded first, but he managed to kill the Boche, which after all is the main thing.
>
> The first night that my company was in the line, we were raided by a patrol. The Americans fired hard and beat them off, but they never reported anything to me. I heard nothing of the affair until about 5.30 a.m. when it was broad daylight, and they told me that they were sure that they had hit somebody and

they had heard him groaning. So I went out and after a bit of crawling round, I found a wounded Boche lying out in a shell hole, about 60 yards from our front line. I got him in and we got some valuable information from him. The whole thing was most exciting.

Gibbs' final comments suggest that while there was much in which the two Allies were in harmony, in other ways there was, and there would remain, a cultural gulf:

The Americans are splendid fighters, but their officers aren't much good at present: much too sympathetic with the men, and inclined to invite instead of order the men to do things.

I quite enjoyed my four days but the food was rather awful.

There had been some surprise that the newcomers took their time to become integrated into the Western Front war, but their commander, General John Joseph Pershing, was firmly against throwing American units piece-meal into the action even under the pressure of the German attacks of early 1918. When they finally came to bear their part, however, they did so with a determination and a commitment that showed that they had come to do serious business, and were prepared to take the knocks as well as the glory for the cause in hand. The staff officer Captain A. J. H. Smith wrote on 2 August:

The USA is now roused and the American people will not I think consider any kind of compromise, they are out for an idea, which may or may not be realisable but which in any case can only be realised by a decisive defeat of Germany in the field.

As they became more effective in the field, joining in the task of pushing the Germans further and further back, respect for their performance grew. Major F. J. Rice, 87th Brigade RFA, wrote enthusiastically to his parents on 14 September, having clearly picked up a buzz-phrase of the time:

Now things are going so well one feels good for almost anything. Isn't the American show 'just dandy'?

The Last Hundred Days: I

'They were a wonderful "last hundred days",' wrote Second Lieutenant R. H. Poynting, Royal Sussex Regiment, to a correspondent in England just before Christmas 1918, when the fighting was all over. 'In 1915 and 1916 – especially after the July push – it was hard to believe that we should ever get to open warfare again and only in the wildest dreams could one imagine the army streaming forward with guns in the open, untrenched country and hysterically grateful civilians.'

The 'Hundred Days' had begun with the opening of a major Allied offensive on 8 August. Over the subsequent weeks advance had almost mutated into rout, in that for the first time a great move forward had not slowed down and stopped, but, on the contrary, had overcome the usual hazards and difficulties and sometimes even gathered pace. It was the longed-for dream at last, war with a following wind. But it was never a walk-over, as Poynting went on to make clear:

> The advance was a very bitter affair, right to the finish, and though we had a comparatively kushi [sic] time, I saw more War in a few hours than in my previous seventeen months in the attack on the Hindenburg Line. Tanks ablaze, mortars ablaze, limbers smashed and strewn over the roads and streams of wounded Yankees and Tommies – and a regular battlefield.

As the offensive began to make progress, however, although there was a sense that the war was finally moving in the Allies' favour, there were few who conceived it might end in 1918. Even that most optimistic of officers, Colonel Bill Murray, would go no further than the hope that 'the balance of both territory and men will be in our favour by the end of the year'. That it should be all over with almost two months of 1918 in hand would seem almost unbelievable. As Captain T. H. Westmacott was to write on 5 November, under a week before the guns fell silent:

> It is difficult to realise what wonderful times we live in. I could not have believed, unless I had seen it, that the same men who were driven back by the Boche in the spring could have so completely turned the tables in the autumn.

Once more the chosen arena for the offensive was the Somme, and, as in July 1916, the British and French would attack side by side. Again it was the Fourth Army which would spearhead the British attack, but apart from such coincidences there was a world of difference between the two campaigns. This was an offensive backed by the most thorough preparation and highly professional staff-work, making intelligent use of tanks and aircraft, and launched with the element so well used by the Germans five months earlier – surprise. Ironically, nature even played the fog card, this time to the advantage of the Allies. The weight of numbers was also in their favour, with the British, for example, deploying twenty-one divisions against the Germans' fourteen. The Canadian and Australian

Corps, both of which had now acquired a formidable reputation for their fighting qualities, were to play prominent roles in the centre of the British attack.

In a much quoted phrase of the German war leader General Ludendorff, 8 August 1918 was to prove the 'black day of the German Army'. It was, also, undoubtedly a good day for the British Army, which was now a most formidable, well-balanced fighting force and, whatever questions there might be over the Haig of the Somme or Passchendaele, the Haig of 1918 was a Commander-in-Chief of grasp and vision – confident that he could win the war within the year. He was, as it were, a better leader of a better team. What makes the British achievement even more impressive is that the bulk of the new soldiers reaching the Western Front in 1918 were conscripts still in their teens.

Moreover, the German Army was now seriously weakened. The long attritional struggles of 1916 and 1917 had taken a severe toll and the huge efforts of early 1918 had in the end been more damaging to the attacker than the attacked. In the words of the British Official Historian, the enemy 'was no longer *ebenbürtig* [i.e., an even match], equal in skill and courage, and it did not require a 3 to 1 numerical superiority – his own calculation – to turn him out.'* A further blow to enemy morale was the fact of the immense and growing strength of the Americans, who now came increasingly into the action, suffering heavy casualties, but displaying that kind of dogged tenacity which had now become virtually a Western Front tradition. The game was up for Germany, in fact, though this was not necessarily apparent in the cut and thrust of battle and as the casualty lists continued to occupy many column inches in the newspapers back home.

Robert Cude, now chief runner to a Brigadier-General, was present at this crucial turning-point of the war. This is from his characteristically lively diary account:

> Early morning of the 8th, we move off across to see Jerry, and within a little while of the commencement of the attack, and while it is still in progress, I go forward with the Intelligence Officer and the General. We find that things are progressing favourably, and Jerry is hopelessly routed. All along the line things are going A1. It is amusing to see Jerry running away, but I will give him his due, he puts up a bit of a scrap before he is compelled to move.
>
> We watch the barrage that is covering the 12th Div slowly advancing, and then we see the men that are following up. It is a good sight, more especially as we can see things that they cannot see, as we are directly behind the front that they are attacking, and we see numbers of the Germans give themselves up. My eyes are on some of the Jerry gun-pits, as we see the Jerrys going in and out. Very soon Capt. Hayfield (Int Off), Capt. Heath (OC TM Batty) and myself are engaged in a race to get to the Jerrys and head them off. I reach the first dugout in advance of the others and find the inmate waiting for me. He offered no opposition to my relieving him of his revolver and his kit. He is a German Officer. The other officers having arrived, and as the 12th Div are coming up the gully, I have a good look through it and find a large fruit cake

---

*Edmonds, *Short History*, p. 361.

A wrecked bridge restored, by Australian Pioneers, at Chipilly; celebratory photograph, 17 August 1918.
(E(AUS) 3909)

that is promptly eaten between several of us. The sum total of my haul consists of Cigs, Cigars, Biscuits, Sweets, Hat, Stick, Gloves, revolver, one of the smallest that I have ever seen, and last, but not least, a small German camera. This latter article, with a bunch of papers that were in the place, I make a present of to Capt. Hayfield. We hand the gentleman over to a Sgt of the 12th Div, and carry on almost through the night, when we go back to Bde for a few minutes. We are off again however within an hour, and we carry on from there almost into Morlancourt, which place is alive with German troops. At 3 p.m. today, 9 August, and after watching one of our Tanks knocking the houses down, we retrace our weary steps homeward, after nearly 36 hours without a break of Intelligence Work, and hard work too.

The fighting soldiers had had little opportunity over the years to catch the whiff of victory, but now they began to show in their letters and diaries a distinct change of tone as the enemy, by fits and starts, fell back from one area after another of the Western Front. Major F. J. Rice, 84th Brigade Royal Field Artillery, gave signs of this in a letter of 21 August, which also told the story of an acutely embarrassing moment:

Two days ago I had quite a lot of excitements, one being that the Boche drew first blood from me and the other being that a horse I was riding was shot in

Capture of Grevillers by the New Zealanders, 25 August 1918; battle traffic at Grevillers, with Mark IV Tanks going forward. (Q 11262)

the near flank and through the wind-pipe while I only got a biff on the left thigh from a pebble or something which didn't hurt. In the first case I was occupying the latrine and the Boche was shelling a road about a quarter of a mile away and yet a bit came buzzing along and just cut my 'knickers', so to speak, or where my knickers should have been. In the second case we had six horsed ammunition wagons on the position, when the Boche put down a burst of field gun HE just over us. As we were ready to start I gave the order 'Walk March' but we had only gone 50 yards when one unfortunate shell fell very short, about 15 yards from me and wounded the horse I was riding (luckily not mine) and the groom's horse behind me (also not my groom or horse).

No more time; we are winning.

P.S. I call the first incident real '*Schrecklichkeit*'!*

Meanwhile, Rice's fellow Artilleryman, Colonel Bill Murray, was entering a period of increasing optimism and elation, even though he was in the Franco-Belgian border country south of Ypres where the German withdrawal took rather longer to get under way than at the centre point

---

*i.e. 'Frightfulness', of which the Germans were constantly accused by the British press throughout the war.

of the attack. Also in positive mood was Lieutenant G. Havard Thomas, 8th Battalion, Sherwood Foresters, who had seen hard and depressing times on the Somme during the winter of 1916–17, but now felt an increasing confidence and satisfaction in achievement. This is evident from these extracts from their letters.

Colonel Bill Murray, 15th Brigade, 13 August:

We keep on pushing out our line bit by bit and it exasperates the Hun beyond words. Last night he attacked us and drove back again a bit but we shall have him out of it tonight again. I wouldn't be a German here for anything. All night long our guns light and heavy pour tons of shells on all his roads, stations, billets and trenches. It must be a life of perfect misery and to feel too that he is taking a bad knock in the south where he hoped to end the war must be terribly galling. None of the prisoners we take know anything at all of what has happened here. They are still told that they are over the Marne and advancing on Paris, and simply won't believe that they have been driven back. This shows that the Higher commands daren't tell them. Which is an excellent sign.

Lieutenant G. Havard Thomas, 8th Battalion, Sherwood Foresters, 23 August:

We are pushing the Boche back all along the line and giving him socks into the bargain though some people think, and I am inclined that way, that he is going back in a lot of places merely to avoid an attack from us. I think the enemy will have another whack at us somewhere before very long, but we have learnt his ways now and he will only smash his horns a bit more.

Colonel Bill Murray, 1 September:

The last time I wrote we had just had a very successful battle. Well, we have followed that up and now have the Huns fairly on the run. Yesterday we pursued him 7 miles right back again to where he started in April. It is curious to look back on those dark days in April when we were hanging on to Ypres by our eyelids and just managing to hold up those furious attacks by which he meant to take his Channel ports. Who would have dreamt then that in four months we should be chasing him back thoroughly beaten?

Lieutenant G. Havard Thomas, 5 September:

I have been on the go for the last 10 days, nothing but hurried orders and moving about. The Hun has been going back and we are helping him to pack up. Yesterday we drove him out of some positions and I advanced about two miles with my company. The Hun fled like rabbits and when we had reached our objective some of them called us bad names from a safe distance! Yelling at us from behind miles of barbed wire, 'Come on Tommy, you ugly pigs.' We go out tonight and I hope to have a good night's sleep, a thing that I have not done since we last came in here. I simply fall asleep standing up. I am absolutely worn out for the time being.

P.S. Can you send me out one shirt, if you please? This one I have on now will walk away on its own when I take it off.

There was a distinct side-effect, however, to such heady momentum: exhaustion. Advances were being made beyond the capacity of those units expected to execute them. Captain Noel Saunders, 8th Battalion Border Regiment, wrote to his wife on 5 September:

> It is a very hard life now, compared to the war a year ago. I saw the Brigadier this morning. He looked worried and tired, like the rest of us. What is so bad is the continual moving over open country, both day and night, usually under shell fire. I wonder how long this kind of warfare will go on.

The speed of pursuit varied greatly. In mid-September Cude noted stiffening resistance on the part of the Germans as the fighting came nearer to the Hindenburg Line. Progress was steady but slow, with the Prussian Regiment opposite adopting new tactics of resistance which drew his admiration:

> The one dominant fact here is that Jerry's style of fighting has undergone a great change. I like it very much, and it is calculated to inflict the maximum of casualties on the advancing parties with the minimum of losses to himself. Every available bit of cover is utilised to screen a field gun or anything up to a dozen MGs and the whole are camouflaged beautifully, so we are unaware of being in their vicinity, until we hear the bark, and a number of men are down. We are paying for our advance here, and dearly too.

But the British too were showing their adaptability and skill:

> Early evening of today, 19 Sept, our boys spot Jerry massing for a counter attack under the cover of 3 fairly decent sized copses, and the SOS is put up and is immediately answered. It was a beautiful barrage, and when one considers that everything is being altered hourly, one marvels that the artillery can put down a barrage at all. This one, however, was a beauty, and the majority of guns are firing at open sights. In a few minutes the place where Jerry was seen has ceased to exist, and as a barrage has been put behind him to prevent him from getting back, he disappeared with the copse. This is undoubtedly the stuff to administer to the troops.

There was an unfortunte postscript to this, however:

> We have some casualties while the stunt is on, for some of the lads were so elated at the turn events were taking that they could not restrain themselves, and rushed forward to help in the work of execution, and incidentally into our own barrage.

The Hindenburg Line now lay immediately ahead, a system of defensive positions ten miles deep interwoven with machine-guns in concrete emplacements, with layer after layer of barbed wire, numerous anti-tank ditches, and artillery placed in carefully sited positions from which an enemy force could be annihilated as it appeared over the brow of the hill. It also incorporated the two canals of the region, the unfinished Canal du Nord and the operational St Quentin Canal – the latter a deep water-filled ravine interrupted by areas of high ground where the canal ran into tunnels. The attack came in late September, following a prolonged bombardment which while it had some effect on the defences also did away

with the element of surprise. In the end the advance was most successful at the point where success seemed the most unlikely. What became in effect an amphibious operation against the St Quentin Canal was assigned to a British Territorial Division which had not greatly distinguished itself on the Somme on 1 July 1916 but which now carried out a most remarkable feat of arms. This was the 46th (North Midland) Division, including the 8th Sherwood Foresters in which Lieutenant G. Havard Thomas – quoted above – was a company commander. His two letters written just after the event tell the story, and carry it forward over the following days:

> 30 September: The big attack went off yesterday morning and we advanced with great success. My company alone captured one Boche colonel and another 100 other ranks. We had a few casualties but not half what I expected. A great mist arose in the early morning and together with the smoke made direction very difficult, but with the aid of compasses I led my crowd to the right places. We had to cross a very large canal and the first waves had life-belts on, like going on leave. My colonel has recommended me for the Military Cross. I hope they give it to me.*

> 6 October: I daresay you have read in the papers of the deeds of the 46th North Midland Div., how we stormed the St Quentin Canal and the whole of the Hindenburg system capturing 4000 prisoners. 3 days after we were again

*They did.

Opposite: Albert, behind the Somme battlefield, as it was for most of the war, with its famous Golden Virgin statue, dislodged by German guns in January 1915, hanging from the tower of the Basilica of Notre Dame de Brebières. It was said that the war would end when the statue fell; it did fall, to British guns while Albert was in German occupation, in April 1918. (E(AUS) 168)

Above: Albert liberated: British cavalry in September 1918 passing the ruined basilica, with its tower and statue down, and the war not far from its conclusion. (Q 11315)

hurled at Fritz at a moment's notice and again we gave him Hell. This time we captured all our objectives and broke right through into new country behind where French inhabitants welcomed us as deliverers.

On the day before the 46th North Midland Division stormed the St Quentin Canal, Captain Dartford returned to Laventie. The town was now abandoned by the Germans but still within the range of their artillery. 'It was intensely interesting', he noted, 'to visit the scene of 9 April and think of all the events that swept over all that ground.' He sought out his former quarters:

> The house has completely fallen in and the brick of the walls has pressed down and obliterated everything. I found no trace of my kit or any objects belonging to the house. The wooden beams that appeared among the debris were all charred so that I think the house must have been on fire at some time. There was hardly a soul about. The main street is not yet used for traffic, being blocked with fallen trees and masonry. The old brigade HQ was still standing but inside was all broken up and any rubbish or papers lying about were German. The only Portuguese souvenir I found was a correspondence block with a note having Montalvao's signature. In the garden of the HQ was a grave with this on a board: '*Hier ruhen 2 Portugesen*' ['Here lie 2 Portuguese'], probably the sentries who were killed by a shell at the entrance there. Looking round at all these ruins it was hard to picture them as I first knew them, full of civilians and estaminets and gramophones.

Soon the enemy guns would no longer be able to reach Laventie, and other places which had suffered many months of devastation would also be freed from the threat of bombardment as the Germans withdrew eastwards. Dartford listed some of them in his diary on 3 October, additionally noting other omens from other fronts which suggested that for Germany and her associate powers the writing was on the wall:

> The Boche has gone back a lot on this front again and everything is moving. Aubers, Bois Grenier, Illies, Salome, La Bassée are all reported taken. Armentières will be next and Lille quite likely. S. Quentin has fallen and Bulgaria has accepted peace unconditionally. Damascus has been taken with 7000 prisoners.

3 October 1918 could also be called the first day of peace for Ypres, since the action in which the British finally broke out from the Salient had ended the day before. Officially known as the Fourth Battle of Ypres and dated 26 September–2 October, it was the shortest of the quartet of grim encounters fought in the town's vicinity which saved it from capture though not from almost total devastation by the enemy's guns. The healing process began soon after. Within a fortnight Major Ronald Schweder was writing to his wife:

> Ypres, I hear, is now quite a popular resort; VADs and nurses are now seen in the streets.

The Last Hundred Days: II

Early in October Captain G. W. Grossmith, a Company Commander in the 1st Battalion of the Leicestershire Regiment, took part in a prolonged and exhausting operation typical of the new war of movement which lasted from '6 a.m. on a Monday to 5 p.m. on a Saturday with no sleep whatever and scarcely once even sitting down.' There were numerous casualties, but at the end there was one of those moments of emotion, even exhilaration, which became increasingly common as the advance moved beyond the zone of guns, tank traps and barbed wire. His unit entered a little village called Bohain:

> As soon as we halted hundreds of civilians came running up the streets towards us and shook hands and kissed us and made a great fuss. It was all rather pathetic. They were chiefly old men, women, and girls, and even young boys were very few. They had been sheltering in their cellars during our bombardment and the German evacuation and were hysterical with joy at their liberation.

The eruption on to the scene of so many liberated citizens was good for the soldiers' morale, but it could cause difficulties, especially since enemy resistance was not yet quite on the ebb. Thus the Artillery officer Major C. E. L. Lyne in a letter of 25 October:

> The war is just at the moment not moving very rapidly, we've come up against rather a snag in front and the Boche is pretty strong, with beaucoup guns, but he can't hold on very long, we believe.
>
> We don't like to do much shooting as there are so many civilians about. It's curious to be mixed up with the civilians in the fighting. The Colonel was out with a BC [Battery Commander] looking for an Observation Post, and pitched on a likely looking house. 'Ah,' said the Colonel, 'here's a good place for an OP', and entered the door; immediately he was surrounded by a bevy of hysterical nuns. '*Vive les Anglais! Nos braves Alliés*', and all wanted to kiss him. It was a convent. 'Most embarrassing,' said the Col.

Major Ronald Schweder, billeted that same week in a comfortable farm-house untouched by shot or shell – 'I can't feel I am at war. Our house is perfectly good, and I have a wonderful bed' – observed that his men soon found willing helpers among the liberated populace:

> Looking out of the window as I write, I see 'Hester', the wench of the farm, helping the limber gunner of No. 1 gun to clean the breech-block, and another female aiding one of the gunners to chop wood.

Altogether Schweder was amazed and elated by the new kind of war, which had even reclaimed a touch of colour and dash:

> We go about nowadays mounted, doing reconnaissance; quite the picture style. A trumpeter toddles after me on a prancing steed.

Men of the 8th Liverpool Irish, 57th Division, photographed during the liberation of Lille, 18 October 1918. 'It wasn't a march that we made,' wrote one officer, 'it was a triumphal entry, amid inhabitants wild with happiness.' (Q 9574)

Cude, now promoted Sergeant ('Some Sgt' was his instant self-deprecating comment), was also to experience what he called 'the Joy of the liberated civis' when he led the way into a small French township after an attack in early November:

> It was with extreme care that I with six men walk down the main road, with rifles at the ready. Soon I see quite small children peering out of the doorways at us, and very soon every house pours out its quota of civis. I was staggered at the reception that I received. One house that I visited, after being invited in, was full of girls, aged 18 to 30 years, and I was embarrassed by the kisses that I had to submit to, but I have as much Cognac as I am able to carry for a while. Am more than unsteady in my walk, but I am considerably lightened by the fact that I gave my Bully and biscuits away to them.
>
> When I leave the place I find that the men of the town are already sawing up the huge trees that had been placed across the roads with a view to stopping our cars and transport.

Captain T. H. Westmacott, formerly Assistant Provost-Marshal to an Indian Brigade [see pp. 97–8], was now Deputy Assistant Provost-Marshal to 24th Division; in this capacity he was engaged full-time in collecting prisoners and contacting liberated civilians. In a letter written on 6–7 November he gave his wife a detailed account, at times humorous, at times poignant, of his demanding and often dangerous duties:

Here I am in the middle of a big battle and having a very eventful time. As you know from the papers the attack was launched yesterday. I was up at 6 and pushed my HQ forward to advanced Divisional HQ at Sepmaries where I made a prisoners' collecting cage in the remains of the school. They began to come in almost at once, and the Division took 15 officers and 311 other ranks in the course of the day, representing 22 different units, which is a good sign, as it shows how mixed the enemy is getting. Some of them were fine fellows but a lot were children of 15; there were some wounded among them and I made a captured German doctor look after them. I was much struck by the callous way he did it. I sent the wounded to our dressing station.

Having got the cage in working order I went out on the roads, where the traffic was very heavy, the enemy having blown up all the bridges behind him. I spent 4 hours at Maresch bridge, where 3 roads met; it was only a one-way bridge and the blocks were dreadful. The Sappers were working very hard to widen the bridge and I turned on a party of prisoners to help. I don't think they liked the idea of being shelled by their own people at all and they worked so hard that they soon had the job finished. I got back to DHQ about 5 and had my tea.

About 6 a message came in to say that a number of French civilians were in Wargnies-le-Grand. This being my job I got a car and went with Bourgeat our interpreter, to the 73rd Brigade, our advanced Brigade, where I was warned that fighting was still going on in Wargnies, but I had no option, and on we went along a road which was being heavily shelled, until we reached the HQ of the Northamptons, where the car had to stop owing to a big crater right across the road. We left the car here, the driver being very cool, while we walked into the village. We had a perfectly loathsome walk up the village, as it was being steadily shelled the whole time. It was pitch dark and we had to put on our gas masks. We searched house after house until at last we were answered in French from a cellar, and there I found the Maire and a lot of old women and children. It was most touching. Bourgeat was the first Frenchman they had seen, and they clustered round him and said '*Mon Dieu! C'est un vrai Français!*' and all kissed him. Then the women kissed me with the tears running down their cheeks. Then the Maire advanced on me. He hadn't shaved for days but I was firm. I shook him warmly by the hand but more than that I couldn't bear.

When the time came for us to go the poor women prayed for us to stay, not as protection to them, but because they feared we might be killed. In fact they all got so weepy and sentimental and I was getting a lump in my throat myself, and I said, in French, 'Ladies, I am married, and I don't know what I could say to my wife if I were to spend a night in a cellar with so many beautiful women.' The eldest was 92 and the youngest about 50, the Germans having carried off all the girls and young women. They all laughed and the situation was saved.

Then we started back down that nightmare of a road. However, we got through the barrage all right. Just before I reached the car I passed a British soldier just killed, so my luck was in. The driver was sitting in the car contentedly smoking a cigarette, though he had been under intense shell-fire for two hours without cover.

A dead German machine-gunner at his post, 20 September 1918, at The Knoll, Hindenburg Outpost Line, where he had been opposing the advancing Australians.
(E(AUS) 3791)

> At last I got home about ten, and I don't think I shall hear the last of the dirty old Maire trying to kiss me.

But the enemy was still fighting hard. Continuing his letter under the heading 'Same day. Evening', Westmacott wrote:

> I saw a German machine-gun turned towards the enemy, evidently used by us against them. The German machine-gunner had fought out to the last, and he had been hit in the throat. He was lying on his back with his head propped on an ammunition box, his right knee drawn up and his left arm raised towards the gun barrel as if he was making a last effort to stop our people from using it. A yard away lay two of our own dead.
>
> Col Hebden, commanding the Royal Fusiliers, was with me, and he said 'By God! that was a brave man, and I shall see that he is decently buried.'

By now the air was full of rumours that the war was about to end. An acceptance of defeat had been evident among captured Germans for some time. In mid-October Sergeant Robert McKay of the 36th Ulster Division, moving his Regimental Aid Post steadily forward, found large numbers of prisoners mingling with the wounded coming back from the fighting zone – mostly dismounted cavalry, the 3rd, 7th and 9th Uhlans. The name 'Uhlan' no longer carried the sense of menace and danger that it had done in 1914. 'Prisoners have lost heart entirely,' noted McKay. 'They admit now that they are beaten and the majority seem glad to be taken. About eighty passed through the 2nd Battalion today.' The wheel was coming full circle. Before long the name Mons would be featuring in operation orders, but as a town to advance to, not retreat from.

Above: The Pity of War: French and British wounded coming in from the battlefield; Battle of the Marne 1918. (Q 6864)

Left: Dead horses, smashed limbers. Almost half a million horses died in the war on the British side alone.

As October moved to its end the tide of German dissolution began to flow. Ludendorff resigned on 27 October to forestall dismissal. On the 29th the German fleet mutinied. On the 30th Germany's eastern ally Turkey signed an armistice with the Allies, while her principal European one, Austria–Hungary, followed suit on 3 November. The Kaiser abdicated on the 9th and Germany became a republic. In a railway carriage in the Forest of Compiègne a Franco–British delegation headed by Marshal Foch offered terms to German delegates who had little option but to agree. Echoes of all this produced a special anxiety among those still engaged in fighting or were within the range of the enemy guns. Entering yet another liberated town, Bavay, with a different interpreter, Luneau, Captain Westmacott suffered quite a jolt:

> As we dismounted at the house of the Maire, a shell hit it and a splinter passed between Luneau and me. Rotten luck if I get done in with the end in view, won't it?

This thought was in countless minds on 11 November, when the news finally broke that hostilities would end that day at 11 a.m. As the last hours ticked away Sergeant Cude wrote:

> If only I can last out the remainder of the time, and this is everyone's prayer. I am awfully sorry for those of our chaps who are killed this morning, and there must be a decent few of them too, for mines are still going up, and will continue to take a price from us for months to come yet.

At last it was eleven o'clock:

> 'Stand Fast' was sounded by bugles, and our minds were taken back to our training days, so many years ago. With the thoughts of the past come thoughts of the good chaps who were with us, but have now departed for all time, having paid the Supreme Price, for the cause of Freedom. When I think of them, I have a keen sense of loneliness come over me, for in my four years out here almost I have missed hundreds of the very best chaps that have ever breathed.
>
> I should have preferred to be in London today, I guess that there is high jinks there, we cannot get a drink to celebrate today except a good issue of Rum!

For most, perhaps, the reaction to the news awaited for so long was low key, without any of the 'high jinks' which Cude correctly guessed would take place in London. Thus Captain T. H. Westmacott on 11 November:

> There was no great demonstration by the troops, I think because it was hard to realize that the war was really over. Shortly before 11 a.m. our Divisional Artillery let the Hun have it with every available gun. I never heard such a roar. A great contrast to the deathly silence which followed at 11 a.m.

The Australian, Corporal Oswald Blows, who had survived many battles since Pozières, wrote the following reflective comment in his diary:

> November 11th: I feel like a soldier who has marched far with his pack and has taken it off for a rest – rid of the burden but the pack is still there. I cannot realise it – it will be long before we realise that peace is for us. Thoughts too

cannot but fly to those who are not with us – who have paid the awful cost that hostilities might cease, as today.

Captain Dartford was with his Portuguese who, after the severe loss of credibility resulting from their performance back in April, were now back in the Allied lines as part of the newly reconstituted 5th Army – though they would be too late to be involved in any serious fighting. The task of reintegration had been carried out by a G.1 (GSO Grade 1) senior staff officer who would win much fame as a commander in the Second World War. Dartford had noted in his diary under 1 November:

> G.1 is Col B. L. Montgomery, a strong personality and he has arranged how the Port are to be attached.

They had moved forward into Belgium and on 10 November had reached the town of Froyennes, near Tournai. His mind as ever had been concerned with the problems which seemed constantly to afflict his 'geese'. When the 23rd Portuguese Battalion had continued its advance on the morning of the 10th, they had left fifteen men behind because they had no respirators, and they had been abandoned without rations or orders. Perhaps it was this, or perhaps it was just an inevitable war-weariness after so many difficult and frustrating months, that produced a less than jubilant diary entry under 11 November:

> As we expected, the Boche has agreed to our armistice terms and at 11 a.m. today we were ordered to cease hostilities. So we have at last reached the Day, and everybody is tremendously pleased.
>
> Division moved to La Tombe, on the other side of the Scheldt and is ordered to concentrate in that area. All troops to stand fast and adopt normal precautions. Nobody knows what ought to be done really and existence seems pointless. Much talk of how and when demobilisation will start.

Not all reactions were muted, however. The following extracts are from the diary of Sergeant Robert McKay (though the 'news' to which he and his colleagues responded on the night before was not strictly true, since the official act of signature did not take place until 5 a.m. on the 11th):

> Nov 10th. 9.30 p.m. News came through that Germany signed the Armistice. Whole country ablaze with Very lights and bands are parading and troops cheering.
>
> Nov 11th. Hostilities ceased at 11 o'clock a.m. today. Guns in the distance kept firing away up to last minute. Great rejoicing.

Colonel Bill Murray too was in buoyant and optimistic mood. He wrote home, happily unaware of what the future might bring:

> No more danger. No more horrors. No more mud and misery. Just everlasting peace. It is a grand world.

Above: Five minutes to go. Irish Guardsmen at their posts at 10.55am on 11 November 1918. Near Mauberge. (Q 3344)

Right: The Colonel and men of the 9th East Surreys cheer the King at St Waast. Near Bavay, 12 November 1918. (Q 3362)

Endings

It was a climax, but it was not quite a conclusion. There was a new subject in men's minds: getting home.

For many quoted in this book there was no homecoming. There would, in time, either be a grave in a military cemetery or a name carved on a memorial for Tom Allen, Philip Brown, A. P. Burke, Harry Dillon, Geoffrey Donaldson, Richard Downing, William Edgington, Valentine Fleming, Kenneth Garry, Reginald Gill, Eric Heaton, W. T. King, J. A. Liddell, Kenneth Macardle, Mick Mannock, Rowland Owen, James Paterson, Alec Reader, Noel Saunders, Harry Stephen, J. R. Webster, Dudley White, A. R. Williams, Irving Wilson, Neville Woodroffe. For others such as B. C. Jones or Frederick Norman there would be the special problems of life as an amputee.

For some categories among those who had come through there was a speedy return. For others the weeks and months dragged on, until, after many protests and even riots, the slow process of demobilization at last released them to rebuild their lives in a world more or less at peace. Some would continue with their military duties. Captain T. H. Westmacott was among those who marched on into Germany to become part of the garrison of the Rhineland. He wrote this account for his wife on 13 December 1918:

> I have seen a sight today which I shall never forget. There are three bridges over the Rhine at Cologne, known as the Mulheim bridge, the Hohenzollern bridge, and the Suspension Bridge. Our infantry began to cross the Rhine at 9.15 a.m., the 9th Div. by the Hohenzollern bridge, and the Canadians by the Suspension Bridge. Until 1.15 p.m. they poured across in three dense columns. So as to do things really well, the German police were told to see that no wheeled German traffic was allowed on the streets, and they obeyed their orders to the letter. There were big crowds of Germans looking on in spite of the rain, but they seemed more curious than anything else. I saw one woman in tears, poor soul, but bar that it might have been almost an English crowd. General Jacob, my Corps Commander, stood under the Union Jack by a big statue of the Kaiser, at the west end of the Hohenzollern bridge, and took the salute of the 29th Div., one of the finest fighting divisions in the British army, being the division which earned undying glory in Gallipoli.
>
> The men marched with fixed bayonets, wearing their steel helmets, and carrying their packs. I wish you could have seen them – each man making the most of himself, and full of pride and *élan*. Then came the guns, turned out as our gunners always turn themselves out. Mind you, the Division was fighting hard all through the last battle, and they have been marching steadily through Belgium and Germany for the last 30 days, but the horses were all fit and hard as nails, and the buckles of the harness were all burnished like silver. The mules were as fit as the horses, and went by wagging their old ears as if they crossed the Rhine every day of the week. A German looking on, said that the

Division must have just come fresh from England. It is difficult to remember what we were like last March and April, during the retreat of the 5th Army, and to find ourselves here as conquerors in one of the proudest cities of Germany.

As for the battleground of the Western Front, it was littered everywhere with the detritus of war. There would be a long task ahead to restore the scarred landscape to some semblance of normality. It could never be quite restored, of course, and there would be many who would not want that outcome anyway. In a letter of 20 December 1918, Second Lieutenant R. H. Poynting wrote: 'The Somme is a vast cemetery. When I hear of people suggesting a monument to Victory in the War I wonder what is wrong with the Somme district for this purpose.' His hopes have been largely realized: the Somme countryside is certainly a monument, if not to victory, then to the men – of all nations, enemy as well as ally – who fought there. So also with the Ypres area, though there the site of so many fearsome encounters reverted with remarkable speed to a busy, prosperous part of Belgium. This much dismayed former Gunner H. A. Coulter when he went there on an early battlefield tour in 1927. He sent his wife a postcard of the ruined Cloth Hall (reproduced on p. 260) with the following message on the reverse:

It has been a terrible disappointment. The war is gone for ever – only a memory now. What we last saw as a vast desert of shell holes, bare tree stumps, mud, filth, smashed guns and tanks and dead men, is all waving cornfield, pretty gardens, brand new villages, noisy estaminets, charabancs, quarrelling children, and flighty girls. It makes one's heart thump. The only things left to remind one that memories once *were* immense realities are the cemeteries and the poppies.

Perhaps he might have been less disturbed now, three-quarters of a century later. The 'immense realities' of which he wrote have not been forgotten. People come in increasing numbers to visit the 'immortal' Salient, wonder at the ravaged ground at Hill 60, walk the preserved trenches at Sanctuary Wood, stroll among the 11,000 graves at Tyne Cot Cemetery, or stand on the ridge at Passchendaele (now spelt Pasendale), from where they can look back towards the towers of the marvellously restored town of Ypres, where every night at eight o'clock at the Menin Gate – a gigantic memorial arch opened in the year of Coulter's visit and bearing the names of nearly 55,000 dead whose bodies were never found – members of the local Belgian community celebrate those realities in the playing of the Last Post.

THE CHANGING FACE OF YPRES

'They may burn Ypres, but they will never take it.'
Diary of Captain T. S. Wollocombe, 4th Middlesex Regiment, 19 May 1915

Right: Ypres: the Market Place featuring the famous thirteenth-century Cloth Hall.

Halles d'YPRES avant la Guerre
YPRES — The Cloth Hall, before the Great War

LES HALLES D'YPRES 1912

Below: Destroyed 1919
(HU 63275)

Ruines d'Ypres
The ruins of Ypres
Ruines des Halles et Grand'Place.
Ruins of the Halls and Market Place.

YPRES   Le Beffroi et les Halles
YPEREN Het Belfort en de Halle
YPRES   The Belfry and the Cloth Hall

Left: Being rebuilt 1927.
(HU 63276)

Below: Restored, 1962.
(photograph taken in 1991)

An Afterword on Attitudes

For many years now the First World War has been a field of conflict between two schools – almost two armies – of thought. There have been those who accept the alleged ethos of the time and see the events of 1914–18 as a hard but heroic struggle in which huge losses were philosophically, even proudly, accepted. By contrast, there have been those who believe that the bravado and cheerfulness shown during the war concealed an increasing sense of futility and disillusion.

Which prompts the question: how did things seem to the soldiers featured here, writing without benefit of hindsight, or with any awareness of the clash of views to come – many of them not living even to have the opportunity of entering into the subsequent debate?

Most offered no comment at all. Rights and wrongs, whys and wherefores did not come within their area of expression. This does not mean, however, that they had no views. On the contrary, there seems to have been a basic feeling shared by the majority of ordinary soldiers that, to put it simply, they wanted the war to be over and they wanted to go home. Hence for example Private Harry Stephen's longing for 'Dear Old Sunny Australia and Home Sweet Home' (see p. 123), or Cude's 'Hurry up Peace. This is undoubtedly the heartfelt wish of all the troops operating on Somme' (p. 153). Similarly Private W. T. King, 2nd Battalion London Regiment, could write on 27 May 1917 (three weeks before he was killed):

> My dear Alf, Here I am again, Old Boy, with my energetic pencil, and as per usual quite gay and hearty, and waiting for a Peace proclamation.

Or there is Bombardier J. W. Palmer's variant written in his diary at Loos in 1915: 'All I long for is home and to get out of this living Hell.'*

However, if there were many who did not commit their thoughts to paper, there were plenty of others who did. Indeed, there was much in the material studied that was notable for its outspokenness and for the seriousness of the questions it raised. More, and surprisingly, critical comments were not confined to the second half of the war – i.e. to the period which followed the slaughter of the Kitchener's volunteer army on the Somme and which for many years has been associated with the 'disenchantment' voiced by writers such as C. E. Montague (in his book of that name published in 1922), or Siegfried Sassoon and Robert

---

*For confirmation of the widespread obsession with peace cf. the statement quoted in my *Imperial War Museum Book of the First World War*, p. 246: 'There was more peace talk to be heard in the line itself than anywhere and it would have been foolish to try and stop it.' This is from a document by a former chaplain, Reverend, later Canon, E. C. Crosse, written as Section I of a History of the Chaplains' Department in the war which was never published. Crosse also makes this interesting comment on what was on the mind of the average Tommy: 'The soldier's ordinary conversation centred round the probable duration of the war, the improbable advent of leave, and the possible arrival of a decent ration, or a move to a "cushy" sector.'

Graves. On the contrary, they began early, during the opening campaigns of 1914 fought by the professionals of Sir John French's BEF. After reading the letters and diaries of some of the members of this first force in the field, it became clear that there were those among them who were soon dismayed and disturbed by what was taking place around them.

'We are getting nearer the Great Event,' wrote Lieutenant Rowland Owen, 2nd Battalion Duke of Wellington's Regiment, to his 'dear M. & F.' – his mother and father – on 23 August 1914, shortly before his baptism of fire in the Mons campaign. He felt almost sorry for his people because they could not be there with him: 'It is not right', he told them, 'that I should have an awfully good time and you not share it.'

Yet it was not long before the experience of action had a sobering effect on his views. There were few hints of enjoyment and distinct symptoms of resignation when he wrote on 6 September:

> I am looking forward to coming home, and I don't mind how soon it is; but I suppose it is one's duty to remain out here to endeavour to smash up the German Empire.

By the end of the month, he had become openly condemnatory about the war, yet there also were the first shoots of a hopefulness that something of permanent value might be achieved because of it, despite the destruction and suffering it entailed:

> I have not met a single man (or horse) of the English, French or German armies who is not dying for the war to finish! John [his Naval officer brother] and the Kaiser alone want to keep on. I often feel that this war has done a lot towards the world's peace. You see: if all goes well, we ought to win the victory which swallows up all strife, like Waterloo; and that ought to keep the peace for, say, 50 years. *By that time I think the really universal feeling against war will manage to make soldiers a thing of the past.* (Author's italics)

This is surely an astonishing statement from a professional officer in the second month of a war to which he had gone with such high anticipation, and for which eventuality he had been training for three years. Yet he was plainly not alone in the hope that what was becoming a very brutal and bloody conflict would be soon over. More, there was a considerable anger at those who had caused the war in the first place. 'Ghastly, absolutely ghastly,' Captain James Paterson, Adjutant of the 1st South Wales Borderers, wrote in his diary on 16 September about the grim stalemate on the Aisne: 'and whoever was in the wrong in the matter which brought this war to be, is deserving of more than he can ever get in this world.'

Most outspoken of all was Captain Harry Dillon, Company Commander of the 2nd Battalion Oxford and Bucks Light Infantry. After his vivid description (see p. 27) of the virtual annihilation of a German Regiment, and of the pathetic cries of its wounded and dying afterwards, during the First Battle of Ypres, he expressed his thoughts to his family in these forthright terms:

> Well, I suppose if there is a God, Emperor Bill will have to come to book some day. When one thinks of the misery of these wounded and later on of wives,

mothers and friends, and to think that this great battle where there may have
been a million on either side, is only on a front of about 25 miles, and that this
sort of thing is now going on on a front of nearly 400. To think that this man
could have saved it all. The proposition is almost too vast to get a grip of. It is
ruining thousands of lives, from the Bay of Biscay through France, Germany,
Russia, India and right to Siberia, poor wives and people are waiting to hear.
It really is the greatest calamity the world has ever seen.

I don't care one farthing as far as I am concerned, but the whole thing is an
outrage on civilisation. The whole of this beautiful country devastated.
Broken houses, broken bodies, blood, filth and ruin everywhere. Can any
unwnding everlasting Hellfire for the Kaiser, his son, and the party who
caused this war repair the broken bodies and, worse, broken hearts which are
being made? Being made this very minute within a few hundred yards of
where I am sitting. Well, them's my sentiments.

Whatever their views, officers like Paterson, Owen and Dillon held firmly
to their duty and, in all three cases, paid the ultimate price. As already
described (see p. 28) Paterson died of wounds on 1 November 1914.
Similarly (see p. 72) Owen was killed in action leading a charge at Hill 60
on 18 April 1915. Dillon, having won the DSO, survived until 1917, then
was invalided back home; he died, of pneumonia, in January 1918.

By contrast, a strongly expressed *positive* view of the challenging
circumstances of the early campaigns occurs in a letter written by Captain E. W. S. Balfour, Adjutant of the 5th Dragoon Guards. He wrote it
on 3 December, when the hard fighting which culminated in First Ypres
was over. While recognizing the awfulness, in normal terms, of what had
taken place, he yet saw glory in it also:

There is some provision of nature with us now which stops us minding
anything as long as the Germans don't get on, and after all if people sat down
and dispassionately, or rather half-dispassionately, contemplated everything
in cold blood, on really bad days, they would proceed to go mad. But when all
is done, and one realises the achievement of the whole, we are all thrilled with
pride at the result and with humbleness and gratitude to the people who have
died, and no one but us out here can realise what willing sacrifices they were,
and that it is really the best and bravest who have died, and all the best soldiers
in this close fighting.

You can't for long go on looking at the sordidness, for romance comes
knocking much too loudly and insistently – the realisation of the ends
involved, the line of guns from here to Belfort which we have heard unceas-
ingly for sixteen weeks: the 11 German Corps against the 4 English ones, but
much more the people who have died.

As the Western Front became institutionalized, what had so shocked – or
moved – these thoughtful professionals was no longer news but commonplace, a fact of life. The very scale of the deadlock war was such that
men became dwarfed by it, and numbed by it, but clearly they also came
to be absorbed into it, and to accept its inevitability, almost its permanence. Many, indeed, came to think of the Front as the only place to
be, finding themselves restive, even alien, in the civilian world they

encountered when on leave. There was a different language spoken in 'Blighty', with too many explanations to be given; back in the trenches everybody understood. From this it was not a long step for some to revel in the fighting, seeing the war as a stage for the display of courage, manliness and gallantry of the highest order. Perhaps the most striking example of such a viewpoint already quoted in this book is the belief expressed by Major 'Mick' Mannock VC that 'strife and bloodshed and physical "exertion" and mental anguish are all good, glorious, wonderfully beneficial things for the human race' (see p. 191).

Yet many men of known gallantry did not subscribe to such views. Another air VC quoted is Captain J. A. Liddell, in his earlier incarnation as a lieutenant and machine-gun officer of the 2nd Argyll and Sutherland Highlanders. When Liddell wrote such comments as (see p. 44): 'It's a war with no glamour or glory such as one expects in a huge world-wide show like this. Modern war is too deadly, and the whole art of war, and all tactics as laid down in the text-books, has been quite altered . . . I'm sure none of the 10,000,000 or so combatants would mind if peace were declared tomorrow', he was aligning himself more with the sceptical officers of the first BEF quoted above than with the philosophy of a Mannock (or with Balfour, also quoted above). In other words, great valour did not necessarily imply a grand, heroic ardour; it might also go hand in hand with the feeling that war, far from being splendid and glorious, was a cruel and wasteful way of settling quarrels between nations.

But what of the balance of views overall? It would seem that where soldiers did express themselves in this context, positive (i.e. more or less pro-war) statements, and negative (i.e. more or less anti-war) statements, occurred in more or less equal proportions.

Here is a small 'anthology of attitudes', from a range of branches, times and situations. It is divided into two sections: 1, broadly favourable comments: 2, broadly critical ones. Each section is printed in date order. It will be noted that most quotations are from officers, especially in category 1. Significantly, two young officers are quoted in both sections, for it should be stressed that it was not uncommon to move between opposing viewpoints, or indeed to hold them both simultaneously; in the words of Second Lieutenant Edward Beddington-Behrens, one of the two officers quoted twice, it was possible to be aware both of 'the mud' and 'the stars'.

Section 1: Favourable Quotations

Second Lieutenant Cyril Rawlins, Transport Officer 1st Battalion Welch Regiment, letter to his mother, 13 August 1915:

> Three o'clock on a wet morning, our machine-gunners coming along from the trenches: they have been eight days in, eight days of deadly peril, of strain, of constant watchfulness, no sleep at night, exposed to the full force of the elements, pestered by flies and lice, and the terrible stench of rotting corpses. They have negotiated a mile of tortuous communication trench, deep in mud,

and marched four miles, encumbered with gear, they are rather wet, too: when they get to their huts, they will have a place on the hard boards, and their greatcoat to cover them: they will lie down all wet as they are, and sleep. Do they grumble or complain of fatigue? Not they. Every man is singing lustily: the front two sections constitute the 'band'. Front section getting a splendid crashing kettledrum effect out of the ubiquitous biscuit tins, slung with string round the neck: second section blowing their mouth organs fit to bust. You wouldn't appreciate the song they sing: it would look silly on paper: but to hear it, another matter. They swing along to their own outrageous clatter, every man happy and jovially blasphemous, hurling coarse wit at their fellows, greeting each guffaw with guffaws of laughter. Doesn't it make a fellow's heart swell with pride to hear them, to be one of them: isn't it a privilege to offer one's life side by side with them? May there be a special Heaven for all of them, and a very special Hell for all those curs at home, fattening in safety behind the protection of their brawny arm, growing rich by their sacrifice.

Lieutenant John Staniforth, after a particularly violent raid by his 7th Leinsters in June 1916, in the course of which no quarter had been asked or given:

We are still holding the line; a little under strength, you will understand, and not quite the same battalion. There are some empty dugouts, perhaps, and some fire-bays without sentries in them, and maybe a platoon or two commanded by a sergeant; but we are still holding the line, and we have not asked for reinforcements. It was the first show the Irish have had, and we have done – not so badly. Wherefore we are proud and 'aughty, and the world is very good.

Second Lieutenant Edward Beddington-Behrens, 126th Battery RFA, 5 July 1916:

You may think by my preceding letter which gave description of night fighting that I only 'see the mud' and 'not the stars'; it is not the case but one cannot help seeing the terrible side of this war, but there are thrills about it that make you feel that life was small without them. Just at the critical moment when life and death are in the balance you suddenly see life in a different light. You have none of the sordidness of everyday life! The finest qualities of humanity are displayed by men who are looked down on as inferior because of their wealth and education but who, when the time comes, show that *original goodness* which we are all born with.

Captain Irving Wilson, Manchester Regiment, from his letter to Captain W. Mulholland (see pp. 112–14), written shortly after the first day on the Somme (Wilson was killed in action November 1916):

I like fighting – as simply the most glorious and exciting kind of game. I don't mean that I would go out of my way to seek it as a holiday amusement, but now when it happens to be business, and duty and pleasure coincide, one may confess that it is fun.

The Kaiser (or whoever it was) I believe to have been right when he called War a 'high and holy experience'. It *is* that – among other things – I mean in the way that everyone is at his best in the face of death, and puts the cause and his neighbour first and himself nowhere. I think it was so, wasn't it? Or is it a figment of my imagination? I had the feeling on the day and night before [i.e. before 1 July] that we all loved each other more than we had ever loved anything before, and more than we loved our own lives; and that we each knew and knew that the rest of us knew, if you see what I mean. I seemed to see it in the men's faces and to feel it under the frivolity with which, being English and damnably sophisticated, we masked our feelings.

Captain Geoffrey Donaldson, 2/7th Battalion Royal Warwickshire Regiment, letter to his mother, July 1916 (killed in action 19 July 1916):

Don't think I'm unhappy or pining because I'm not, and this is a great experience. There have been moments of excitement, too. I wouldn't have missed it for anything. So don't worry, it's a long lane that has no turning.

E. G. de Caux, a French officer of the 3rd Regiment of the Line and for many months Official Interpreter to the Post Office Rifles: extract from a letter to Lieutenant-Colonel Eric Gore-Browne, formerly an officer with the battalion, written in September 1916 after the battalion had taken part in the capture – with heavy losses – of High Wood:

I wish some great French artist would paint a picture of the Roll Call of a British Regiment after one of those devastating yet splendidly victorious engagements on the Somme: a hollow square of jaded muddy figures standing in an orchard open on one side to the after glint of a Sun that set red: mist begins to float up the valley, but the glint of light on some clouds high up still has the hardness of silver. A strong voice such as Vince's calls one name after another from a Roll lit by a fluttering candle shaded by the hand of the one remaining Sergeant-Major. A dark mass of tall trees in the background. There should never, never be anything but a brotherly feeling amongst Frenchmen for their English Comrades after the War. And you do it all so simply. On the eve of battle one would think you were preparing for a football match. Compared with earlier experiences of operations, what one meets on every side here is admirable.

Second Lieutenant E. F. Chapman, 20th Battalion Royal Fusiliers, letter home dated 14 February 1917:

As you say, life can never be the same again as it was before August 4th 1914. But I think it will be *better* after the war than it ever was before. We must have learned a wisdom that nothing else would have taught us. And when we get home again we shall have the happiness of men who have seen terrible things, who have been in hell, and have come back to a blessed heaven of peace. Different from the old happiness, but more permanent.

Lieutenant Kenneth Mackenzie, 9th Battalion, Duke of Wellingon's West Yorkshire Regiment, undated letter c. 1917 to a young doctor about to join the RAMC:

The Army is an exacting master and will take everything you can give, and more. Yet it is a splendid and noble job we are on, and the Huns *must* be crushed.

Private Andrew Munro MM, 50th (Calgary Bn) CEF, July 1917, in a letter to his parents (already quoted, see p. 143):

> Yes, dad, we all heartily wish it was over, but it is just as you say. Not one of us wants peace until we get the right peace, and everyone knows what that is.

Section 2: Critical Quotations

Captain Eric Gore-Browne (see above), Post Office Rifles, letter to his wife, 7 August 1915:

> Sometimes I think this war must end soon as there are so many people who hate it so. I have met nobody who was not sick of it though everybody is cheerful and quietly confident.

Second Lieutenant Cyril Rawlins (as quoted above), Transport Officer 1st Battalion Welch Regiment, letter to his mother, 12 October 1915, after his battalion had suffered in the Battle of Loos:

> You once sent me a little poem, saying that war was not altogether bad, but it is, it must be, a thing accursed, altogether devilish, as if the spirit of Evil had laid hold upon this world in this terrible form: perhaps it is God's judgement upon the world for our complex and vicious civilization, and yet it is hard to see how to kill all the best men of Europe is going to mend matters: all the degenerates, all the criminals are left. I will try to go on writing my letters: if I can: I feel better now, but I was sick at heart and broken in spirit after the battle, and could not think: I saw the faces and forms of my dead comrades: how they looked: their jokes and last words only a few short hours before: I almost wished myself with them, out of it all: only for your sake: there was no good in the world: a world of death, and blood and filth unspeakable: England, and home, and you, and all things peaceful and beautiful, a dim remembrance of past existence.

Second Lieutenant Edward Beddington-Behrens (as quoted above), 126th Battery RFA, letter of 16 July 1916, after finding the unburied bodies of some soldiers recently killed:

> Well one can really see the other side of this frightful war. The cold-blooded murder of all these fine fellows and waiting out there a fortnight to be buried. I found them by the horrible smell. Thank goodness I don't drink as the rum I took did me a lot of good. I think we will all return with Peace at any Price after the war.
>
> It is all very well for people at home to sit in armchairs and jaw but if they came out here just for one night they would have their eyes opened and would not want any more.

Corporal Oswald Blows, 28th Battalion, AIF, on the fight for Pozières on the Somme (see p. 119ff), diary entry, August 1916:

> Why should men slaughter one another like this? Out there is wholesale slaughter. The number of our men who returned is about 160 – out of the 500 who went in.

Second Lieutenant S. Wilkinson, 9th Battalion, King's Own Yorkshire Light Infantry, letter to Miss Lewis c. 14 August 1916:

> The worst part of a war is *memory*. Thoughts on one's people and friends in England come round whenever military matters can be put aside for the time being. Then one realizes the hideousness of war – the waste of time, brains and money and what is far more important the opportunity of carrying on with one's life work.

Sergeant Richard Downing, RFA, letter to his parents April 1917 (died of wounds May 1917):

> God! How I long to have it all over! One gets so fed up to think one is wasting the best part of one's life owing to that Archdevil the Kaiser, when I ought to be assisting dear Father and making things easier for him!

Major Ronald Schweder MC, RFA, letter to his wife, 2 May 1917:

> Who was the person who told your father 'Peace in two months'? How I wish it could be true. The casualty lists are awful. The results of the war and all the sacrifice will be sweet nothing, I expect.

Lieutenant Harry Graham, Staff Officer, 40th Division, letter to his wife during the Battle of Cambrai, 28 November 1917:

> War is perfectly horrible, and I am rapidly becoming a Pacificist. I would sooner we sank to a 5th Rate Power than that my grandchildren should have to undergo these experiences again.

Corporal D. L. Rowlands, 15th Battalion Durham Light Infantry (who later won the MM), letter to his future wife, 5 February 1918:

> Perhaps you would like to know something of the spirit of the men out here now. Well, the truth is (as as I said before I'd be shot if anyone of importance collared this missive) every man Jack is fed up almost past bearing, and not a single one has an *ounce* of what we call patriotism left in him. No one cares a rap whether Germany has Alsace, Belgium or France *too* for that matter. All that every man desires now is to get done with it and go home. Now that's the honest truth, and any man who has been out within the last few months will tell you the same. In fact, and this is no exaggeration, the greatest hope of a great majority of the men is that rioting and revolt *at home* will force the government to pack in on *any* terms. Now you've got the *real* state of affairs 'right from the horse's mouth' as it were.
>
> I may add that I too have lost pretty nearly all the patriotism that I had left, it's just the thought of you all over there, you who love me and trust me to do *my* share in the job that is necessary for your safety and freedom. It's just *that* that keeps me going and enables me to 'stick it'.

In the light of such forceful yet contrary opinions it seems absurd – even with so small a sample as is here offered – for one school of thought or the other to claim that it holds the true doctrine about the Western Front war. Doubtless on the one hand most soldiers accepted the nature and purpose of the fighting unquestioningly, but on the other there was certainly much serious concern at the waste of life and the destructiveness of the war, and it is surely a matter of sheer common sense that this should have been so. The men who fought the First World War were not a race of unthinking automata but a mass of individuals with their own instincts and responses. To acknowledge that there were those who raised doubts and questions about what they witnessed or experienced is not in any way to detract from or denigrate the commitment or the achievement of the soldiers of the Great War. It is to recognize their right to the kind of freedom of thought that we in our generation automatically claim for ourselves. It is surely time that a truce was declared between the opposing camps, in that both sides clearly have a part of the truth, but neither can lay claim to the whole of it.

It should perhaps be emphasized that these quotations were not neatly stacked like so many shells in carefully balanced files, but were found virtually haphazardly while researching collections of letters or diaries in pursuit of other subjects. They were noted over many months: only as the research came to an end did it seem that there was enough material to make a worthwhile contribution to the debate that has divided historians of the Western Front for so long.

There is perhaps space for a personal word in conclusion. It has been a moving as well as a fascinating experience to spend so many months in the company of the soldiers who are quoted in this book – and of numerous others, who for one reason or another were not included. Reading their accounts, often written with their authors not knowing whether they would survive to write the next letter or turn the next page in their diary, one came to see them, not as objects of research, but as people whom one might have known and with whom one might have become friends. Their youthfulness was particularly, and poignantly, apparent too, in that by concentrating on accounts written at the time there was no risk of hearing the veteran's tone of the later memoir or of a tape recording made in old age. From so much rich material, it would be almost invidious to pick out one statement with which to finish, but if there is a keynote sentence which has lingered longer in the mind than most it is that in which Private, later Sergeant, Robert Cude, the free-thinking battalion runner of The Buffs, expressed his basic philosophy of Western Front life: 'Must grumble, but carry on.' This, surely, is the authentic accent of the Tommy of the First World War and, quite as much as the process of trial and error which turned the British Army into the formidably successful force it eventually became, helps to explain why the war ended as it did in 1918.

Index of Contributors

This index serves two purposes: it lists those whose writings are here quoted and gives due acknowledgement to the copyright owners who have kindly allowed the publication of material held in the Museum's collections. Their names appear in round brackets after those of the contributors with whom they are associated. Every effort has been made to trace such copyright owners; the Museum would be grateful for any information which might help to trace those whose identities or addresses are not known.

Ranks are as they were at the time of the experiences described. In the case of fatalities, the place of burial or commemoration is given in square brackets; these details have been supplied by the Commonwealth War Graves Commission, whose help is gratefully acknowledged. Figures in italics refer to illustrations.

Gunner W. R. Acklam 122; Second Lieutenant Tom Allen Killed in Action 26/2/15 [Cuinchy Communal Cemetery] 50–1, 91, 94, 258; Private Harold Anderton (Mr Donald Anderton) 64; Corporal C. A. Ashley 77–9; Captain E. W. S. Balfour (Mr P. E. G. Balfour CBE, Mr J. Balfour OBE MC) 33, 264, 265; Captain J. W. Barnett (Mrs C. Robertson) 49, 72, 74; Second Lieutenant Gordon Bartlett (Mr Arthur Crane) 70–1, 179; Captain Hadrian Bayley (Mr James Collier CB) 82; Second Lieutenant Edward Beddington-Behrens (Dr Stephen Kane) 95, 265, 266, 268; Captain W. Bell 96; Sapper Hugh Bellew (Mrs Jean Ashenhurst, Mr Christopher Wright) 6, 15; Corporal Oswald Blows (Mr C. R. Rush) 120, 254–5, 268; Reverend J. F. Bloxam 195–6; Private J. L. Bramley 213–14, 215–16, 218; Sapper Harold Brooks (Mr D. E. A. Brooks) 90, 100, 156–7; Second Lieutenant Philip Brown Killed in Action 4/11/15 [Ration Park Military Cemetery, La Chapelle d'Armentières] 51–3, 258; Private A. P. Burke Killed in Action 9/10/17 (Tyne Cot Memorial, Belgium) (Mr Francis A. Fogarty) 139, 258; Brigadier-General F. M. Carleton DSO (Mrs J. B. Carleton) 125–30, 125; E. G. de Caux 267; Lieutenant E. F. Chapman (Dr R. E. Chapman) 68, 267; Lieutenant Dougan Chater (Mr Michael Chater) 44, 46; Captain Cosmo Clark (Mrs J. M. Clark) 216, 219–20; Sergeant F. E. Collins 172; Second Lieutenant H. E. Cooper (Mr Peter Cooper, Miss Patricia Cooper) 105–7; Gunner H. A. Coulter 104, 220, 259; Brigadier-General E. Craig-Brown (Mrs Katherine Dean, Mr John Martin) 171–2; Sergeant T. H. Cubbon 19, 32, 137; Private, later Sergeant Robert Cude MM (Mrs Susan M. Ashton) 108, 150–3, 153, 154, 234, 239–40, 243, 250, 254, 262, 270; Lieutenant, later Captain R. C. G. Dartford MC (Mr James Dartford) 165–8, 167, 221, 248, 255; Captain, later Major

Harry Dillon DSO Died (of pneumonia) Alexandra Hospital, London 13/1/18 [All Saints, Spelsbury, Oxfordshire] xi–xii, 18, 19, 20, 27, 31–2, 134, 189, 258, 263–4; Sapper David Doe 182, 228; Captain Geoffrey Donaldson Killed in Action 19/7/16 [Ploegsteert Memorial] (Miss Hilary Hamilton) 41, 116–19, 116, 137, 258, 267; Sergeant Richard Downing Died of Wounds 11/5/17, [Duisans Cemetery, nr Arras] (Mrs Carole Sherwood) 59, 61, 258, 269; Corporal William Ebsworth (Mrs Stella Skinner) 175; Lieutenant T. C. Eckenstein (Miss Genevieve Eckenstein) 174; Sergeant, later Lieutenant William Edginton Killed in Action 8/5/15 [Menin Gate, Ypres] (Mrs Anne Shakeshaft) 5, 13, 17, 25, 28, 47, 74–5, 75, 258; Captain Valentine Fleming DSO MP Killed in Action 20/5/17 [Templeux le Guerard Cemetery, Somme] (Mr Nicholas Fleming) 28–30, 33, 258; Private, later Second Lieutenant Kenneth Garry Died of Wounds 18.6.17 [Grevillers Cemetery, Bapaume] 53–5, 258; Major F. S. Garwood (Mr James Osborne) 31–2; Lieutenant John Gaussen 121; Sergeant Albert George (Mrs Barbara Horwill) 9–11, 13–15; Captain Arthur Gibbs MC (Mrs Jennifer Keeling, Mr Christopher Palmer) x, 236–7; Captain Reginald Gill MC Died of Wounds 28/9/17 [Lijssenthoek Military Cemetery, Belgium] 104–5, 119–20, 258, 269; Captain, later Lieutenant-Colonel Eric Gore-Browne DSO (Mrs F. Hugill) 59, 66–7, 96, 102, 267, 268; Corporal J. W. Gower (Mr G. Gower) 65; Private Maurice Gower (Mr A. Gower) 229–30, 234–5; Lieutenant Harry Graham (Mrs Laura Dance) 269; Private Raymond Grimshaw (Mr Brendan Grimshaw) 189; Captain G. W. Grossmith MC (himself) 249; Bombardier Dudley Gyngell (Mrs Phyllis Wilmott) 214–15; Captain A. H. Habgood (His Grace the Archbishop of York) 15, 20; Lieutenant G. Havard Thomas MC (Mrs G. Havard Thomas) 146, 155, 236, 242, 245, 248; Second Lieutenant Eric Heaton Killed in Action 1/7/16 [Hawthorn Ridge No 1 Cemetery, Somme] 55, 56–7, 64, 258; Brigadier-General the Hon A. M. Henley CMG DSO (Mrs Juliet Daniel) 236; Private Walter Hoskyn (Mrs B. Rudge) 184; Private W. A. Hoyle 216–17; Private Albert Johnson 171, 174–5; Bombardier B. C. Jones 87–8, 88, 139, 258; Lance Corporal Jim Keddie 73, 74; Private W. T. King Killed in Action 16/6/17 [Arras Memorial] (Mrs A. Chesher) 258, 262; Second Lieutenant Gilbert Laithwaite (The President and Fellows of Trinity College, Oxford) 206–8, 209–10, 217–19, 228; Lieutenant B. L. Lawrence 146–9; Captain J. A. Liddell VC MC Died of Wounds 31/8/15, [Basingstoke (South View or Old) Cemetery, Hampshire] (Mrs Gillian Clayton) 44, 48, 258, 265; Lieutenant L. S. Lloyd (Mr Michael Lloyd) 66, 83, 154–5; Brigadier-General Lord Loch CMG MVO DSO (Lady Loch) 114–5,

114n, 159–64, 159; Captain C. J. Lodge Patch MC (Mrs Jean Hewitt) 208–9, 212; Major C. E. L. (John) Lyne x, 198–9, 249; Captain P. H. B. Lyon MC (Miss Elinor Lyon, Miss Elizabeth Lyon) 225–6; Second Lieutenant Kenneth Macardle (served as Callan-Macardle) Killed in Action 9/7/16 [Thiepval Memorial, Somme] 99, 102, 258; CQSM Robert Scott Macfie (Mrs M. S. Paton) 46–7; Captain A. M. McGrigor (Mr P. M. McGrigor) 178–9, 233–4; Sergeant Robert McKay (Mrs M. Middleton) 186–8, 252, 255; Lieutenant Kenneth Mackenzie (Dr Andrew Mackenzie) 154, 180, 217, 267; Second Lieutenant G. Macleod Ross 180; Captain Arthur Maitland 20; Major Edward (Mick) Mannock VC DSO MC Killed in Action 26/7/18 [RFC/RAF Memorial Arras] 190, 191, 258, 265; Sapper G. J. Matkin (Mrs Ruth Henderson) 78, 79–80; Lieutenant A. G. May (Mr E. Linholdt Jnr) 89–90, 137, 138, 172–4, 176; Captain Charles May (Mr H. W. Karet) 109–10, 157–8; Lieutenant I. L. Meo 123–4, 123; Captain H. Meysey-Thompson 87, 99–100, 108; Private H. J. Milton 25–6; Private T. G. Mohan (Mrs Dorothy G. Mohan) 180; Captain P. Mortimer 48; Captain Will Mulholland 112–14, 266; Private Andrew Munro MM (Mr Donald A. Munro) 91, 93, 140–4, 140, 268; Major, later Lieutenant-Colonel William Murray (Mr George Murray) 72, 182, 185, 223, 225, 238, 241–2, 255; Private Frederick Norman (Mr R. Norman) 87, 258; Captain C. L. (Neville) Overton MC (Mr Richard Overton) 89, 183–4, 222–3, 228; Lieutenant Rowland Owen Killed in Action 18/4/15 [Menin Gate, Ypres] (Captain C. H. H. Owen RN) xi (quoted anonymously), 5, 15, 19, 20, 38–9, 38, 72, 258, 263, 264; Captain F. E. Packe (Mr A. H. Packe) 48–9, 93; Bombardier J. W. Palmer (London Borough of Waltham Forest; Archives Collection, Vestry House Museum) 41, 61, 82, 87, 262; Major-General Sir Archibald Paris 111; Captain James Paterson Died of Wounds 1/11/14 (Ypres Town Cemetery, Menin Gate) 1, 5, 6, 7, 17–18, 19, 25, 27–8, 258, 263, 264; Sister Jentie Paterson (Mr A. Ian Buchanan) 36–7; Battery Sergeant-Major Douglas Pegler 60, 64, 89, 115, 169, 189; Private Edward Penny DCM (Mr Malcolm Fife) 119; Miss (later The Hon) Dorothy Pickford (Mrs C. H. Pickford) 230–2, 232; Major-General Reginald Pinney CB (Group Captain P. G. Pinney CVO RAF) 233; Second Lieutenant R. H. Poynting 238, 259; Second Lieutenant S. H. Raggett MC (Mr P. N. R. Raggett) 93, 94, 99; Second Lieutenant Cyril Rawlins (Mrs Beryl Ridley) 78, 83, 91, 95, 180, 265, 268; Private Alec Reader Killed in Action 15/9/16 [Thiepval Memorial, Somme] (Mr Roger Goodman) 65–6, 122–3, 122, 137, 258; Sergeant Bert Reeve (Mr Peter Reeve) 5, 15–16, 17; Major F. J. Rice (Miss Jennifer Rice) 91, 93, 237,

240–1; **Private S. T. H. Ross** (Mr and Mrs L. J. H. Ross) 30, *30*; **Corporal D. L. Rowlands** (Miss J. Rowlands) 269; **Captain George Samuel** 200–1; **Captain Noel Saunders** Killed in Action 20/10/18 [Amerval Communal Cemetery Extension, Solesmes] 243, 258; **Captain, later Major Ronald Schweder MC** (Mrs Andrina F. Tritton) 55, 67–8, *68*, 89, 99, 137, 138, 149, 154, 203, 228–9, 248, 249–50, 269; **Private E. C. J. Sheppard** 75–6, *76*; **Sergeant Albert Slack** 210–12; **Captain A. J. H. Smith** (Lady Darwin) 233–4, 237; **Lieutenant, later Captain John Staniforth** (Mrs Rosamund du Cane) 50, 51, 55, 58–9, 89, 91, 93–4, 100, 102, 134–5, 178, 203, 210, 266; **Private Harry**

Stephen Killed in Action 11/4/17 [Australian National Memorial, Villers-Bretonneux] 123, 258, 262; **Second Lieutenant P. D. Stewart MM** (Mrs Janie Howard) 210; **Private Charles Tames** 177–8; **Staff-Sergeant F. R. Thornton** 21–4, *22*; **Major H. E. Trevor** 95; **Private G. Ward** 135–7; **Major J. R. Webster DSO MC** Killed in Action 22/3/18 [Pozières Memorial] 194–5, 258; **Captain T. H. Westmacott** (Mrs Elizabeth Hughes) 97–8, 238, 250–2, 254, 258–9; **Corporal Dudley White** Killed in Action 9/10/17 [Tyne Cot Memorial, Belgium] (Mrs V. M. Collins) 131–2, 258; **Second Lieutenant S. Wilkinson** 269; **Private, later Second Lieuten-**

ant A. R. Williams Killed in Action 16/8/17 [Tyne Cot Memorial] (Mrs Dorothy Beddows) 94, 180–1, 258; **Captain Irving Wilson MC** Killed in Action, 28/11/16 [Anchor Cemetery, Beaumont-Hamel] 258, 266; **Lieutenant T. S. Wollocombe** (Mr Richard Wollocombe) 6, 8, 9, 11–12, 260; **Lieutenant Neville Woodroffe** Killed in Action 6/11/14 [Menin Gate] (Brigadier J. H. P. Woodroffe DSO) 1, *34*, 34–5, 137, 258; **Captain Oliver Woodward** 94–5, 169, 171; **Lieutenant, later Captain J. D. Wyatt** (Mr J. H. Wyatt) 46, 64, 67, 69–70, 107; **Lieutenant, later Captain Harry Yoxall MC and Bar** (Mrs Lindsey Pietrzak) 93, 109, *184*, 185, 192–4.

General Index

Figures in italics refer to pages with illustrations.

Abbeville, 67
Aerial photography and observation, 59, 69, 160
Air warfare, xii, 50, 162, 188, 189–91, *190*, 194, 213, 238
Aisne, Battle of the, xi, xiii, 3, 18–20, 25, 35, 263
'Alberich', 147–8
Albert, 25, 119, 121, 214–15, 217, 218, 220, *244*, *245*
Allenby, General Sir Edmund, 159, 160, 163
American forces, 233–7, *234*, *235*, 239, *see also* United States
Amiens, 67, 125, 129, 212, 219–20, 221
Amputations, 37, 87–8, 139, 258
Anzacs, *half-title*, *61*, 178, 234
Argyll and Sutherland Highlanders, 44, 48, 265
Armentières, 25, *33*, 227, 248
Armistice, ix, 24, 36, 88, 139, 254–5
Arras, 147, *161*, *162*
  Battle of, 25, 123, 139, 142, 149, 159–64, 178, 198
Artillery, ix, 13–14, *26*, *58*, 58–63, *60*, 160, *161*, 183, 185, 206, 214–15, *224*, 243
Ashwell, Lena, 154, 232
Australian forces,
  Bullecourt, 123, 159; last 100 days, 238–9, *240*, *252*; Messines, 169, 171; mules, *63*; night fighting, 163; no executions, 97; patrols, 104; Pioneers, *240*; Pozières, 119–21, *119*, *121*, 268; reputation, xiii, 121, 178, 238–9; style, 120–1, 141; Third Ypres, *197*, 269; trench life, 123; Tunnelling Company, 94, 169; *see also* Anzacs

Bayonet fighting, 31–2, *85*

Beaumont-Hamel, 180, 217
Bellewaarde, 176
Béthune, 66, 67, 88
Billets, 46, 55, *64*, *65*, 223
Birdwood, Lieutenant-General Sir William, 178, 233
Blaney, Norah, 154
'Blighty', 69, *197*, 265; wounds, 69, 89, 216
Border Regiment, 243
Boulogne, 6, 36, 38
British Expeditionary Force (BEF), xiii, 3–4, 7, 11–12, 17, 25, 28, 165, 205, 263
Brothels, 158
Buffs, The, (East Kent Regiment), 108, 150, 270
Bullecourt, Battle of, 139, 159
'Bullring', *84–5*
Byng, General the Hon. Sir Julian, 200

Cambrai, 66, 200
  Battle of, 69, 200, *201*, 269
Canadian forces,
  Cologne, 258; Concert Parties, *157*; executions, 97; last 100 days, 238–9; Munro, 91, 140–4, 268; reputation, xiii, 121, 178, 238–9; Second Ypres, 73–4; Somme, 140–1; Third Ypres, *181*; Tunnelling Company, *170*; Vimy Ridge, 142, 159
Canal du Nord, 206, 243
Capper, Major-General Thomas, 31
Casualty Clearing Stations, 4, 36–7, *37*, 88, 124, 134, 186
Cavalry, *1*, 7, 8, 12, 13, 28–30, 59, 75–6, 78, 82–3, 97, 114, 161, *245*, *see also* Horses
Cavell, Nurse Edith, 21
Cemeteries, 90, 230, 259
Censorship, 67, 141–2, *172*, 177
Chaplains, xii, 95–6, 98, 134, 195–6, 262n
Chemin des Dames, 225
Cheshire Regiment, 97
Christmas Truce (1914), 47–9, *49*, 168

Churchill, Winston, 134, 219–20
Clemenceau, Georges, 220
Clements, General, 233
Conscripts, xiii, 180, 239
Contalmaison Château, *100*
Crosse, Reverend E. C., 262n
Croy, Prince Réginald and Princess Marie de, 21

Devonshire Regiment, 113
Dragoon Guards, 29, 33, 264
Dressing Stations, 70, 134, 174, *183*
Duke of Wellington's (West Riding) Regiment, 5, 15, 38, 217, 263, 267
Dunkirk, Dunquerque, 29, 158
Durham Light Infantry, 51, *193*, 225, 226, 269

East Surrey Regiment, 194, *257*
East Yorkshire Regiment, *105*
Enemy, attitudes to, 48, 72–3, 107, 123, 147, 152, 168, 179–81
Entertainments, 154–8, *155*, *156*, *157*, 213, 232
Escape organizations, 21
Essex Regiment, 20
Etaples, xiii, *84–5*, 88
Executions, military, 96, 97–8

Fatalism, 93–5, 134
Fatigues, 64–6
Feilding, Lieutenant-Colonel Rowland, 108
Festubert, 71, 93
Field Ambulance, 15, 20, 186–8
Fifth Army, 159, *183*, 192, 205, 208, 212, 213, 216, 220, 233, 255, 259
Fifth Army, German, *11*
First Aid Posts, 134, 186, *187*, 187–8, 208
First Army, xiii, 69, 159
Flers-Courcelette, Battle of, ix, 132, *139*
Flesquières, *210*
  Salient, 207
Foch, General (*later* Marshal) Ferdinand,

205, 223, 254
Fog, 205, 206, 238
Football, 157–8
Fourth Army, 159, 238
French, Field-Marshal Sir John, ix, xiii, 17, 43, 83, 104, 263
French forces,
    Arras, 159, 162–3; Artillery, 37; *Cuirassiers*, 37; Cycle Corps, 37; Divisions, 12, 28, 73; Dragoons, 37; government, 17; mutinies, 160; senior partner in alliance, x–xi; Somme first day, 112; Verdun, 71; wounded, 253
Frezenberg Ridge, Battle of, 75–6
'Friendly fire', 18, 34, 243
Fromelles, Battle of, 116, 119, 137

Gangrene, 20, 87–8
Gas, gas warfare, 72–3, 74, 77–82, 79, 117, 174, 186, 199, 206, 207, 208
GHQ, xiii, 6, 160, 164
'Going Over the Top', 134–9, 135, 142, 175
Gordon Highlanders, 44, 71, 113, 214, 228
Gough, General Sir Hubert, 159
Graves, Robert, 262–3
'Green cross' envelopes, 141, 142, 177
Grenadier Guards, 146, 159
Guns, *see* Artillery

Haig, General (*later* Field-Marshal) Sir Douglas, xiii, 69, 77, 83, 111, 126n, 131–2, 137, 151, 223, 232, 234, 239
Havrincourt Salient, 206
Hazebrouck, 36
High Wood, 123, 127–8, 267
Hill 60, 38, 71–2, 73, 169, 171, 259, 264
Hill 70, 80–1
Hindenburg Line, 147, 148, 149, 200, 238, 243, 245, 252
Honourable Artillery Company (HAC), 53, 176–7
Horne, Lieutenant-General (*later* General Sir) H. S., 126, 159
Horses, 10–11, 17, 44, 61, 177–8, 201, 202, 215, 217, 240–1, 249, 253
Hospitals, 36, 88, 124, 134, 213, 218, 228
Howitzers, 58, 60
Humour, 99–102, 100, 101, 154–6, 228
Hussars, 8, 9, 16, 19, 26, 29, 32, 45, 66

Indian troops, xiii, 29, 48, 72, 97
Intelligence, 59, 69, 108, 160, 225, 239–40
Irish Guards, 4, 34, 50, 91, 93, 94, 256

'Kaiser's Battle', ix, 108, 205, 206–12, 207, 209, 211, 215
King's Liverpool Regiment, 46, 70, 184
King's Own Royal Lancaster Regiment, 126, 183, 222
King's Own Scottish Borderers, 72
King's Own Yorkshire Light Infantry, 95, 269
King's Royal Rifle Corps (KRRC), 99, 108, 109, 184, 192
Kitchener, Lord, xiii, 17, 33, 43, 152–3, 159
Kitchener volunteers, xi, xiii, 33, 113, 115

La Bassée, 78, 248
    Canal, 88, 223
La Boiselle, 110–11, 119, 152
Laboureur, Jean-Emile, 103
Lancashire Fusiliers, 206, 217, 219, 228
Lancers, 28, 98
Landon, Major-General H. J. S., 126–7, 129
Langemarck, 27, 72
    Battle of, 186, 195
Laventie, 221, 248
Le Cateau, Battle of, xiii, 3, 13–15, 95

Le Havre, 5–6, 13, 77
Leicester Yeomanry, 76
Leicestershire Regiment, 249
Leinster Regiment, 50, 91, 178
Lens, 78, 182
Liaison officers, 165–8
Liberation, 249, 250
Lice, 37, 102, 265
Lille, 248, 250
Liverpool Irish Regiment, 250
Liverpool Scottish, *see* King's Liverpool Regiment
Lloyd George, David, 171, 182
London Regiment, 64, 65, 165, 172, 262
London Rifle Brigade, 79
London Scottish, 28, 30
Loos, Battle of, 43, 61, 65, 69, 77–83, 79, 80–1, 87, 91, 96, 115, 179, 262, 268
Loyal North Lancashire Regiment, 21, 184
Ludendorff, General Erich von, 239, 254
Lys, Battle of the, 222, 224

Machine-Gun Corps, 131, 234
Machine-guns, 9, 12, 45, 120, 132, 176, 185, 193–4, 216, 243, 265
Mametz, 113, 217
Manchester Regiment, 99, 109, 113, 158, 217, 218
March attack (1918), *see* 'Kaiser's Battle'
March Retreat (1918), 213–20
Maricourt, 213, 215
Marne, Battle of the, 3, 17–18, 20
Medals and awards, 104, 108, 120, 152, 153, 164, 172, 192, 209, 212
Medical services, *see* Casualty Clearing Stations, Dressing Stations, First Aid Posts, Hospitals, Nurses, RAMC, Stretcher-bearers, Wounded
Mellish, Reverend E. N., 96
Menin Gate, 75, 259
Menin Road, 31
    Battle of the, 192–6, 193
Messines,
    (1914), 28–31
    (1917), 43, 137, 169–75, 172, 175, 176, 186
Middlesex Regiment, 6, 8, 11, 15, 55, 128, 185, 216, 219
Mines and mining, 72, 169–73, 170, 175, 176
Moltke, Helmuth von, 3
Monchy-le-Preux, 161
Mons, 3, 7, 8, 23, 252
    Battle of, 4, 8–12, 25, 263
    Retreat, 1, 4, 12, 21, 34, 74
Montague, C. E., 262
Montgomery, Colonel Bernard Law, 255
Mud and rain, 33, 44, 46–7, 62–3, 146–7, 152, 182, 184–5, 193, 196, 198–9, 265–6
Mules, 63, 217
Murray, Lieutenant-General Sir Archibald, 12

Nantes, 6, 17, 36
Nerve, loss of, 123–4, 137–8, 194, *see also* Shell-shock
Neuve Chapelle, 117, 165
    Battle of, 69–71, 71, 87
New Zealanders, xiii, 85, 97, 171, 178, 190, 241; *see also* Anzacs
Night fighting, 163, 266
Nivelle, General Robert, 159, 162–3
No Man's Land, 50, 59, 99–100, 104–10, 114, 116–17, 119, 139, 166, 207, 215
North Somerset Yeomanry, 75–6
North Staffordshire Regiment, 146
Northamptonshire Regiment, 67
Northumberland Fusiliers, 55

Nurses, xii, 36–7, 228, 229

Observation Points (OPs), 59–60, 61, 82, 207, 249
Owen, Wilfred, 94
Oxfordshire and Buckinghamshire Light Infantry, 18, 27, 31, 135, 263

Passchendaele, 63, 150, 182, 198–9, 199, 259, *see also* Ypres, Third Battle
Patrols, 104–7, 105, 117
Periscopes, 54
Pershing, General John Joseph, 237
Pétain, General Henri Philippe Omer, 164
Peyton, Major-General W. G., 130
Pilckem Ridge, Battle of, 182, 183, 186
Pill-boxes, 186, 187, 187–8
Ploegsteert ('Plugstreet'), 51, 61, 108
    Wood, 53, 169
Plumer, General Sir Herbert, 171, 192
Poppies, 117, 143, 259
Portuguese forces, xiii, 165–8, 166, 167, 221–2, 248, 255
Post Office Rifles, 59, 66, 122, 267, 268
Pozières, 119–21, 121, 268
Prisoners, 8, 31, 37, 69, 108–9, 119, 160–1, 176–81, 177, 179, 181, 209, 210, 225, 226, 227, 242
Prussian Regiment, 243

Queen Alexandra's Imperial Military Nursing Service Reserve, 36
Queen Mary's Army Auxiliary Corps, 228
Queen's Own Oxfordshire Hussars, 28
Queen's Royal West Surrey Regiment, 208, 212
Queen's Westminster Rifles, 48

'Race to the Sea', 25, 26
Raids, 104, 107–10, 107
Railways, 68, 69, 78, 206
Rawlinson, General Sir Henry, 126
Refugees, 15, 211
Religion, 91–3, 95–6, 125, 134, 142
Richthofen, Baron von, 190
Rifle Brigade, The, 91, 146
Royal Army Medical Corps (RAMC), 15, 20, 36, 267
Royal Artillery (RA), 18
Royal Engineers (RE), 6, 8, 77, 78, 128, 180, 182
Royal Field Artillery (RFA), 5, 9, 13, 43, 58–9, 67, 72, 75, 82, 87, 93, 95, 104, 198, 200, 240
Royal Flying Corps (*later* Royal Air Force), 144, 189
Royal Fusiliers, 68, 128–9, 133, 175, 180, 185, 216, 252, 267
Royal Garrison Artillery, 58, 199
Royal Horse Artillery, 5, 13, 28, 58, 75, 202, 223
Royal Horse Guards, 76
Royal Irish Rifles, 177
Royal Naval Division, 111
Royal Scots, 177–8
Royal Sussex Regiment, 123, 238
Royal Warwickshire Regiment, 105, 116–18, 121, 137, 267
Royal West Kent Regiment, 171
Runners, 150–3
Rupprecht, Crown Prince, 182

St Eloi, 28, 169, 170, 219
St Omer, xiii, 29, 77, 88, 190, 230
St Quentin, 15, 205, 209, 248
    Canal, 243, 245, 246–7
Sassoon, Siegfried, 262

Scarpe, Third Battle of the, 163
Schlieffen Plan, 3
Scots Guards, *frontispiece, 33*
Second Army, xiii, 192
Self-inflicted wounds, 19, 35, 137
Shell fire, 10, 19, 173, 199, 206–8, 243
Shell-shock, 124, 138, 173
Sherwood Foresters, 100, 146, 194–5, 242, 245
Siegfried Stellung, 147
Smith-Dorrien, General Sir Horace, xiii, 13, 83
Snipers, 19, 34, 184
Soissons, 17, 35, 147
Somme,
    (1916), 43, 98, *100,* 104, *110–11,*
        111–21, *112,* 123, 125, 130, *133,* 134,
        141, 143, *144–5,* 152–3, 159, 161,
        177, 180, 186, 266
    (1918), 217, 238, 259
South Lancashire Regiment, 174, 177
South Wales Borderers, 5–6, 27, 263
Souvenirs, *5,* 143, 149, *175,* 240
Staff officers, x, 151–2, 164, 209
Stretcher-bearers, 136, 174, 184, 186–8, 208–9
Suicide, 19, 34, 137
Swinton, Colonel Ernest, 131

Tanks, ix, *40,* 131–2, *131,* 174, 184, 185, 200, *201,* 225, 238, *241*
Tennyson, Major Lionel, 91
Territorial Army, xiii, 28, *30,* 37, 46, 70

Third Army, 114, 159, 160, 205, 206, 209–10, 217
Tower Hamlets, 192
Training, 68, *84–5*
Trenches: alternative civilization, x;
    communication, 50, *56–7,* 184, *207;*
    descriptions of trench world, 50–5, *52, 54;* digging, 29, *33,* 53, 56, 65–6; first
    experiences, 3, 4, 18–20; first winter,
    44–9, *45;* flooded, 62; German, 148–9,
    172; Messines, 29; organization, *56–7;*
    siege warfare, ix
Trones Wood, *144–5*
Tyneside Irish Brigade, *110–11*

Uhlans, 8, 252
Uniforms, 36, 47, 141
United States of America, 111, 227, 237, *see also* American forces

Vermelles, *65,* 178
Vimy Ridge, 83, 142, 159

WAACs (Women's Army Auxiliary Corps), 205, 228–32, *230, 231, 232*
War, attitudes to, 35, 68, 122–3, 198, 262–70
Weapons, 30, 43, 44, *see also* Artillery, Machine-guns, Tanks
Weather, *see* Fog, Mud
Welch Regiment, 48, 78, 265, 268
Welsh Guards, 236

West Yorkshire Regiment, 189, 207, 210, 217
Wieltje, 186, 187
Wilhelm, Crown Prince, 11
Wilhelm II, Kaiser, 31, 32, 147, 254, 263
Wiltshire Regiment, 35
Wimereux, 229
Wire, 29, 64–5, 109–10, 117, 159, 166, 173, 243
Women,
    medical role, xii, 36–7, 228, *229;*
        soldiers, *see* WAACs
Worcestershire Regiment, 62, *112,* 177, 213
Wounded, care of, 20, 36–7, 76, 86, *88,*
    186–8, 196, *see also* Amputations,
    Blighty, Gangrene, Medical services

Yorkshire Regiment, 46, 64, 69
Ypres, 25, 72, 169, 186, 188, 223, 233,
    248, 259, *260–1*
    Salient, *half-title, 40,* 63, 71, 75, 169,
        176, 186, 189, 233, 248, 259
    First Battle of, xiii, 4, 25–37, *29, 30,* 44,
        263, 264
    Second Battle of, 72–6, *74,* 176
    Third Battle of, 43, *63,* 93, 142, 143,
        154, 159, 178, 182–8, *181, 183, 187,*
        192, 198
    Fourth Battle of, 248

Zillebeke, *45*